KU-187-690

WITHDRAWN FROM STOCK

SOURCES AND ANALOGUES OF OLD ENGLISH POETRY

The Major Latin Texts in Translation

Translated by
Michael J. B. Allen
and
Daniel G. Calder

D. S. Brewer • Rowman and Littlefield

Published by D. S. Brewer Ltd
240 Hills Road, Cambridge, England

ISBN 0 85991 013 X

First published in the U.S.A. 1976
by Rowman and Littlefield
81 Adams Drive, Totowa, New Jersey 07512, U.S.A.

Library of Congress Cataloging in Publication Data

Allen, Michael J. B. comp.
Sources and analogues of Old English poetry

"The most important Latin sources and analogues for Old English poetry, presented in a modern English prose translation."

Bibliography: p.

1. Christian poetry, Latin—Translations into English. 2. English prose literature—Translations from Latin. 3. Anglo-Saxon poetry—History and criticism. I. Calder, Daniel Gillmore, joint comp. II. Title.

PA6164.A5 871′.01 75-2240

ISBN 0-87471-687-X

Printed in Great Britain
by Redwood Burn Ltd, Trowbridge & Esher

To

Charles R. Forker

doctrina sed vim promovet insitam

CONTENTS

Preface

From the beginning of Anglo-Saxon studies, scholars have looked for Latin parallels to Old English poetry. Initially, they searched for specific sources and prominent analogues, but their emphasis has shifted to assembling materials which illustrate various themes, major and minor, in the Christian background. This book attempts in a modest way to gather the fruits of their scholarship so one tradition can be aligned with the other: the intellectual milieu of Christian Latinity and the splendid, if idiosyncratic, transformation the Anglo-Saxon scops wrought upon it. The book includes all the Latin sources (and the only extant non-Latin source may be found in Appendix II), but it also contains analogues clearly relevant to each poem as a whole. The criteria for selection and omission of analogues alternate from poem to poem: *Durham*, for instance, belongs to a highly stylized rhetorical genre whose classical and medieval antecedents are well-known, while *Christ III* presents a bewildering array of possible analogues from a range of ecclesiastical texts.

The point of departure has been the work of the Fathers. Though the literate Anglo-Saxon must have known some of the Augustan poets, there is no direct impress of Virgil, Ovid or Horace in the surviving poems. At the other extreme, material written after 1066 is excluded, except in the cases of *The Battle of Maldon* and *The Battle of Brunanburh* where the post-Conquest notices form a significant part of the historical record.

For practical reasons we have omitted biblical passages and the following poems: *Beowulf* and the *Finnsburg* fragment (good modern translations of their sources and analogues already exist); various liturgical pieces which expand familiar parts of the Mass; the several paraphrases of the Bible; and minor legendary-historical items like *Waldere* (to deal with these sixty-three lines would mean the inclusion of a lengthy and distant analogue, Ekkehard's *Waltharii poesis*). However, Appendix I contains pertinent information on the omissions with a Latin background, except *Beowulf* and *Finnsburg*.

Some overlapping occurs among both poems and analogues. The elegies partially gloss each other and much else besides; gnomes are ubiquitous; many narratives describe or allude to the Harrowing of Hell; and one need only glance through J. D. A. Ogilvy's *Books Known to the English, 597-1066* (Cambridge, Mass., 1967), let alone Migne's *Patrologia Latina* to realize that the quantity of homiletic material on such recurring themes as the world's mutability, the Last Judgment, or the wages of sin, cannot be circumscribed. The reader should consult the headnotes for cross-references to selections serving multiple purposes.

We have tried to bring the study of the sources and analogues of Old English poetry into line with recent research on the ascription and dating of patristic texts, even though scholars have yet to embark on the task of identifying the manuscripts and versions actually used by the poets. The translations are our own (though we have consulted those that do exist), and are based on modern editions where available. Poetry has been rendered as prose, and biblical passages which crop up in the midst of a text have been left unrevised; also unrevised are the occasional shifts in syntax and speaker. Bracketed Latin words or phrases either indicate deviations from the adopted text or else clarify the translation. The order and titles are those of the *Anglo-Saxon Poetic Records*.

Many people have been generous with their assistance. We would like to acknowledge the aid of Professors Peter Clemoes, Stanley B. Greenfield and Robert D. Stevick in the planning stage. We also wish to thank Professors Henry A. Kelly and Fred C. Robinson for reading the first draft of the typescript; their numerous suggestions have been incorporated into the text. Professor Thomas D. Hill kindly advised us on the sources and analogues for *Christ III* and gave us his discovery of the antiphonal source for Lyric VII of *Christ I*. Several scholars have checked sections in which they had special expertise: we wish to thank Mr. Ian D. Mackenzie for his work with Avitus, Professor

Bengt Löfstedt for his reading of *The Acts of Andrew and Matthew among the Cannibals*, Professor A. N. Doane for his advice on the sources of the *Genesis* poems, Professors Rowland L. Collins and Charles R. Sleeth for their comments on the sources of *Christ and Satan*, Father John O'Neill for help with the source of *Juliana*, Professor Roy F. Leslie for kindly discussing the problem of the analogues to the elegies, Ms. Rachel Rogers for sharing the preliminary results of her researches on *Christ III*, Professor Paul Sellin for alerting us to the existence of the two Gerardus Vossiuses, and Professor Terence Wilbur for looking over our translation of the Old Saxon *Genesis*. Many of the translations were reviewed by Professor Donald Jackson, and to him and to Dr. Carol D. Lanham we owe a special debt. Mr. Robert E. Bjork, Mr. Edward J. Chittenden and Dr. Sherron E. Knopp provided diligent research assistance, and Ms. Jane Abelson and Ms. Sandy Migliaccio worked tirelessly in checking references and proofs. To all these scholars and assistants we offer our sincere appreciation, while accepting full responsibility for the errors which persist.

This project was funded in part by the Center for Medieval and Renaissance Studies and by the Research Committee of the Academic Senate at UCLA, and to both we are very grateful. Finally, we would like to acknowledge the cooperation we received from the staffs of the University Research Library, UCLA, and the Henry E. Huntington Library in San Marino.

ABBREVIATIONS

AnM	— *Annuale Mediaevale*
Archiv	— *Archiv für das Studium der Neueren Sprachen und Literaturen*
ASPR	— *The Anglo-Saxon Poetic Records*
Bonner Beiträge	— *Bonner Beiträge zur Anglistik*
CC	— *Corpus Christianorum*
CL	— *Comparative Literature*
CPL	— *Clavis Patrum Latinorum*, ed. E. Dekkers and A. A. Gaar. Sacris Erudiri, III. Rev. ed. Bruges, 1961.
CSEL	— *Corpus Scriptorum Ecclesiasticorum Latinorum*
EETS	— Early English Text Society
ELH	— *Journal of English Literary History*
ELN	— *English Language Notes*
JAF	— *Journal of American Folklore*
JEGP	— *Journal of English and Germanic Philology*
JTS	— *Journal of Theological Studies*
K-D	— Krapp-Dobbie (see *ASPR*)
MAE	— *Medium Aevum*
MGH	— *Monumenta Germaniae Historica*
MLN	— *Modern Language Notes*
MLQ	— *Modern Language Quarterly*
MP	— *Modern Philology*
MS	— *Mediaeval Studies*

Neophil	— *Neophilologus*
NM	— *Neuphilologische Mitteilungen*
N&Q	— *Notes and Queries*
PBA	— *Proceedings of the British Academy*
PL	— *Patrologia Latina*
PLS	— *Patrologia Latina: Supplementum*
PMLA	— *Publications of the Modern Language Association of America*
PQ	— *Philological Quarterly*
PRM	— *Pour Revaloriser Migne*, P. Glorieux. Lille, 1952.
RB	— *Revue Bénédictine*
RES	— *Review of English Studies*
RHE	— *Revue d'histoire ecclésiastique*
RHS	— *Revue d'histoire de la spiritualité*
SN	— *Studia Neophilologica*
SP	— *Studies in Philology*
VL	— *Vetus Latina*, I, 1: Fischer, Bonifatius. *Verzeichnis der Sigel für Kirchenschriftsteller*. Freiburg, 1963.
ZDA	— *Zeitschrift für Deutsches Altertum und Deutsche Literatur*

I

GENESIS

The "Caedmonian" *Genesis* is a composite poem, with a later piece interpolated into an earlier: *Genesis A* comprises lines 1-234 and 852-2936, and *Genesis B*, lines 235-851. *Genesis B* is an obviously incomplete and fairly literal translation of an Old Saxon poem, itself extant as a twenty-five and a half line fragment corresponding to lines 790 (791)-817a. Interestingly, the Vatican MS containing the Old Saxon *Genesis* also has two other fragments dealing with the stories of Cain and Lot respectively; but they are not sources for the corresponding passages in *Genesis A*.

Genesis A

Bernard Huppé outlines the first two hundred and thirty-four lines as follows:

> It begins with the exhortation to praise God, then describes how the angels lived with God in joy until Lucifer was cast into hell, while the faithful angels remained in concord. It tells of the empty places in heaven, and of how God determines to fill them with a new creation. . . . In these first 111 lines the poem has advanced only through the first verse of Genesis, as that verse was understood in the hexameral commentaries to include the creation of the angels. In lines 111-234, the poem settles to a closer paraphrase of the biblical verses dealing with the works of the days (*Doctrine and Poetry: Augustine's Influence on Old English Poetry* [New York, 1959], pp. 132-3).

This paraphrasing continues, in fact, through lines 852-2936: from God's visit to Adam and Eve after the Fall to the sacrifice of Isaac. Huppé later points to a specific source for the opening exhortation to praise God in the [Common] Preface to the Mass (pp. 132-4). Actually, Laurence Michel had made that same connection sometime earlier ("*Genesis A* and the *Praefatio*," *MLN*, 62 [1947], 545-50), following Sir Israel Gollancz (*The Caedmon Manuscript of Anglo-Saxon Biblical Poetry* [Oxford, 1927], p. lxii) and F. Holthausen (*Die ältere Genesis* [Heidelberg, 1914], p. 91).

Genesis A thus presents us with three distinct categories: 1. an opening with a definite source, the Common Preface to the Mass; 2. an expanded narrative describing the fall of the angels and God's decision to create a new world, and depending on the hexameral commentary on the first verse of Genesis; and 3. the rest of the twenty-two hundred odd lines which closely paraphrase Gen. 1.1-2.14 and 3.8-22.18. We have translated the source (under Entry VII, XIB), and the Bible is excluded as a matter of policy. There remains the question of the hexameral exegesis.

J. M. Evans' caveat that "the background of a poem written on a biblical theme is necessarily complex" ("*Genesis B* and Its Background," *RES*, 14 [1963], 1) cannot be taken lightly. Even Huppé, who has written the only significant critique of *Genesis A* which draws upon the Fathers, is forced to admit that the two thousand or so later lines are "on the whole closer" in method to lines 112-234 than they are to the first one hundred and eleven lines (p. 147); though he does argue for "small modifications or alterations which have as their purpose the inclusion of exegetical material" (p. 148). These modifications, he says, "may be readily explained as designed to make the biblical story clearer or more dramatic" (pp. 147-8); that is, they are still paraphrasings of a kind. Huppé's argument thus turns on itself, and we must conclude that while the *Genesis A* poet may well have been aware of and even utilized materials from the hexameral tradition, there is no need to include scattered annotations which are neither formal nor material analogues for the poem as a whole. We note, however, some of the main works in that exegetical tradition during the early Middle Ages:

1. Ambrose, *Hexameron, CSEL,* 32, 1.3-261.
2. Basil of Caesarea, *Hexameron;* see Eustathius, *Ancienne version latine des neuf Homeliés sur l'Hexaéméron de Basile de Césarée,* ed. Emmanuel Amand de Mendieta and Stig Y. Rudberg (Berlin, 1958); also *PL,* 53.867-966.
3. Augustine, *De Civitate Dei, CC,* 48, esp. Books XI-XIV. ———, *De Genesi ad Litteram, CSEL,* 28, 1.3-456.
4. Isidore of Seville, *Mysticorum Expositiones Sacramentorum, seu Quaestiones in Vetus Testamentum (In Genesin), PL,* 83.207-88.
5. Bede, *Hexameron, PL,* 91.9-190.
6. Alcuin, *Interrogationes et Responsiones in Genesim, PL,* 100.515-66.
7. Hrabanus Maurus, *Commentariorum in Genesim Libri Quatuor, PL,* 107.439-670.

Genesis B

The twenty-five and a half line Old Saxon fragment is the direct source for a part of *Genesis B,* but their joint Latin background can only be reconstructed from various apocryphal works, hexameral exegesis, and Christian Latin poems of the fourth, fifth and sixth centuries.

A long tradition stretching from Sievers and Ten Brink to Evans maintains that the literary influences on *Genesis B* were more direct than the theological. All have singled out Avitus' *Poematum de Mosaicae Historiae Gestis Libri Quinque* as the most relevant poem among those dealing with the theme of the Creation and Fall in Latin poetry (E. Sievers, *Der Heliand und die angelsächsische Genesis* [Halle, 1875], pp. 17 ff.; B. ten Brink, *Early English Literature,* trans. H. M. Kennedy [London, 1883], p. 84; Evans, pp. 13-6). However, Rosemary Woolf and others maintain that there is a lost apocryphal source ("The Fall of Man in *Genesis B* and the *Mystère d'Adam,*" in *Studies in Old English Literature in Honor of Arthur G. Brodeur,* ed. Stanley B. Greenfield [Eugene, 1963], p. 188n), and the controversy continues to be lively. Still, it is undeniable that Book Two of Avitus' poem does describe Satan's defiance and unconquerable desire for revenge in a way remarkably like the description in *Genesis B* and, incidentally, in Milton's *Paradise Lost.*

Since Evans himself concedes that the handling of Adam and Eve's temptation in *Genesis B* differs from that in Avitus (p. 15), we must look elsewhere for information on its several deviations from the orthodox account. These are: *I.* the temptation is undertaken not by Satan himself, but by a subordinate devil; *II.* this devil masquerades as an angel of God rather than a serpent; *III.* he tempts Adam first, claiming he has been sent by God; *IV.* the forbidden tree in paradise is an obvious tree of death; *V.* Eve eats the fruit in the belief she if fulfilling God's will, and then has a vision of God on His throne surrounded by angels; *VI.* after the Fall there is an unusual emphasis on the immediate repentance of Adam and Eve.

Numerous scholars have attempted to explain these differences. Biblical and apocryphal works help clarify the first two. *I.* C. Abbetmeyer (*Old English Poetical Motives Derived from the Doctrine of Sin* [Minneapolis, 1903], p. 16) and A. D. McKillop ("Illustrative Notes on *Genesis B,*" *JEGP,* 20 [1921], 30) suggest that Satan's dispatch of a subordinate demon to destroy Adam and Eve derives from a fusion of the story of Lucifer's fall with Christ's binding of Satan during His descent into hell (see Entry XVII); while Evans finds a simpler explanation in Jude 6. *II.* Both Evans and Woolf note that a phrase in II Cor. 11.14 clearly authorizes the idea that Satan often disguises himself as an angel of light (Evans, p. 7; Woolf, p. 191). The image recurs in the apocryphal *Vita Adae et Evae* and in the *Apocalypsis Mosis* where the devil as angel is confused with the devil as serpent (see F. N. Robinson, "A Note on the Sources of the Old Saxon *Genesis,*" *MP,* 4 [1906-7], 389-96). *III.* Unless we are willing to suppose Woolf's lost source, we must concur with Evans' conclusion that "the devil's prior approach to Adam is completely without precedent" (p. 9). *IV.* Evans finds convincing descriptions of a tree of death in various Christian Latin poems: Prudentius' *Liber Cathemerinon,* Dracontius' *Carmen de Deo* and Cyprianus Gallus' *Heptateuchos* (p. 10). *V.* But he finds no correspondence in any of them which would explain Eve's belief that she is fulfilling God's will in eating the apple. Evans' explanation of Eve's post-lapsarian vision has been questioned by John F. Vickery who interprets it as a proleptic and ironic glimpse of the Last Judgment ("The

Vision of Eve in *Genesis B*," *Speculum*, 44 [1969], 86-102). *VI.* Finally, Evans' unsettling tentativeness in referring the emphasis on Adam and Eve's immediate repentance to yet another of the Latin Fall poems, Claudius Marius Victor's *Alethia*, only underscores the remoteness of all these analogues.

In short, Evans' claim that the poet depended upon a tissue of reminiscences from the Christian Latin poets is no more reasonable than Woolf's insistence on a lost apocryphal source. Although the Latin poets were known to some of the insular and continental Saxons (see Evans, *Paradise Lost and the Genesis Tradition* [Oxford, 1968], p. 142), we cannot be sure whether they were known to the Old Saxon poet or his translator. Readers should also consult the valuable supplement to Evans' work by Michael Benskin and Brian Murdoch, "The Literary Tradition of Genesis," *NM*, 76 (1975), 389-403.

With all these cautionary notes in mind, we have, nevertheless, translated portions of the long biblical poem by Alcimus Avitus, Bishop of Vienne (c.450-c.519), since it is the closest of the admittedly distant analogues for *Genesis B*. The Old Saxon fragment is translated in Appendix II.

Alcimus Avitus, *Five Books of Poetry on the Events in Moses' History*

Book II, *Original Sin*

Text: *MGH, Auctores Antiquissimi*, 6, 2
(Berlin, 1883), 212-19; 223-4.

Meanwhile Adam and Eve were free and at peace, unaware of their impending fall; they made use of the garden's good things and enjoyed its blessed abundance. The ready earth offers up a plentiful store of food, and they constantly pick down fruit from the rich tree's slender spray. If the branches, curving from the weight of the crop, allow the ripe apples to fall from the tree-top, the bare shoot immediately begins to swell into flower and to give promise of fruit in the new buds. Should Adam and Eve wish to take a sweet sleep, they lie down on the painted meadows' soft grass. Though the sacred grove gives them every opportunity to enjoy themselves and presents them with a plenitude of strange delights, hunger does not force them to take their meals or look for food: no maw in need of pampering commands the tired entrails to fill themselves. Unless they had actually wanted to try the food given them, hunger would not have known what kind to ask for, and there would be no nourishment to sustain continuous life. They regard their naked bodies and are not ashamed to see each other's limbs: simple honesty considers nothing ugly. By nature man is modest not sinful; for the good Creator formed the body to be chaste and afterwards the demands of the flesh defiled it. At that time the radiant mind preserved an uncorrupted view of the kind of glory which exists in the angels' starry homes, and which Christ promises to restore to the redeemed after the time of death. Sex will not be there to worry them nor will fleshly union join the warm genitals in base intercourse. Mourning will cease, together with profligacy, fear, wrath, pleasure, fraud, pain and deceit, sadness, discord and envy. No one will be in need; no one will yearn for anything. But under the reign of peace Christ's glory will suffice for all the saints.

In the sacred beginning the original human beings understood and embraced these goods, until they were overthrown in their first battle against the false enemy and then conquered by sin. The enemy was once an angel, but then he became inflamed with his own evil and burned to attempt arrogant deeds. Thinking he had made himself and was his own creator, as it were, he went mad in his fierce heart, denied his Creator and said, "I will acquire God's name and build an eternal throne above the sky like the Most High; with my vast power I shall be a match for Him." While he thus boasted, the Supreme Power hurled him from heaven, and as he fell stripped him of his former honor. Satan, who once shone at the head of the created order, will be the first to pay the penalty when the Day of Judgment comes; because one could hardly imagine him falling, he will receive the harshest sentence. For the distinction of the criminal augments the crime: an ordinary sinner is less guilty, but the evil an important man does must be treated more harshly. Yet, because the ardent nature of the devil's angelic power uses its vital capacities to probe into secrets, sees what will happen and unfolds universal mysteries, it is superior to ours. Here is a story of portentous horror attended by notable signs and wonders. Every terrible deed enacted in the whole world results from the devil's teaching. He guides the hands and knives which commit crimes: a hidden thief, he strikes through public misdeeds. Often he changes into the fierce faces of men, then of wild beasts: deceitfully, he switches from face to face. Sometimes he suddenly takes on the false semblance of a winging bird, and then again he feigns an honest garb. When he appears like a girl in a beautiful body, he draws men's burning gazes to lewd delights. For greedy men, he often makes the cruel silver glisten and sets their souls alight with desire for cheating gold; as he flees away, he deludes their grasp with an empty phantasm. No one can trust appearances or beauty. For the devil, however by doing harm he may seize and retain a man, assumes an outward mask with a false face, a mask prepared for tricks and fit for secret fraud. Still greater is the power permitted this dire spirit to feign what is holy. Thus the nature which was joined to man and which the Creator fashioned to be upright stayed whole for a time; then the devil perverted its use.

Satan perceived how these new humans led a blissful life without danger in that quiet place. He saw how they ruled the subject world under the law given to them, calmly and gladly enjoying what they governed. When he spied them, a spark of envy surged through his blood and his hot malice burst into raging flames. It had not been long, perhaps, since he fell from heaven and dragged a line of followers bound to him in his descent. As he contemplated this recent fall, it weighed upon his heart: he was deeply pained that someone else should own what he himself had lost. Then his shame was mixed with bitterness. A complaint unfolds from his heart, and with the following words he thus gives vent to his sighs.

"Woe is me! that this creature molded [from clay] should be suddenly exalted above me, that a hateful race should spring from my downfall. Courage once kept me on high, but, behold, I am now rejected and exiled. Mere clay has succeeded to angelic honor; earth inhabits heaven; dust has been raised in the form of this base creature and now holds sway; and my power, transferred away, is perishing. It has not wholly perished however; a large part, renowned for its power to do great harm, retains its special strength. I shall not delay; I shall fight them at once in a battle of flattery while their pristine well-being and simplicity, inexperienced as it is in guile of any sort, makes them vulnerable to my cowardly attack. Better too that my fraud take them while they are alone before they dispatch their fertile children down through endless ages. It is insufferable that anything immortal should come from earth. Let this race die at its source: its defeat and overthrow will be the seed of death. At its very beginning let life breed death's calamities; let all men be struck down in the person of one man. The dead root shall not produce a living point. In my ruin the only consolations left to me are these: if I cannot climb up again to the closed heavens, let them also be closed to Adam and Eve. If this new substance can be destroyed in a disaster like mine, I will take my own less seriously. Let me have a companion in my defeat; let a fellow being suffer the punishment with me and share the fires which I foresee. It is not difficult to find a pretext for deceiving them. I must show them the way I have just hurried down in my headlong fall of my own accord; the vaunting which expelled me from my kingdom will also hurl man from the threshold of paradise." Having spoken thus, his voice was choked with groans and lamentation.

The serpent was perhaps the most cunning of all living things; it was envious and skillful in its clever heart. From all the rest the transgressor chooses to assume its shape. He wraps his airy body in its skin and thus altered he strives to be a darting snake. He becomes the serpent with its long neck: he paints the shining coils with speckles; he roughens and arms the length of its curving back with bristling scales. The same emerges in early spring when the summer sends ahead its blessed warmth in the months that first succeed the numbing cold. With movements renewed, it escapes from the old year: shedding the dry skin from its sleek body, it leaves behind the secret caves of the earth and sets out. Its terrifying form bears a fearful beauty; its eyes flash balefully, then learn to accustom themselves joyfully to the bright light and the longed-for sun. At this time it pretends to be gentle: its jaws move in constant play as if they were singing, and the three-forked tongue darts out from its throat.

After the treacherous demon had maliciously and deceitfully assumed the viper's shape and entered into it completely, he flew towards the grove. It so chanced the happy young couple were plucking rosy apples from the green boughs. Then the serpent feared he would be unable to undermine the man's heart and steadfast mind by injecting his poison. So he stretched his rippling coils to the top of a tall tree and balanced his length along its lofty branches.

In a low voice he stung the woman's willing ear, "Most beautiful and fortunate maid, the world's glory, radiant loveliness adorns you with the modesty of a rose. You will be the parent of the race; the mighty world awaits you, its mother. You are man's first and surest pleasure and comfort; without you he cannot live. Though he is larger, he is subject to your love by law. As his sweetest partner, you will bear him a progeny through union. Given you at the height of paradise is a worthy seat, and the world's substance trembles before you as servant and slave. All that heaven and earth create, all that the sea produces from the great deep is bestowed on you to use. Nature has denied you nothing. Behold, you have been granted power over all things. I am not envious; I am full of wonder. But still I would like to know why you freely refrain from touching one sweet tree. Who gave such dire orders? Who is jealous of such gifts? Who introduced fasting into these delights?" He hissed the wickedly enticing words at her. Woman, what stupidity clouded your mind, making you speak with a serpent and converse with a beast? Aren't you ashamed that a wild brute should presume to speak like you? Will you suffer the monster and even reply to him?

When Eve, who was easily seduced, received the deadly venom in her ears and surrendered to the wicked praise, she spoke to the serpent in her foolishness, "O mighty snake, most sweet with your delightful words, God does not require us to be hungry, as you think; nor does He forbid us to take care of our bodies with plenty of food. Look, see the feasts the whole world offers us. Having supplied us with every pleasure from the beginning, the Father has allowed us to use them lawfully. He has loosened life's every rein. Only this tree in the middle of the grove, the tree you see, is forbidden as sustenance. These apples alone must not be touched; but man can take all the rest of the abundant food to eat. Yet if we violate the law by misusing our liberty, the Creator swore to us in a terrifying voice that we would expiate our guilt immediately with a sort of 'death.' Learned serpent, please show me now what God calls 'death,' for in our ignorance we do not know what it is."

Then the clever dragon, death's master, gladly taught her about death, and thus spoke to her captive ears, "Woman, you are frightened of a word which is empty of terror. You will not be sentenced with instant death. Rather, the Father, who is your enemy, has not dealt fairly with you; He has not allowed you to know the high secrets He keeps to Himself. What good is it for you to lay hold of the universe or see the world when your minds are blind and shut up in a miserable prison? Nature also created the beasts with bodily senses and with eyes that see; one sun serves all things; and the beast's mode of seeing is not very different from man's. Take my advice, rather, and direct your mind to higher things: stretch your lofty understanding up to heaven. For this forbidden apple which you fear to touch will allow you to know every secret the Father has kept hidden. Don't hold your hands back now; they are poised to take the fruit. Don't let pleasure be restrained any longer; don't let it be captive to the law. For when your mouth has sampled the divine taste, your eyes will be purified, and forthwith you will see like the gods. You will know sacred and sinful things, and discern wrong from right and false from true."

The credulous woman lowers her gaze and marvels at the serpent promising her such gifts as he treacherously whispers to her. She begins to hesitate longer, to waver in her mind and to turn her uncertain thoughts more and more towards death. When he saw her overcome by the imminent danger and had told her again about the name and citadel of the gods, he plucks an apple from those on the deadly tree. He blends its beauty with a sweet savor and makes its color pleasing. While she still falters, he offers it to her. To her cost, the credulous woman does not despise the wretched gift; seizing the lethal fruit, she takes it in her hands. Without prompting, she brings it to her nose and her open lips. In her ignorance she plays with future death.

O, how many times did she draw back, stung with remorse, when she raised the fruit to her mouth; did her bold hand stop, trembling with the apple's weight; did she shrink in agitation from enacting the crime? But she yearns to be like the gods and the poison slowly creeps through her, destroying her with vanity. Contrary feelings prey upon her mind: first desire, then fear. Her pride beats down the law and then the law comes to her aid. In fearful conflict the tide boils back and forth in her divided heart. But the enchanter serpent does not cease beguiling her. As she hesitates, he shows her the food and complains of her delay. He rejoices that she is about to fall to impending ruin.

When Eve had been overcome at last and was determined by the grievous decision to tempt eternal hunger by taking the food of crime and to satisfy the serpent by eating it, she yielded to deception: herself devoured, she bit into the apple. The delicious poison enters and with the food she swallows horrid death. At first the clever snake contains his joy; fierce victory conceals its brutal triumph.

Knowing nothing of her deed, Adam was blithely returning from another part of paradise through the grasses of a wide meadow; he sought his wife's embraces and her chaste kisses. Eve ran up to him and for the first time temerity fanned the female furies in her violent heart. And thus she began to speak, for she carried the deadly half-eaten apple, guarding it for her poor husband: "Dear husband, accept this food from the seed of life: perchance it will make you like the Thunderer in heaven and equal to the gods. I do not present you this gift in ignorance; I know about it already. The first taste has reached my stomach and dissolved [God's] covenants; I have braved the danger. Please believe me, it is criminal that your manly mind should have hesitated to do what I, a mere woman, could do. You were frightened perhaps to go first. At least, follow me and raise your dejected spirits. Why do you turn your eyes away? Why do you postpone your best hopes for so long and steal time from honor that is to come?"

Having said this, she offered him the food of death, the future victor; for when the soul dies, sin feeds death. The wretched man hears her words whispering the counsel of evil, and casts behind him all his steadfast sense of right. He is not shaken by anxiety or fearful trepidation, nor does he delay as much as the woman when she took her first bite, but follows her quickly. The irresolute man resolutely seizes the poison from the mouth of his miserable wife as if it were her dowry, and lifts the deadly food to his own. Scarcely had his shuddering jaws taken one bite of the apple, scarcely had the fruit released its full flavor, when, lo, a sudden blaze surrounded their faces and a mournful light was splashed across their new vision. Nature did not create men blind, nor did the perfection of the human form produce a face deprived of the use of light. Adam, it was no longer sufficient for you to know what the great Creator wished you to know. Now you will be much more blind. The power to see was granted you to perceive life; of your own accord, however, you also see death. Then the pair groan because their eyes have been opened; for rebellious sin flamed in them and their bodies felt lewd desires. Whether it was just dead or just born, I am not sure I can tell, but they felt a sense of shame for the first time as they surveyed their naked limbs. Already conscious of its own guilt, the mind was appalled; fighting it was the law of the flesh imposed upon their limbs.

[Two digressions follow on magicians and Lot's wife]

(408) Then the victorious serpent came jubilantly from the battle and brandished the purple crest on his scaly head. He no longer hid the triumph he had previously concealed. Vehemently he exults over the defeated pair and thus begins, "Behold, the divine glory of the praise I promised awaits you. Believe me, whatever my knowledge amounted to is now yours. I have shown you everything; I have led your senses through secrets. Whatever evil wise nature has denied you I have established for you; I have given my left hand to join with your right. Accordingly, I have consecrated you and your fate perpetually to me. Although God first made you, He has no more right to you now than I. Let Him hold onto His creations. What I have taught is mine; the bigger share remains for me. You are in debt to your Creator for many things, but to your teacher for still more." He spoke and left them quaking in the midst of the gloom. His counterfeit body vanished as he fled through the clouds.

Book III, *God's Sentence*

By then the sun had passed its zenith and was sinking down, leaving the summit of heaven's height behind; at the approach of night it had abandoned the upper air. But a greater heat than the sun's raged within them, the heat of cares and burning pains possessed their guilty hearts. Their senses were enslaved. Shame turned their eyes from each other's body and repelled their miserable gaze. No longer may they look contentedly at flesh, branded now with the fixed stigma of sin. They both search for clothes so they can cover their limbs with soft leaves, though this will reveal their naked evil.

Nearby stood a fig tree with shady boughs and a canopy of leafy foliage. Adam grabbed it quickly. He tore out the moist inner rind from the bark he had stripped away and sewed it together: he assuaged his shame with a garment of green. With equal skill, his tearful wife clothed herself. Having seduced them with a wretched apple, their treacherous madness dressed them with a leaf; having used a pitiless tree to render them naked, it used a comforting tree to smother them with clothes. Yet the time will come when a new Adam will use a tree to heal and purge away the sins of a tree: He will make the very material which gave death its power into the medicine of life. Death, you will be struck down by death. The Heavenly Serpent will hang from the lofty tree-trunk. Though imitating the venomous one, may He purge away all venom; may His form destroy the dragon of old.

II

ANDREAS

Although a single source for *Andreas* once existed (whether in Greek or Latin has been a moot point), all that survives are other versions of the legend. Jakob Grimm, the first editor, did not know the two long Latin versions (*Casanatensis* and *Vaticana*) and insisted that the Greek Πράξεις 'Ανδρέου καὶ Ματθεία εἰς τὴν χώραν τῶν ἀνθρωποφάγων (*The Acts of Andrew and Matthew in the Land of the Cannibals*) was the source (*Andreas und Elene* [Cassel, 1840], p. xviii). Later commentators rejected this attribution and claimed that a Latin translation of the Greek must have served as the Anglo-Saxon poet's guide. After more than a century of debate neither the Greek nor the Latin alternatives have been established as the source, though scholars now generally agree it was probably some Latin text no longer extant (see Claes Schaar, *Critical Studies in the Cynewulf Group* [Lund and Copenhagen, 1949], pp. 12-24).

Nine MSS of the Greek tale (commonly designated P) survive, along with five Latin recensions of differing value: 1. the "Bonnet" Fragment, which corresponds to lines 843-954 of *Andreas*; 2. the *Recensio Casanatensis*; 3. the *Recensio Vaticana;* 4. the compressed account in MS 1576 at the University of Bologna, which covers the same ground as lines 1-339; and 5. the even more truncated late version printed by Fabricius in 1719 as part of the Pseudo-Abdias collection (see Kenneth R. Brooks, ed., *Andreas and the Fates of the Apostles* [Oxford, 1961], pp. xv-xviii).

After a careful comparison of all the versions in both classical languages, Schaar decides that, since *Andreas* most closely resembles the Greek P, the Latin text used by the Old English poet must also have been very similar to P. In the treatment of certain details, however, *Andreas* resembles *Casanatensis* (pp. 20, 23). Brooks concurs and adds that, while none of the extant versions "can be the immediate source, . . . [*Casanatensis*] fulfills more of the conditions than any other" (p. xviii). The Latin of *Casanatensis* is, to say the least, irregular.

The Acts of Andrew and Matthew among the Cannibals

(Casanatensis)

Text: Franz Blatt, ed., *Die lateinischen Bearbeitungen der* Acta Andreae et Matthiae apud anthropophagos (Giessen and Copenhagen, 1930).

At that time all the apostles were gathered together and they divided the regions among themselves, casting lots to see which area each was to be assigned for preaching. The province called Mermedonia, which is inhabited by wicked, evil men, fell in the lot to blessed Matthew. There they ate nothing except human flesh and drank nothing but human blood. In the middle of the city they had built an oven and also a tank next to the oven. They put men to death in the tank in order to collect the blood. Hard by this tank was another and in it they sprinkled the blood from the first tank, ... and it flowed out, purified as it were, ... for drinking. Their law was such . . . . that from all sides they would converge there on weary pilgrims or strangers and seize them quickly. Holding them by force, they would ruthlessly imprison them, pluck out their eyes and give them a harmful draught of poison to drink. This drink had been prepared through the evil spells of magic, so that all who took it lost their senses and were no longer in their right minds; thrust back into prison, they ate hay like oxen or cattle.

2. When Matthew entered the city of Mermedonia to preach the word of salvation, he was immediately seized by the wicked men of that city. According to their vicious custom, they plucked out his eyes, gave him the harmful draught to drink and shut him up in the prison where they held many other men. But when he drank the harmful draught, it did not hurt him: neither his mind nor senses were taken away or changed. Then blessed Matthew knelt down; bathed with tears, he began to pray faithfully to the Lord, "Lord Jesus Christ, good Master, I am praying to you because we left everything and followed you, just as you told us. That is why, if you have prepared these tortures for me and surrendered me to this city's wicked people to be devoured as food, I will not run away from your command. May it not be as I want, but as you do; for I am ready to suffer everything for your sake. Only most of all I pray you of your mercy that you grant me the light of my eyes so I may see how they tear my flesh."

3. When he had finished praying, suddenly there was a great light in the middle of the prison and from the midst of the light came the Lord's voice saying to him, "Matthew, our beloved, do not be afraid, for I am with you. I will not desert or leave you; but I want you to suffer here for twenty-seven days so that through you and because of you the many souls of the men imprisoned with you in great torment may be guided towards me. When you have spent these twenty-seven days, I will send you the apostle Andrew, your brother, to rescue you and all those with you. Peace be with you." After the Lord had spoken to him, He returned to heaven. Comforted by the Lord's words, Matthew said, "May your grace remain with me, my Lord Jesus Christ." And Matthew began to sing psalms in the middle of the prison and to meditate on the Lord's words. In his hand every prisoner held a writing-tablet, which the evil, vicious murderers had put into their hands when they thrust them in. The number of thirty days was written on each tablet. Daily the murderers came to the inmates in the prison and looked at the writing on the tablets to find out who had been shut up (like animals for fattening) for the full thirty days. People who had finished their thirty days they cast out and killed immediately; and they and their judges prepared their flesh to eat and their blood as a draught to drink. When the murderers came into the prison, to

throw out a man for the slaughter, blessed Matthew closed his eyes so none of the murderers would realize he had his eyes open. When they took the tablet out of his hand, they didn't know his eyes could see; and looking at the writing on his tablet, they found the thirty days were not yet finished. They said among themselves, "He still has three days left. Then we shall lead him out from this prison to the slaughter, so we can give his flesh to our princes to eat."

4. Then the Lord Jesus came down to a city in Greece and taught His disciples there. He said to blessed Andrew, "Go down to the city called Mermedonia and enter it, because wicked, evil men who drink men's blood live there. I shall send you to them to preach the saving word and to rescue from prison both Matthew—whom I sent there before you—and the rest of the men who dwell bound in the prison with him. For, look, only three days remain before they take him out to kill and eat." Andrew replied, "I am ready, Lord. I pray you, do not be angry with your servant if I dare to speak a word in the ears of my Lord. How can I accomplish this in three days, when it will take me three days to get there? For, Lord, you know all things, and you know I am a man of flesh and I don't know the way. So, Lord, if it is your will, send your angel there; he can quickly cross over the sea and speedily rescue your apostle Matthew from prison." Then the Lord called to blessed Andrew, "Andrew, what did you say? What you ask for is nothing. Only listen to me who made you. I tell you truly that if I gave the word, if I ordered [the angels] who mingle the winds, my word would bring the city into my presence at once. I command you to rise in the morning. Go down to the seashore with your disciples and you will find a little boat. Board it so you can set out on the journey, as I have commanded you."

5. When the morning came, blessed Andrew went down with his disciples and began to walk along the seashore as the Lord had commanded him. While he was walking along looking intently across the waves, he saw a little boat riding through the middle of the waves. Only three men were sitting in it. The Lord provided it through His holy power. The Lord Himself was in the boat with two angels and He had transformed both them and Himself into the image of men. In a little while, after the Lord had guided the boat ashore, blessed Andrew, thinking the

men were merely sailors, said to Jesus, "Brothers, where are you going in such a small boat?" In reply the Lord said to Andrew, "We are going to the province of the city of Mermedonia where there are men who eat other men." Andrew replied to Jesus, "We want to cross over there too. So, brothers, lead us to the city you are heading for." Jesus said to him, "Brother, why do you want to go there? Every man flees from that city; why are you in a hurry to travel there?" Andrew replied to Jesus, "We have a little business to do there and we have to finish it. If you want to take us along, I pray you, tell us at once; otherwise we will go and perhaps find another boat." Jesus said, "If you really must go, board this boat and set out with us."

6. When blessed Andrew had boarded the boat with his disciples, the Lord immediately tested him, saying, "What are you going to give us for passage money?" Saint Andrew replied, "Believe me, brother, I don't have gold or silver to pay you the fare, nor even bread as provision." The Lord replied, "Brother, what's this you're saying: you don't have gold or silver to give us for the crossing, nor even provisions and supplies? Why did you board then?" Andrew said, "Good brother, listen to me. Perhaps you think it was either pride or a clever trick to cheat you? We cannot give you the fare. We have nothing else but our souls and even they are not in our power, for we have given our souls and bodies into the hands of our Lord Jesus Christ, the great Man of God. He chose us as the twelve apostles and He gave us this rule: when we go out to preach His Gospel, we are not to carry money or a bag with us, or bread, or shoes on our feet, or a staff in our hands, or two tunics. If you want to show pity on us, tell us at once; but if you don't, show us how we can leave." When He heard this, the Lord said to him, "If your Lord and Master ordered this, then by all means keep the rule as you received it." Andrew replied, "Brother, I tell you truly that the Lord and Master is our God, the God who made all things. The rules of our Lord Jesus Christ, which I have just described, I have always kept and observed." When the Lord heard this, He said, "Come with joy." Andrew said to Jesus in reply, "Brother, forgive me. May the Lord grant you His grace and guide you always on the sea and everywhere." Then blessed Andrew boarded and sat down near the pilot with his disciples.

7. So the Lord called one of His angels (He had them with Him in the boat as sailors) and said, "Get up and go down to the boat's hold and bring three loaves here. Put them in front of all the brothers for them to eat so they won't be hungry; for they have come a long way." When He had done this, Jesus said to Andrew, "Get up; eat with your disciples. Refresh them so you may be strong enough to endure the sea's waves." For a great tempest of sea and surge had risen against them. Blessed Andrew immediately called to his disciples gently and said calmly to them, "My children, the Lord our God has shown us great mercy. He has given us such a humble and gentle pilot, for I see great humility in this man. Now get up and refresh yourselves with a little bread so you will be strong enough to endure the stormy sea." But because they were being tossed around too much by the stormy sea, they could not answer him and were greatly troubled. The Lord, however, wanted them to take a little bread to refresh themselves. Andrew was wholly incapable of recognizing that the pilot was the Lord Jesus, and he said to Him, "Brother, may the Lord grant you celestial bread from His kingdom; only let them be, for you see they are infants and terror of the sea's motion has exhausted them." The Lord said, "Perhaps these brothers are not used to sailing. If you wish, ask them whether they want to get down onto land and wait till you have finished the business on which you were sent by your Master. Then you will come back to them. Perhaps I can get the boat to shore if I row." Blessed Andrew said to his disciples, "My children, do you want to alight on land and wait for me till I return after I have finished the mission I was sent on? For, as I see it, this pilot is strong enough to get us back if he rows, and then you can alight on land." His disciples answered the blessed Andrew, "If we leave you, we may be forced to give up everything you've taught us, and there will be nothing left. As for us, wherever you go, in life or death, we shall not desert you."

8. Then Jesus said to Andrew, "I see your disciples love you, for they are ready to go with you in life and death. If it is true you walked with your Master and you know what sort of miracles He did in the presence of men, refresh your disciples with telling them about the miracles you saw Him perform;

filled with the sweetness of His miracles, they may then rejoice in their hearts and not be so dreadfully afraid of the sea's waves. For now we are some distance from land." Blessed Andrew comforted them at once, saying, "My sons, act like men and be strong of heart. You have all given your souls to serve the Lord Jesus Christ. Don't be afraid, for the Lord will not desert His servants and all those who hope in Him. For there was a time when we went with the Lord Jesus Christ and boarded a ship with Him. He stretched Himself out as if in a deep sleep: He pretended to be asleep to test us, but He was not asleep at all. Suddenly a mighty wind arose and there was a great storm. The whole sea was whipped up and the surge rose so high it came over the boat's side. We were dreadfully afraid and cried out impulsively with a loud voice, 'Lord, save us.' The Lord arose at once and gave orders to the wind and sea; they became silent immediately and there was a great calm on the sea." Andrew also recounted many of his Master's other works to them. "Now, my children, don't be afraid, for our Lord will not desert us." Meanwhile blessed Andrew prayed to the Lord secretly in his heart for his disciples to be put to sleep so they would no longer fear the sea's waves. Andrew was heard immediately and his disciples were overcome by a heavy sleep.

9. Andrew turned towards Jesus and said, "There is something I want to say to you." And the Lord said, "Say what you wish." "Sir, please show me and teach me your technique of steering; for I have been watching you steer from the time I boarded till this very hour, and am full of admiration. I have been to sea and in a boat many times, but never once have I been able to watch anyone at sea steer a boat as I now watch you. For I tell you that it certainly seems to me as if we were crossing over dry land in this boat. So I beg you to teach me, a novice, your technique of steering, because I want to learn it very much." Jesus answered, "It is not as it seems to you. Steering like mine only seems skillful to you because we have sailed more often and been exposed to dangers at sea. But since you are a disciple of the Saviour called Christ, the sea knew you were a just man and a disciple of the Highest Power; therefore its waves could not overwhelm us." When Saint Andrew heard this, he cried out with a loud voice and blessed him, saying, "May the Lord bless you; and blessed be the Lord for joining me with a good man."

10. Then the Lord Jesus tested him and said, "I have heard your Master did all His miracles openly in the presence of His disciples. So I want to hear about His great miracles now from your own mouth, just as you saw Him doing them. Why do the faithless Jews say He is not God, but only a man. If He were only a man and not God, how could He do God's wonders and perform His great miracles? You who were with Him as His disciple, describe the miracles to me now, just as you saw them." Andrew replied, "Brother, it is true our Lord and Master told us openly He is God; and you must believe, brother, He is God and man, for He made man." Jesus said, "How is it, then, the Jews do not believe; perhaps He did not perform signs and wonders among them." Andrew retorted, "Haven't you ever heard how many wonders and miracles He performed in their sight? He made the blind see, the lame walk. He cleansed the lepers and cured the paralyzed. He turned water into wine. He took five loaves and two fishes and made the people sit down on the grass; He blessed the bread and broke it and satisfied more than five thousand men. Afterwards they collected twelve baskets of fragments, and the Jews saw everything but still did not believe in Him." Jesus said, "He wrought these signs only among the common people; their chief priests did not see them, so they rose up against Him."

11. Andrew replied, "Brother, He did even more in the presence of the chief priests and yet they did not believe in Him." Jesus said, "Tell me about the wonders He did among them." Andrew responded, "Sir, I see you have a great and wise spirit; how long are you going to test me?" Jesus said, "I am questioning you so my soul may rejoice and my spirit be exalted, and not only mine, but all those souls who have heard about His miracles." Then Andrew said, "Son, may the Lord fill your heart with every joy for persuading me so forcefully to tell you [*ut enarrarem*] the wondrous signs my Lord Jesus Christ did in their sight.

12. "The following event occurred when the twelve of us were walking with Him. We entered with Him into the Jews' temple where they openly showed us their idols. When the chief priests saw us following our Lord Jesus Christ, our Master and God, they cried out to us with one voice, 'You wretched men, why do you follow and walk with the man who says he is the son

of God? Who says God has a son? For who ever saw God talking with a woman? Isn't he the son of Joseph the carpenter? Isn't his mother Mary and isn't one of his brothers called Jacob, and the other Simon?' When we heard these words of unbelief, we did not reply to them; but our hearts held fast to the word of His truth. Then He took us up to a desert place and the unbelieving chief priests followed behind us to see if He would perform some miracle, for His name was now widely known. Before everyone He showed us His power, so we would all know He is God. There He performed great miracles, which no one could do except God alone. Unless He were God Himself, He could not have done any of them.

13. "Now we went into the Jews' temple with the Lord Jesus before us, and we behind Him; thirty chosen men and four chief priests followed us. Inside it had been made to look like heaven. The Lord showed us how to know if everything were true or not; He looked to the right and to the left and saw two marble sphinxes resembling cherubim, which the idols' priests worshipped and adored, one on the right, the other on the left. Jesus then turned round and said to us, 'Look and see, all this has been made with a workman's hands to look like heaven; likewise these sphinxes have been shaped like the cherubim and seraphim in heaven.' Then the Lord looked at the sphinx on the temple's right side and told me He was going to give it orders. He called out, 'Statue, which a workman's hands have formed, tear yourself away from the place where you stand and come down. For the Lord will give you a mouth to speak with, so you may verify and make known to these chief priests, who trust and worship you, whether I am God or man.'

14. "At once the sphinx came down from its place, and, having received a spirit from the Lord, spoke with a loud voice, 'Sons of fools, why are you so stupid that you won't be satisfied with the blindness of your own hearts, but also want to make others as blind as we are! You say this man, our Lord Jesus Christ, is only a man, not God. But this is the God who made heaven and earth, and who made man in His own image and likeness, and all the earth's foundations. This is He who spoke with Abraham; who loved Abraham's son, Isaac; who led Jacob back to his own land and appeared to him in the desert and did many good things for him. This is He who led [the Israelites

from Egypt] and gave them water which flowed from a rock. Therefore, this is He who has prepared [the Day of] Judgment and Rewards. But the Jews have not believed in Him. Now, do not presume that I am anything [divine]—for you made us from marble, and we are stones not gods—when you say, "we are offering to our gods." You also seduce many other people when you say we are gods. Our priests, the ministers of our temple, indeed purified themselves and [abstained] from women for seven days for fear of demons. Thus purified, they entered the demons' temples to see them perform a true miracle; they themselves thought the idols would say something true. But the priests are fornicators when they break the law: they enter the synagogue and sit down and read, but they do not understand or see the word of God's truth. For this reason I tell you your temples and synagogues will be hated, and churches will be erected in the Name of the only-begotten Son of God.'

15. "Now, in the sight of the priests and before all those who were present there, the Lord ordered the sphinx to go up and stand in the place it had occupied before. The sphinx went up at once and returned to its place. The chief priests of the law saw and knew all that had happened and yet they did not believe in Him. Indeed, He showed many miracles to them and to us who were there. Even if you wanted to hear about them, I do not know if you could put up with [my telling] them." When the Lord heard this, He said to Andrew, "A wise man is reluctant to talk. If he asks a fool a question, he is wasting his speech: it is as if he were throwing a stone down a well."

16. After the Lord had said this, He leaned on one of His angels and inclined His head, pretending to sleep. When blessed Andrew saw this, he started to do the same as Jesus, thinking Jesus was truly asleep; having inclined his head on his disciple, he was instantly overcome by a deep sleep in the same way. Then the Lord Jesus summoned His angels and said to them, "Take up this Andrew and his disciples. Carry them off in a cloud straight-away and set them down before the city gate of Mermedonia." And it was done as the Lord commanded them.

17. When blessed Andrew woke up, he looked all around thinking he was still at sea, but the sea had vanished. Then he saw his disciples lying on the ground fast asleep; casting his eyes about, he also saw the city gate of Mermedonia. He was very

surprised and hurriedly woke his disciples, saying, "Get up, my brothers and children, get up quickly and let us bless the Lord Jesus Christ. Get up. See the great miracles He has done for us; know now for certain that the pilot in whose boat we came here and to whom we talked was the Lord Jesus Christ. He possessed our eyes so we shouldn't recognize Him, and therefore we did not." Then his disciples replied, "Father Andrew, you knew we understood nothing when you spoke with Him in the boat, and that we were transported in a heavy sleep. Eagles descended at that time, took up our souls and led us into the heavenly paradise. There we saw great miracles: we saw the Lord Jesus Christ sitting on His throne of glory and all the angels round about Him singing hymns, with Abraham, Isaac, Jacob, and David accompanied by his lyre. The twelve apostles stood in a circle and the Lord's voice was heard, saying, 'Everything you ask of my Father will be given you.' But when you woke us up, then we returned to ourselves."

18. When blessed Andrew heard this, he rejoiced greatly and looked up to heaven at once and said, "Lord Jesus Christ, good Master, show yourself to me, for I now know you are not far from your servants. I beseech you, forgive me for thinking you were a man when I talked with you in the boat and for speaking to you accordingly. I ask you now, Lord, to forgive me, your servant, since I sinned in ignorance." After blessed Andrew had said this, the Lord immediately appeared to him in the likeness of a handsome young man and said, "Our Andrew, be glad." When Andrew recognized Him, he immediately threw himself prone on the ground and worshipped Him, saying, "Please, forgive me, Lord Father. Forgive me, Lord Jesus Christ, because I thought you a man. Spare someone who is ignorant; spare someone who didn't believe; spare your servant's soul. My lips sinned when my spirit did not recognize you; my tongue sinned when my eyes did not recognize you. Therefore I spoke to you as a man; I dealt with you in my simplicity as someone confronting a man. So I pray you to forgive me; I implore you to spare me; I beg you to pardon me. I am the servant, you the Lord. I am the disciple, you the Master. I am a man, you are God. I was created by you; you are the Creator. I am the one who listens; you are the one who commands." The Lord said, "Andrew, I shall no longer call you a servant, but a faithful friend; for I have

revealed to you everything I heard from my Father. I will pardon you completely, spare and forgive you completely, because you have acted faithfully, spoken faithfully and remained most faithful. I made you endure all those things on the sea because of what you told me when you said, 'Lord, I cannot go to the city of Mermedonia quickly.' I have shown you all this so the whole earth may know I am the Lord and that I do everything which is possible in heaven, earth, the sea and the ends of the world. Now, most faithful of men, get up quickly; get up with faith; get up like a man; take comfort and be strong. Go into the city. Go into the prison. Rescue my other servant, Matthew, and all those staying there with him. You are going to suffer many physical tortures and all for my Name's sake. Your hairs and your blood will be scattered through the city's squares and streets and you will be killed. But be faithful and strong. Don't be afraid of them, for they cannot kill your soul. Don't give in to them, nor do what they want. Remember me, for I suffered before you; remember the time they spat on my face, struck me with blows and assigned demons to throw me to Beelzebub, the prince of demons. For your sake I suffered many things; I have told you all about them so you should not be afraid to suffer for my Name's sake, as I suffered for you. Go and bring forth fruit and your fruit will last. When I endured everything for you and suffered at the hands of the wicked, do you think I was unable to ask my Father to call out the vast hosts of angels for me? But in that case how were the writings of the prophets to be fulfilled? I had to suffer like that to show you how to endure and so how to enter eternal life with the martyr's palm, offering your fruit to God. For through the great triumph of your glorious preaching you will capture many men from this city in your net, and they will believe in me." Having said this, the Lord returned to heaven.

19. Andrew was greatly comforted by the Lord's words. With his disciples he entered the city, passing through the middle of the people, whose eyes were possessed so they could not see him. When he came to the prison where blessed Matthew was, he looked up to heaven and prayed; stretching his right hand towards the prison, he made the sign of the Holy Cross. Immediately all the prison guards died and fell down; the prison doors opened for them and its iron melted. All the chains of

those who had been bound melted as well. Then blessed Andrew entered the prison. Casting his eyes about, he saw blessed Matthew in the middle of the prison, sitting quietly by himself in the silence. But when blessed Matthew saw him, he got up at once and they kissed each other. Andrew said to him, "What's this I see, brother? You have only three days left before you must be taken out to be slaughtered and eaten." Matthew replied, "My brother, didn't you hear the Lord when He said, 'I send you now like sheep in the midst of wolves.' When I entered this prison, I prayed to our Lord Jesus Christ to have mercy on me. He appeared to me and said, 'Stay here twenty-seven days and I will send your brother Andrew to help you. In this way I will rescue you and all those in torment with you.' And now it has happened. Please, brother, tell me what we should do."

20. Then Andrew cast his eyes about and saw that all the men in the prison were chained and standing naked, eating hay like oxen or other animals. Then blessed Andrew struck his breast and said secretly in his heart, "Woe to me a sinner. What sort of evil crimes has this wicked human race inflicted on these men! When the Lord created man, He fashioned him in His own likeness; but now the devil has made them like beasts of burden." Andrew turned and began to rebuke Satan, saying, "Satan, woe to you; how many wars have you waged against the human race, vicious evil one, enemy of God and His angels? What harm have these unhappy pilgrims done to you that you inflict them with such crimes, wickednesses and evils? Unhappy one, how long will you fight against humanity? Until you are exalted over them? It was you in your rottenness who tricked Adam, the first man, so he was thrown out from the delights of paradise; you saw to it that the loaves on his table would be turned to stones. Furthermore, you entered the hearts of God's sons [the angels] and made them lie with [mortal] women; and their sons were made into giants on earth. In anger the Lord brought a flood upon them and destroyed all their sins and then saved Noah. Now you have entered this city and through your wicked encouragement you have made men eat others like themselves and drink their blood; as a result they are cursed and damned. Do you think God will destroy His image? Evil one, didn't you hear the Lord when He said, 'I will not send another flood upon the earth?' For each crime you commit against

mankind now, a similar torment is reserved for you on Judgment Day."

21. Blessed Andrew rose immediately with blessed Matthew. After they had prayed, they laid their hands on the eyes and hearts of the men who had been blinded; at once their eyes were opened and their senses returned to them and they gave thanks to God. Then Saint Andrew said to them, "Get up. Don't be frightened any longer now. Go into the lower parts of the city and when you find a figtree on the way, sit down under it. Eat as much fruit as you wish until I come to you. If by chance I get delayed, simply remain there; for you will find a lot of fruit on the tree. So that you won't be in any need at all, the more you eat, the more the tree will bear fruit. The mouth of the Lord has commanded this." But they said to him, "We won't go anywhere unless you go with us, lest we be seized again by evil men." Andrew replied, "Go, set out safely; you no longer have reason to be afraid. Not even the dogs will bark at you." Then, together with Andrew's disciples and blessed Matthew, they all departed as the blessed apostle Andrew had bid them. The number of prisoners was about two hundred forty-eight, not including forty-nine women. Through the power of our Lord Jesus Christ, blessed Andrew commanded the clouds of heaven: they lifted up his disciples along with the blessed apostle Matthew and deposited them on a mountain. The blessed apostle Peter was there and they stayed with him.

22. Andrew began to walk around the city. He came to a spot in the city and, raising his eyes, saw a tall statue standing on a marble column. There he waited for something to happen to him. Now the murderers went to the prison so they could bring out a man to carry off for their food. But after they found the gate open and seven guards dead, they dashed off quickly to their leaders. They said, "Masters, we found the prison open, and when we went in, we found no one there except the prison guards, dead." When the city's leaders heard this, they puzzled among themselves and said, "What does the news of this occurrence mean? Such things have never happened or been heard of in this city till now. Perhaps the time has come for this world to change. Indeed, it has come, for now we have no food left. What should we do, since we have nothing to eat and no food left? Go quickly and prepare something for us to eat from

the seven guards, because the blood-storage tank is empty." The murderers departed and brought the seven dead guards and put them on the tank's rim. They took up their swords to slit them. Suddenly the Lord's voice came to Andrew, saying, "Don't you see the evil they are doing?" Andrew said, "Lord, now I see." And he turned back to the Lord and said, "O my Lord Jesus Christ, who created me in my mother's womb and made me come forth into the light, I beseech you through your mercy (you who made me enter this city), don't let them do such things here; instead, may the sword fall from their hands and their hands become like stones." Immediately the sword fell and their hands withered. When the leaders saw this, they wailed aloud, "Woe to us, for there are magicians in this city. They have gone to the prison, freed all the prisoners and killed the guards. Now they have struck the executioners' hands. What else shall we do? We shall all starve, for we have no food left."

23. After they had gathered together all two hundred and seven of the city's old men, they led them into council, to decide by lot which of them to use as food and whose blood to drink. They cast the lot and it fell on seven old men. When they led out to slaughter one of the old men on whom the lot had fallen, he said to the executioners, "I beg you, don't kill me. I will give you my son to kill in my place." They replied, "Unless we check with the leaders, we dare not do anything." When they consulted the leaders, they said, "Go, take his son and put him on a scale. If he is heavier than his father, take him and kill him for us. But if he is lighter, don't take him." This was done, and the young man was found to be lighter. Then the old man said, "I have a daughter. If you are willing, I will give her to you. Kill her, but let me go." He handed his children over to the assembled executioners and they let him go unharmed. But when they led the children to the place to kill them, the infants began to cry bitterly. They wallowed in supplication at the executioners' feet and implored them, "We beg you, we beseech you, pity our youth! Don't kill us, for we are only children. Spare us for a little while, so we can grow bigger, and then kill us." But the executioners did not give in to the children. With outstretched hands they seized a sword to kill them. Now blessed Andrew turned and saw all they were doing. He looked up to heaven and said, "Lord Jesus, just as you heard me the first time and did not let them eat the dead guards, so

now hear me quickly. Don't let these children be killed, but stay the executioners' swords. May they melt in their hands." And it happened accordingly. When the executioners saw this, they were very afraid. But Andrew was overjoyed and praised the Lord.

24. However, when the leaders saw that the swords had melted, they were greatly shaken with tears and said, "Now we are dead men." Straightway the devil appeared to them in the likeness of an old man. He said, "Woe to us, for now we shall perish since we haven't found food. What shall we do? We don't have sheep or oxen that can supply us. But, if you are willing, listen to me. Inquire diligently. One of the pilgrims here is called Andrew. Take him and kill him. If you don't kill him, he will never let you do what you want with the men we have in prison. He is spreading the word about all our deeds. He is the one who dispersed our prisoners in all directions, through the districts and towns. So let's find this stranger and eat him; he has emptied our temples and homes with the result that no one offers up sacrifices." In the meantime, they did not bury any of the men who departed this world, but ate them all.

25-26. With the devil urging them on, they all rose up against blessed Andrew to kill him. Having looked for him, they found him.

27. When they turned towards him, they saw the sign of the Holy Cross on his forehead and they fell back. But Satan, mankind's most wicked [foe], said softly to them, "My children, why didn't you kill our enemy?" They said, "Because we saw the Cross fixed on his forehead. Therefore we were scared and fell back and did not go near him." Then the devil said to them, "Why were you afraid? So many of you went out against one man." They answered, "Go yourself, you who urge us so strongly, and kill him if you can." The devil replied, "I can't prevail against him without you. But listen and mark my words. If we can't manage to kill him, seize him and lock him up. Let's mock him with torments and great tribulation." They seized Andrew and threw him into prison. Together with the wicked devil they began to mock him and say, "Andrew, why did you come here to be mocked by us? If we afflict you with all these horrible torments, who can rescue you from our hands?" When Andrew heard this, he gave them no reply. He only turned his

face to heaven, wept in his heart and prayed to the Lord. But the devil transformed himself, and, pretending to be a voice come from heaven, said to him, "Why do you weep, Andrew?" Andrew replied, "I wept when I recalled the words of my Lord Jesus Christ, who commanded us to endure all the evils inflicted on us." The devil said, "Andrew, listen to me: do only what seems useful to you. Take counsel lest you suffer greater torments in vain." Andrew replied, "Even if you kill me now, I'll not do your will, but the will of my Father and Lord who is in heaven, Jesus Christ. However, at the time it pleases my Lord to visit this city, I will impose on you the sort of punishment He demands." When the devil heard this, he and his minions departed from Andrew.

28. Another day the city's leaders sent to the prison. They led blessed Andrew out from the prison, put ropes around his neck and dragged him through the city's streets and squares. His flesh, blood and hair were scattered through the streets and he was brought to the point of death. Blessed Andrew then recognized that everything the Lord had told him earlier he would suffer was now fulfilled; he cried out with a loud voice to the Lord and weeping said, "O Lord Jesus Christ, this is enough torment for me. As you told me to suffer all things, so I did. My spirit weakens; you know what my enemy and his minions have inflicted on me. My good Lord and Master, remember when you cried out on the Cross to your Father, 'My God, my God, why have you forsaken me?' I am your servant. For three days they have dragged me through all this city's streets and squares. My hairs have been pulled out and scattered through the streets; my flesh has been stripped and my blood scattered through the squares. Everything you commanded has been fulfilled. Nothing remains but that you receive my spirit, if it is your will; for I am worn out and my soul fails. You know that mankind is frail. Lord, where are the sayings and the sweet words you used to comfort us with, when you said, 'If you hear me and follow me, the smallest hair on your head will not perish.' But Lord, now I suffer all these unbearable torments. Why haven't you at least shown yourself to me to comfort my heart so it shouldn't fail?" When blessed Andrew had thus prayed in his heart, he heard the Lord's voice saying to him in Hebrew, "Andrew, I tell you truly, heaven and earth will pass away before my word has no power. Look back now and see what has become of your flesh

and hair. When blessed Andrew looked back, his flesh and hair appeared to be trees, flowering and bearing fruit. Seeing this, Andrew gave glory to God and said, "Lord, I know now you are not far from your servants." When evening came, the leaders, seeing he was now failing, took him back into the prison and said, "Since his flesh and hair have now been destroyed, perhaps he will die in the night."

29. A blinding light appeared to blessed Andrew in the prison and out of the light the Lord stretched forth his hand and lifted up Andrew sound and whole. Blessed Andrew immediately fell down and adored him, saying, "My Lord Jesus Christ, I thank you." Then he saw a tall marble column with a marble statue standing on it. He made the sign of the Holy Cross in front of it and said, "Through the power of our Lord Jesus Christ, before whom heaven and earth tremble, I command you to pour a flood of water through your mouth to fill this whole city to the very top." The statue immediately poured forth vast torrents like a raging flood through its mouth and the water came up to the very top. (The water was salt so it would eat men's flesh, just as the men themselves had done before.) Because of the water many people and beasts of burden were killed.

30. At once everybody began to take flight in all directions. But Saint Andrew raised his eyes to heaven and said, "Lord Jesus Christ, I undertook to perform this first miracle on the city through your power. Hear me, send your angel directly with clouds of fire and encircle the city so no man nor beast can escape." Immediately the angel of the Lord came down with clouds of fire and surrounded the city. When blessed Andrew saw this, he gave thanks to God and blessed God for hearing him quickly. They all cried out convulsively and said with great weeping, "Woe to us for all these things which have come upon us. This flood has occurred because of the pilgrim we imprisoned and all the evils we inflicted on him unjustly. Look, we will perish in these flood waters; and we are surrounded by fire from heaven. Whether we want to or not, let us believe in him, in the words he has preached to us, in all his doctrine and also in his God, whom he invokes daily. Perhaps God will change His mind about us and remove this evil so we won't perish." They all ran in haste to Andrew in prison, crying out, "Holy man of God,

Christ's apostle, free us through His power." They threw themselves down, prostrated themselves on the very earth at his feet and begged him. When Saint Andrew realized they all believed in the Lord Jesus, he gave praise to God and said, "Statue, forbear; leave off and close your mouth. In the Name of the Lord, I order you not to pour water through your mouth any more." As the apostle left the prison, the water immediately receded before him. All the people cried out with one voice, "Apostle of our Lord Jesus Christ, have mercy on us, have mercy on us and do not exact retribution from us for the evils we have done you."

31. Then the old man who had given over his children to be killed in his place came to Andrew, saying, "Have mercy on me." Blessed Andrew replied, "Why do you, an old man, ask for mercy for yourself, when you had no mercy on your children, but handed them over in their innocence to take your place. I tell you therefore: when the water has returned to the abyss, you will die, together with the other fourteen executioners who slaughtered men every day, and you will remain in hell until Judgment Day. So go now to the abyss where you will die, to your place of execution, along with those who did not spare their children." Saint Andrew turned to the people and said, "Come and follow after me." They went after him and the water opened up to the right and left before Saint Andrew, until he came to the mound where they used to kill men and where the blood ran down. Then blessed Andrew looked up to heaven and prayed before all the people. Forthwith the earth opened its maw and swallowed the water along with the executioners and the old man who had handed over his children; and they departed into the abyss. When everyone there with him saw what happened, they were very afraid. They said among themselves, "Woe to us in our misery. For all this has been done to us by God. If Andrew wants to, he will destroy us and exact a terrible retribution from us for the things we inflicted on him. For, as we saw, everything he said to the old man and the executioners occurred. Now the fire from heaven will burn us, if he tells it to. This just man really is from God and he is God's worshipper. Everything he said has certainly come to pass." And inwardly they began to be very afraid. But when Saint Andrew realized all this, he comforted them, saying, "My children, don't be afraid, for everything that

has been done was for your sake, so you would know the true God, who is in heaven, the Lord Jesus Christ, who has power in heaven and on earth, in the sea and the abyss."

32. Then blessed Andrew commanded them, "Bring before me the men who died in the water." They could not carry them in, since a great many people had died, including women, infants and beasts of burden. Immediately Saint Andrew prayed, "Lord Jesus Christ, send your Holy Spirit from heaven and raise up all the souls which died in this flood, man and beast, so everyone may believe in your Holy Name." When this was said, all the dead rose at once and the people all believed in the Lord Jesus Christ. After this was over, blessed Andrew built a makeshift church in that same place and gave them the precepts of Christian law, baptizing them in the Name of the Father and the Son and the Holy Spirit. He ordained one of their princes bishop over them and blessed them: "Thrive and remain in the holy ministry as I have delivered it to you. Guard the mystery of my Lord Jesus Christ as I have given it to you, for His power is great. I have to go on a journey. I am going to return to my disciples and to Him who sent me." Then all those who believed began to ask, "Lord Father Andrew, stay with us and don't desert us now until you have confirmed us in the whole faith of the Lord"; and they wept bitterly, beseeching him. He replied, "Allow me to go now. When I have seen my disciples, I will quickly return to you." He set off and they wept even more bitterly.

33. As he was going along, the Lord suddenly appeared to him and said, "Andrew, why are you walking off like this? You have let great work slip fruitlessly away from you. Why didn't you listen to the men you taught? Why didn't you listen to them when they wept and besought you? You must realize you didn't hear them when they begged; but when they wept I heard them, for their cry reached up to me. So I command you to return to them at once and stay with them seven days until you establish and plant in them the whole Christian faith. When these seven days [with them] are complete, go back to the city to raise up all the men who departed from that city into hell." Having said this, the Lord went away into heaven. Andrew turned back towards Mermedonia, blessing the Lord: "I thank you, my Lord Jesus Christ, you who want all souls to be saved and to come to know

the truth." When the people saw him return, they met him with exultation and rejoiced with great gladness, giving thanks to the Lord, who had heard them when they wept and cried aloud to Him. Blessed Andrew stayed with them seven days, proclaiming and teaching them the Lord Jesus Christ's words of salvation. He confirmed them in the whole catholic faith as he had been ordered by the Lord Jesus Christ. After the seven days had passed, he set out and departed. But all the people of Mermedonia, from the greatest to the least, went with him for a short way out of great joy. Then they returned to their own city, blessing and praising the Lord, saying, "There is one God. The blessed Andrew, His apostle, has shown Him to us. He is our Lord Jesus Christ, to whom be honor and glory, world without end, Amen."

III

THE FATES OF THE APOSTLES

Despite Cynewulf's assertion that he gathered the material for this poem "far and wide" (line 1) "from holy books" (line 63b), scholars have searched diligently for a single source which would contain the same information about the apostles in precisely the same order as the poem. Such a catalogue has not come to light, though similar martyrologies describing the apostolic missions and deaths had wide circulation from the fifth century on (see George Philip Krapp, ed., *Andreas and The Fates of the Apostles* [Boston, 1906], p. xxx).

Kenneth R. Brooks suggests that the sequence in the poem "is closest to that of Jerome's *Notitia de Locis Apostolorum*" (*Andreas and The Fates of the Apostles* [Oxford, 1961], p. xxx). But the *Notitia* forms part of the introductory material to the *Martyrologium Hieronymianum* and neither should be considered authentically Jerome's, even though the manuscripts are early (see *CPL*, 2031). Cynewulf's poem also corresponds in certain respects to the Pseudo-Isidore, *De Vita et Obitu utriusque Testamenti Sanctorum;* but, as Lipsius asserts, this is itself dependent, for the most part, on the *Breviarium Apostolorum* (Richard Adelbert Lipsius, *Die Apokryphen Apostelgeschichten und Apostellegenden* [Braunschweig, 1883], I, 213).

Krapp believes that "all the details in the poem . . . may be derived, with one exception, from the martyrology of Bede and from the *Breviarium Apostolorum*" (p. xxx). The one exception is

Thomas' miraculous revival of Gad, an event recorded in the apocryphal *Acts of Thomas* (see M. R. James, *The Apocryphal New Testament* [Oxford, 1953], pp. 373-4). Whether or not we should continue to regard Bede's *Martyrology* as a legitimate analogue to *The Fates of the Apostles* is problematic. Krapp wrote before the publication of H. Quentin's *Les martyrologes historiques du moyen âge* (Paris, 1908), pp. 17-119, which traced the various layers and accretions that had become part of Bede's work. Bede himself does not mention the apostles. More than fifty years have passed since George L. Hamilton reminded Anglo-Saxon scholars that "The passages cited by Professor Krapp and his predecessors as from the *Martyrologium* of Bede, are taken from an enlarged text of the *Martyrologium* of Usuardus, whose work, written about 875, is an abridgment of Ado's developed text of the *Martyrologium* of Florus of Lyons, itself an expansion of Bede's original work" (*MLN*, 35 [1920], 387). If we accept the usual dating of Cynewulf's poems as early ninth century, then we must accept the probability that Cynewulf could not have used Bede's *Martyrology*.

With the *Breviarium Apostolorum* we are on safer ground. This work exists in a MS that was once part of the Gelasian Sacramentary; most scholars assign the MS to the early eighth century, and the text undoubtedly derives from ancient liturgical practices (see *Liber Sacramentorum Romanae Aeclesiae ordinis anni circuli*, ed. Leo Cunibert Mohlberg, in conjunction with Leo Eizenhöfer and Petrus Siffrin [Rome, 1960], p. xxxv). We have followed Lipsius' authority for the emendations and location of place names in the *Breviarium*.

Kenneth Sisam tentatively suggests that the order of the apostles may be derived from some Litany of the Saints ("Cynewulf and His Poetry," *PBA*, 18 [1932], 327); and Daniel G. Calder recently argues that these litanies left a marked impression on the poem ("*The Fates of the Apostles*, the Latin Martyrologies, and the Litany of the Saints," *MÆ*, 44 [1975], 219-24). An example of a litany, from the Stowe Missal, may be found in Edmund Bishop, *Liturgica Historica: Papers on the Liturgy and Religious Life of the Western Church* (1918; rpt. Oxford, 1962), p. 139; see also *PL*, 72.626-30 and 101.522-4, 591-6.

A. *Concerning Places Associated with the Apostles*

Text: Hippolytus Delehaye, Paulus Peeters and Mauritius Coens, eds., *Acta Sanctorum, Novembris, Tom. II, Pars Posterior* (Brussels, 1931), p. 2.

29 June. The feast of the holy apostles Peter and Paul in Rome.

30 November. The feast of the holy apostle Andrew in the city of Patras in the province of Achaia.

27 December. The feast of the holy apostles James, the Lord's brother, and John the Evangelist.

24 June. The feast of the death of Saint John, apostle and evangelist, in Ephesus.

21 December. The feast of Saint Thomas the apostle in India, and the translation of his body to Edessa.

25 July. The feast of the apostle Saint James, brother of John the Evangelist, in Jerusalem.

1 May. The feast of Saint Philip the apostle in the city of Hierapolis in the province of Asia.

24 August. The feast of Saint Bartholomew the apostle, who was beheaded in India by command of King Astyages [= Astrages].

21 September. The feast of Saint Matthew the apostle, who suffered in the province of Persis.

28 October. The feast of the apostles Simon Cannaneus and Simon the Zealot, who were killed by temple priests in the Persian city of Suanis[?].

B. *The Breviary of the Apostles*

Text: *Liber Sacramentorum Romanae Aeclesiae ordinis anni circuli*, ed., Leo Cunibert Mohlberg, in conjunction with Leo Eizenhöfer and Petrus Siffrin (Rome, 1960), pp. 260-1.

Simon, which in Hebrew means "the obedient," surnamed Peter, was the son of John and the brother of Andrew; he is said to have been born in the village of Bethsaida in the province of Galilee. Because of Simon Magus, although it was God's hidden will, Peter came to Rome. He preached the Gospel there and was pontiff of the city for twenty-five years. But in the thirty-sixth year after our Lord's Passion, under the Emperor Nero, he was crucified, as he himself wished. His feast is celebrated on the 29th of June.

Paul, which means "the devout," was born in the tribe of Benjamin and was the apostle to the Gentiles. He was baptized in the second year after the Lord's Ascension, and was beheaded under Nero on the same day as Peter and buried in Rome.

Andrew, which means "manly or handsome," was Peter's brother. He preached in Scythia and Achaia and was crucified and died in the city of Patras on the 30th of November.

James, which means "the supplanter," was the son of Zebedee and brother of John. He preached in Spain and the west and was executed by the sword under Herod. He was buried in Achaia Marmarica on the 24th of November.

John, which means "the grace of God," was an apostle and an evangelist, the son of Zebedee, the brother of James and the Lord's beloved. He preached in Asia and was buried in Ephesus on the 27th of December; but another of his feasts is the 24th of June, when the feast of Saint John the Baptist is also celebrated.

Thomas, which means "the abyss," was called Didymus [the twin], that is "similar to Christ." He preached to the Parthians and Medes; he then left for the eastern shore and preached the Gospel there. He died in the east, pierced by a lance, in the Indian city of Kalyan [*Caliminica*] and was buried with honor on the 21st of December.

Philip, which means "the mouth of the lamp," was born in the town of Bethsaida where Peter was also born. He preached Christ to the Gauls. Then he was crucified and stoned in the province of Phrygia, where he rests with his daughters. His feast is celebrated on the 1st of May.

James was the Lord's brother and the first bishop of Jerusalem. While he was preaching Christ, the Son of God, in Jerusalem, he was hurled down from the temple by the Jews, stoned to death and buried there near the temple. His feastday and ordination are the 27th of December.

The apostle Bartholomew, whose name derives from the

Syriac and means "the son of him who holds up the waters," preached in Liconia. Eventually he was flayed alive by barbarians in Albanopolis [*Albano*], a city in Armenia Major, and beheaded at King Astrages' command. He was buried there on the 25th of August.

Matthew, apostle and evangelist, whose name means "he who has been given," also received his surname from the tribe of Levi. Christ chose him while he was living as a publican, and he first preached in Judea and afterwards in Macedonia. He suffered in Persis and rests in the Parthian Mountains [*Pastorum*]. The 21st of September.

Simon the Zealot, which means "the zealous," was first called Cananeus ("blazing with God's zeal"). He shares his name, Simon, with Peter and is likewise honored. He received the lordship of Egypt and is said to have been the next bishop of Jerusalem, following James the Just. After a hundred and twenty years he was found worthy to receive a martyr's passion and was crucified under Hadrian. He lies in the Bosphorus [*Porforo*]. His feast is celebrated on the 28th of October.

Jude, which means "the confessor," was the brother of James. He preached in Mesopotamia and the interior regions of Pontus. He was buried in Beirut [*Merito*], a city in Armenia. His feast is celebrated on the 28th of October.

Matthias was one of the seventy disciples and he became the substitute for Judas Iscariot among the twelve apostles. He was chosen by lot and is alone in not having a surname. He was assigned to preach the Gospel in Judea.

IV

SOUL AND BODY I and *II*

Various scholars have suggested various provenances for the Soul and Body legend. Th. Batiouchkof traces it back to the early Eastern church ("Le Débat de l'âme et du corps," *Romania*, 20 [1891], 1-55; 513-78); and Louise Dudley discusses the importance of the Christian Coptics and their knowledge of the Egyptian *Books of the Dead (The Egyptian Elements in the Legend of the Body and the Soul*, Bryn Mawr College Monographs, No. 8 [Baltimore, 1911]). But in the Latin West, as Eleanor K. Heningham emphasizes, "the Body and Soul legend was made familiar . . . primarily as an *exemplum* in the *memento-mori* sermons" (*An Early Latin Debate of the Body and Soul* [New York, 1939], p. 52). In a later article she writes that most of the debates "go back at least as far as the homilies . . . of Ephraem Syrus who died shortly before 375 A. D.; many of them seem to have been spread in the West by Latin homilies like Batiouchkof's [Nonantola version] and the pseudo-Augustinian collection, *Sermones ad Fratres in Eremo*" ("The Precursors of the Worcester Fragments," *PMLA*, 55 [1940], 299n).

Despite the late date of the surviving MS, scholars feel certain that the Nonantola version is early (see Louise Dudley, "An Early Homily on the 'Body and Soul' Theme," *JEGP*, 8 [1909], 225-6). Of the sermons selected by Heningham as pertinent—*Sermons 49, 58* and *69*—only *69* does not definitely precede the Old English poems (see J. P. Bonnes, "Un des plus grands prédicateurs du XIIe siècle: Geoffroy du Loroux, dit Geoffroy

Babion," *RB*, 56 [1946], 174-9). Because of the uncertainty in dating *Sermon 69*, and also because it duplicates the Nonantola homily in many respects, we have excluded it. *Sermon 68* is also of interest and is included under Entry XIII.

These texts should be read as analogues for both the Old English poems on the Day of Judgment (see Entries IX and XXI) and for the Elegies (see Entry XIII).

A. Nonantola Version

Text: Th. Batiouchkof, ed., "MS Bibl. nat., no. 2096 (52)," *Romania*, 20 (1891), 576-8.

Dearest brothers, since the description of divine miracles instructs us in humility and goodness, let us hear what Macaris, who exercised the care of souls in Alexandria, told some people in a conversation. He is said to have heard the story from a brother monk who had been in a state of ecstasy. There was a very rich man who abounded in crimes as much as he overflowed in riches. When he saw his life's end approaching, he was at last terrified that he had committed such crimes. After his soul had pushed its way to the mouth of the wretched body, it was greatly stricken with grief and did not dare leave. In front it saw a ready crowd of menacing demons who said, "What's this? Why are we waiting? Perhaps the angel Michael is coming with a host of angels to overwhelm us and snatch away the soul which we've kept bound in our chains for many years." Then one of the wicked crowd of demons added, "Don't be scared; the soul is ours. I know its works. I stayed with it always night and day." Then the poor soul began to say in anguish, "Alas for me, alas for me, why did I ever deserve to enter that gloomy, wicked body! (Woe to you, wretched soul, why did you carry off the money and belongings of others and the goods of paupers and accumulate them in your own home! You drank wine then and over-adorned your body with the most glorious and beautiful clothes.) Flesh, you were fat and I was thin; you were vigorous and I was wan; you were merry and I was sad; you laughed and I always wept. Now you will be food for worms and dust's decay. You will rest for a little while, but you have led me with weeping to hell." Then the body began to change color and the face to sweat . . . towards the body's mouth. Then the guards who were there said, "Seize that soul and stab its eyes, because it lusted after whatever it saw, whether right or wrong. Stab its mouth, for it never held back from what it wanted to eat, or drink or say. Stab its heart; neither piety, mercy, charity nor goodness ever got up that far. Stab its hands and feet, for they were in a hurry to do evil." Then the demons dragged the wretched soul from the body while it groaned and grieved, and they lifted it onto their black wings. While the soul was on the journey [to hell], it saw a great brightness and said, "Where is that brightness?" The demons replied, "Don't you recognize the home you left when you started on this pilgrimage? When you were here, you didn't renounce us and our vanities through baptism and the sign of Christ. You heard the prophets, you heard the apostles, you heard the priests, but you never stopped doing evil things. Christ was never mentioned on your lips at all, for your heart was far from Him. Now you are passing near your very own [*privatam*] home; but you will not stop there, nor will you have joy in the good things there present. Now you listen to the angelic choirs; now you hear the bright [song] of the saints, but you don't live there, just as we who were thrown out of paradise into perdition don't live there either. From now to eternity you will be with us. To this point you have been on a pilgrimage; now you will be in perdition where you will remain in the company of many wicked men." Then with grief and groaning, with weeping and tears, the poor soul began to say, "Alas for me in my misery, why was I ever born; why did I go to Egypt and abandon the brightness from which I sprang immaculate? I see now the broad way one reads about in the Gospel and which leads to the valley of perdition." The devil was ready there in the likeness of a dragon. When he had opened his close-set jaws, he swallowed the soul and vomited it up into the hottest fire where it would await the future Judgment with others like itself.

After the monk had awakened, he was weighed down again by sleep. Having been led into a monastery of brothers, he saw a sick monk whom nobody cared for—a pauper wrapped in the oldest tatters, thin and pale. He was neither an extremely young nor old man; he was very patient. Then the brother [who was dreaming] heard angels' voices approaching and surrounding the sick monk. Then the soul, which belonged to the Lord, came to the mouth [of the sick monk's] body, and said, "Behold, now we are going to be parted; behold, now we are going to leave the world; behold, now our Lord and Father is going to raise us up from this state of great poverty. Patiently you waited for this hour when affliction and hunger, thirst and cold would end. When you were hungry and thirsty, I was full of food and happiness. When you were lean and pale, I was merry and glad. I give thanks to my Lord now that through you I escaped the fiercest torments. Now you will rest for a little while in the dust and I in peace, until we rise together again in glory." Then the body began to change color: it had been the color of ashes before; now it began to be ruddy, for its face was merry. One of the brothers came and announced to the others, "The pauper has died." A few of the monks came back there, but they didn't wash or clothe him since he stank. Then the soul went off and met Michael the angel who touched it because it had harmed no one. The angels raised the soul on their splendid wings and Michael and the soul softly chanted a spiritual song together. While the soul was being carried along like this by the angels, it saw a great bright light from afar and said, "What is that light?" Then the angels responded, "Recognize your own sweet homeland; you left it immaculate and immaculate you are indeed going to return. Now you listen to the angels' song; now you see the glory of the saints; now you perceive the reward, the sweetness of your [good deeds]." Then with joy and gladness the soul said, "How has it come to pass that I now enter so great a brightness, so sweet a joy, so rich a homeland?" The angels replied, "It is because of your goodness and gentleness; because you kept on doing all that was good; because you never complained in your poverty; because you did not disparage your brother; because you did not indulge in drunkenness, lust or commit murder or any other crime; because you ate your bread and water joyfully; because, in praying to the Lord, you did not shed tears only for yourself, but for everyone; because you restrained your tongue from evil; because you didn't do to another what you didn't want for yourself; and because you not only feared hell, but yearned for Christ the Lord with exceeding love." Then the angels led the joyful soul into the place of consolation [*refrigerii*] where many are at peace, and the kind angel Michael, who was bringing the soul, remained there where he had come from.

The monk awoke and related all he had seen and heard to the brothers. May we also deserve to attain that peace through the offering [*praestante*] of our Lord Jesus Christ, who lives and reigns, world without end.

B. Pseudo-Augustine, *Sermon 49*

Text: *PL*, 40.1332-4.

The Misery of the Flesh and the Falsity of the Present Life.

O life, you deceive so many men; you have seduced them so much from what is proper; you have blinded so many! When you flee, you are nothing; when you appear, you are a shadow; when you rise, you are smoke. You are sweet to the stupid, but bitter to the wise. He who loves you, does not know you; those who despise you, they understand you. You should be feared and shunned. Woe to those who believe in you; blessed are those who despise you. You are not the true life you pretend to be. You seem long to some in order to destroy them in the end; short to others to prevent them from repenting when they wish to; broad to others so they can do what they want; narrow to others so they cannot do good. Therefore, wise man, flee what flees. Our life is like a man in someone else's house: he does not know the hour or day when the head of the house may say, "Get out, for the house you are in is not yours." Vain world, why do you promise us so much while you deceive us? He who wants to be your friend will be considered God's enemy; friendship for this world is enmity towards God. The flesh is what destroys the soul; the flesh is what receives the enemy and his vices. Again, it is the flesh which engenders murders, fornication, concupiscence, strife, lust, theft, idolatry, avarice, pride and fraternal discord, envy and blasphemy against God. It is the flesh which provokes schisms, incites heresies and introduces divisions in God's church, erects barriers between Christians, creates wars between nations and makes kinsmen curse one another. What is worse, it introduces all kinds of conflicting thoughts into the hearts of God's servants and everything which is evil in this fallen, wicked and abominable world. And just as the flesh arose, so in all haste it passes away. The devil has power over the flesh, but not over the soul, as the Lord said to the devil about blessed Job, "I surrender him, but not his soul, into your power" (Job 2.6). The miserable flesh weighs the soul down; in its inconstancy it plunges the soul into hell. The flesh is the soul's enemy; if it were not the enemy, it would certainly not delight in this world's vanity, nor enjoy life's emptiness. Most hideous life, you which the humors swell, pains torment, the airs infect, foods pass through, fasts make lean, jests dissolve, sorrows consume, care constrains, carelessness dulls, riches make arrogant, poverty humiliates, youth raises up, age bows down, disease crushes, grief consumes—besides all this, you succumb to hideous death in its fury. O flesh, weighed down with deformity, you should have embraced the life which remains steadfast in eternity. There life is without death, youth without age, light without darkness, joy without sorrow, goodness and desire without harm. There is a kingdom which never changes. These are the seven things you ought to have attained; miserable flesh, why did you reject them while you lived? If you had persevered in doing good and had done it well, you would not have been deprived of good at all; for you would have remained where there is eternal joy and unfading glory; where there is imperishable and unequalled gladness and Christ is the delight of the apostles, prophets and all the saints; where there is the greatest pleasure with the angels singing God's praises and all good things are enjoyed. You have scorned all these delightful goods because of this world's depravities. But behold, after death, even though you have been made over into clay of the earth, you will have enemies—corruption, foulness and the worm. You will endure stinking decay, so that the living may take you as an example—what you were and what you are and that you are eaten by worms. But at the very end of the world when your soul, your life, returns to the body where you were before, you will be handed over to eternal punishments and damned along with the soul.

Miserable soul, persecuted by the flesh! What the flesh wants, the body does. But when it is sated with the richest foods, drinks and pleasures, the flesh urges the body on to all manner of evil. The flesh provokes murders, the flesh commits adulteries, the flesh joins in quarrels and scandals, the flesh induces drunkenness, the flesh is entirely in love with this world. Miserable flesh, what have you got, what are you doing? Why do you weigh the soul down so heavily, when it only wants to serve God? O miserable flesh, isn't your own perdition enough for you without still attempting to drag the unhappy soul down with you? Alas, soul, you have taken on your enemy, the flesh. Wicked flesh, what are you looking for, what do you want? On Judgment Day the soul cannot be judged without you as well. Miserable, decaying flesh, full of all the filthiness of sin, when you were alive, you were beautiful like the sun and bright like the moon; your eyes shone like stars and your hair was long; you anointed yourself with precious ointments; you wore the best clothes and you seasoned your food and drink with an array of spices. But, when you refreshed and pampered the shadowy, disgusting body, understand soul, that you were preparing food for worms. You should have remembered what you heard from your Maker and Creator when you first committed sin, "You are earth, and to earth you will return" (Gen. 3.19). Listen also to Job, "Naked I came from my mother's womb and naked I shall return there" (Job 1.21). Also listen to Isaiah when he prophesied, "Man is as grass" (Isa. 40.6). Miserable and abominable flesh, listen to the famous preacher, Paul the apostle, "We brought nothing into this world and we cannot take anything out of it" (I Tim. 6.7). The miserable flesh carries nothing with itself but a load of sins. The soul does not sin, except through the flesh: let the soul see, insofar as it can. Our soul suffers in prison; the flesh holds it shut up. The soul, not the flesh which persists in its wickedness, cries to the Lord. There is no other recourse for the soul unless it rises up from the flesh and the flesh is reduced to dust; unless wine is taken from it and it is given water; unless its blood is removed and it receives the earth's moisture. Miserable flesh, what will happen to you when I leave you and life departs? You will lie alone in the womb, in the bosom of the earth, and never be delivered to anything else. You will have the worst legacy inside you—corruption, decay and worms. Look at all the things you acquired when you were alive, and look at what you will possess when you lie in the grave. Couldn't you make yourself lean by fasting, and, besides fasting, humble yourself in ashes and a hairshirt? You would have been saved forever with the soul if you had believed it and understood that you cannot do good unless you do good to others.

Unless you mortify the body with abstinence, you cannot save the soul. Listen to what our Creator says to the flesh, "My creature, I took you up beautiful and bright from the clay of the earth; I created you in my image; I gave you the breath of life; I granted you an invisible soul; I clothed you in the tunic of immortality; I put you in the paradise of pleasure. You enjoyed the life of the angels; you contemplated the foods and the delights of gladness. Everything I created I put under your control and I gave you overflowing riches. Moreover, all the trees of paradise were subject to you, and, except for one I had prohibited, you could eat whatever was there. Look from where you have fallen—from paradise into hell, from light into darkness, from the place of pleasantness and gladness into chaos and all the darkest evils. Now you are given over to decay and rottenness, instead of delightful sweetness. Instead of eating the food of angels, you will be food for worms; instead of the attire of immortality, you are wrapped in a garment of corruption. Behold, I have taken the life I gave you and carried it away." Thus, miserable, decaying flesh, you are consigned to hell, where there is weeping, wailing, lamentation, the gnashing of teeth and terrible torments. What is worse, after death you will be reduced to corruption, and after the worms, the decay and wasting away, you will then be reduced to dust. Flesh, you who will be surrendered to the inextinguishable fire, listen to the soul when it says to the body, "I came from heaven as God's gift to you, for you come from the earth. It is better if you ascend to heaven with me than drag me down to hell. While we live and are together, let us set our hands to doing good—to giving alms and to pure fasting, to providing charity for the needy and clothing for the poor and to doing all good works—so we can ascend to heaven through the good work we do. There we shall no longer be clothed in the body's dissolution, but in the garment of incorruption. There is no more decay there, but the sweetest fragrance; no more darkness, but the shining of perpetual light; no more legions of worms, but bands of angels; and countless thousands of saints and the choir of all the prophets, together with the holy angels, who sing a hymn to God unceasingly." May Christ grant us to possess eternal joys with them; who with the Father and the Holy Spirit lives and reigns forever and ever. Amen.

C. Pseudo-Augustine, *Sermon 58*

Text: *PL*, 40.1341-2.

The world's glory is nothing.

Dearest brothers, the text from the apostle [Paul] reads as follows, "Time is short; therefore those who have wives should be as if they did not have them . . . and those who use the world should be as if they did not use it; for the fashion of this world passes away" (I Cor. 7.29, 31). The day of the Lord will come like a thief. Therefore, soul, whatever you hear or read, may holy Daniel's advice come to your aid, "Take my advice and redeem your sins with almsgiving" (Dan. 4.24). If you neglect this advice, you knock at heaven in vain. Soul, you who live within the fragile walls of the flesh, keep watch and knock, seek and ask. "When you knock and seek, it will be opened to you," the Lord says. "If you pass through fire, I am with you and the flame will not burn you." When you seek something in prayer, you will find it; when you knock and ask, Christ will open the doors for you so you can enter as the owner of paradise. Brother, if you still think you will have anything left at the world's end, consider your own end. It is written, "Naked I came from my mother's womb and naked I will go under the earth" (Job 1.21). You brought nothing with you, brother, when you entered the world, and you will take nothing with you when you leave. All you people who do not know, listen; you who are negligent at any time, learn. Go to the tombs of the dead and see paradigms for the living. The bones are lying there, but the man himself has perished. Nevertheless, his trial is reserved for the Judgment Day. At one time he was a man like us, a man living in vanity, studying the ways of the world. He increased his estates with his wealth; he planted vineyards; he filled the bins in his many granaries and rejoiced in his abundance. And suddenly, behold, all this was snatched away from his eyes. He used to congratulate himself on his many schemes; he dressed himself in silken garments; he provided himself with pomps and luxuries; he indulged in rich banquets; on drunken occasions he danced and joked; he prolonged his lunch to dinner, and scarcely saw an end to his happiness. And behold, all this was snatched away from his eyes. Where did it all go—the pomps, the schemes, the exquisite banquets? Where are they now—the throngs that pressed around him in a frenzy, the men who praised him at home and abroad? Where are the ornaments of his [various] homes and the precious luxuries of his clothes? Where is the display of his gems and the immense weight of his silver? And where, finally, is that desire which does exactly what it wants every day? Doesn't it know about the time when it must lose everything? Where are the wisdom and the profound explanations [he gave] in public? Where are the laudatory applause and the constant adulation of friends? Where are the subject flocks of servants and the radiant lights of lamps? Where is the crowd of clients who walked before him? All this has passed from his eyes and no one will remember him anymore. He lies in his grave, reduced to dust. His flesh, which was nourished by delicacies, has dissolved; the nerves have fallen away from his joints. The bones alone remain and serve as examples for the living so they can recognize the relics of the dead. Presumably, the dead man's body is at rest, but his soul lives in hell, and it will no longer see the light. For many shadows encircle him; trembling and affliction seize him; worms and fire consume him; and his eyes never cease crying. Since he is wracked by terrible pains, his teeth gnash repeatedly; his soul never stops being punished. Now he repents that he lived so badly in this world, that he was negligent and did not love piety and mercy. He will look for mercy now and he will not find it. He repents that he possessed and kept great riches and did not give them away to the poor; he repents that he lost the time for repentance and did not amend his daily life so he would not meet with such punishments. Thus the great resurrection waits for him so it can hand him over to a punishment even worse. For then the angels will harass him and reproach him because he did not love to give alms. Therefore, mercy is denied him. Burning Gehenna waits for him because, when he was alive, he did not extinguish [the burning pangs] of the poor. Everlasting worms will consume the belly of the man who did not feed the hungry pauper. O what a value the Lord sets on the mercy one shows in this world's life; the person who delights in showing mercy here will find it remembered at the Last Judgment. For it is written in the Gospel, "Blessed are the merciful, for they shall obtain mercy" (Matt. 5.7). Hurry, while you have life's light, so that death's darkness does not take hold of you. Be merciful in this world, for merciful deeds cancel your sins and come to your aid on Judgment Day. What you eat, you lose, and what you strive for, you leave behind; but what you give away to the poor, you will have forever. On the Day of Judgment your mercy goes before you. This mercy will intercede for you in the Lord's sight, so that you, who have been merciful, may obtain mercy when you stand before our Lord Jesus Christ, to whom is honor and glory, world without end. Amen.

V

THE DREAM OF THE ROOD

The cult of the Cross, long an established part of Christian worship, received renewed emphasis in England as a result of Pope Marinus' gift of a fragment of the True Cross to King Alfred in 885 (see C. L. Wrenn, *A Study of Old English Literature* [New York, 1967], p. 137). Whether the composition of *The Dream of the Rood* was connected with this revival remains unresolved, but the poem does stand curiously detached from the many devotional expressions accompanying the Cross from the fourth century on (see Michael Swanton, ed., *The Dream of the Rood* [Manchester, 1970], pp. 42-52). No other text in any language, the runic "quotations" from the poem on the Ruthwell and Brussels Crosses excepted, resembles it. Rosemary Woolf writes, "It is almost certain that this uniqueness of conception is the Anglo-Saxon poet's own, and that he did not have before him a source which he followed closely" ("Doctrinal Influences on *The Dream of the Rood*," *MÆ*, 27 [1958], 137). Nevertheless, there are a few intriguing comparative items.

For the idea of a tree speaking Margaret Schlauch returns to classical models and cites the Ovidian *De Nuce* as a possible analogue, though she admits it is "not in any sense a source," merely an item that might clarify the relationship between the Old English poem and pagan literary modes ("The *Dream of the Rood* as Prosopopoeia," in *Essays and Studies in Honor of Carleton Brown*, ed. P. W. Long [New York, 1940], p. 34). But there is no need to go to Ovid. Woolf (p. 149) and P. L. Henry (*The Early*

English and Celtic Lyric [London, 1966], p. 236) have each identified examples in Christian literature of the Cross itself speaking, though Woolf's Pseudo-Augustinian sermon would seem to be a far closer analogue than Henry's brief sentences excerpted from the apocryphal *Gospel of Peter*. The Latin sermon is of early date (see *PLS*, 2.881) and belongs to the Roman tradition; the *Gospel of Peter* exists only in Greek fragments not discovered until 1886, and there is no evidence that its peculiar account of the Crucifixion was ever known in the West (see James Hastings, ed., *A Dictionary of the Bible* [New York, 1923], Extra Volume, p. 428; and Wilhelm Schneemelcher, ed., *New Testament Apocrypha*, trans. R. McL. Wilson [Philadelphia, 1963], I, 179).

For its retelling of the Crucifixion the poem follows Matthew 27, though additional possibilities may have influenced the poet. H. R. Patch stresses the importance of hymns, in particular the famous *Vexilla regis* and *Pange lingua* by Venantius Fortunatus, who was a sixth-century bishop of Poitiers; and in passing Patch also mentions an antiphon of the *Magnificat* for the Feast of the Invention of the Cross, *O Crux, splendidior cunctis astris* ("Liturgical Influence on *The Dream of the Rood*," *PMLA*, 34 [1919], 233-57 and especially 245n). F. E. C. Dietrich first suggested the poem might have some relation to the riddles; he later received support from G. Sarrazin (Dietrich, *Disputatio de Cruce Ruthwellensi* [Marburg, 1865], p. 11; Sarrazin, *Von Kädmon bis Kynewulf* [Berlin, 1913], pp. 128 ff.). We have included two Latin Cross riddles written by two Englishmen, Hwætberht (Eusebius) and Tatwine, in the first half of the eighth century. Finally, we have chosen selections from the apocryphal *Passion of Saint Andrew the Apostle* and from Ambrose's *Exposition of the Gospel according to Luke* that both show the heroic aspects of the Crucifixion as it appears in early Christian literature (see F. J. Cassidy and Richard Ringler, eds., *Bright's Old English Grammar and Reader*, 3rd ed. [New York, 1971], pp. 309-17; and John Fleming, "*The Dream of the Rood* and Anglo-Saxon Monasticism," *Traditio*, 32 [1966], 53). For the legend of the Invention of the Cross, see Entry VI.

A. Pseudo-Augustine, *Sermon IV*

Text: *PL,* 47.1155-6.

Then Jesus came to the tree from which death's laws had sprung. When He ascended this citadel of sin, He brought down the keystone of the enemy's power. The tree, which had formerly been the mother and source of torments, unknowingly received the Just Man. It pierces and afflicts Him. He is not guilty and yet His punishment is savage. O [Satan], cruelest of murderers, you have lost the props of your cause. The Cross itself cries out against you; the very instrument of death and pain rejects you. "I do not recognize that the man I punish is a criminal," the Cross says. "These apples are not of my seed; this man is not mine. You are deceived, for you graft alien fruit onto me. He derives nothing from me. Why does He hang upon me? I see only the image of my apples' shape, for I do not recognize my native poison in Him." Then the Man—strong in battle, righteous on the gibbet and innocent in the hostile torment—crushed the horns of sin with His spotless hands. When He fastens Himself completely to the wood, He blunts death's sting and kills the sin which a tree created. Then the blood, pouring from His side, washed away whatever sin had earlier stained; shining from its sullied mesh of branches, the Cross beamed forth radiantly. The innocent blood ran through the wood's fibers, once the instrument of punishment and suffering. With this medicinal blood the fibers in turn prepare the sacraments of salvation, where previously they had provided death's food for those about to live.

B.1. Venantius Fortunatus, *The King's Banners*

Text: *MGH, Auctores Antiquissimi,*
4, 1 (Berlin, 1881), 34-5.

The King's banners go forward. Blazing is the mystery of the Cross: there the Creator of the flesh was hanged in the flesh on a gibbet.

His body was pierced with nails, His hands and feet extending; for our redemption's sake, the Victim was sacrificed here.

Here He was wounded too by the dread spear's point; to wash away our sin, He dripped with water and blood.

What David prophesied in a song of faith is now fulfilled; He said to the nations, "God reigned from a tree."

Beautiful, resplendent tree, decked with royal purple, you were chosen to carry such holy limbs on your worthy trunk.

Blessed [tree], from your arms hanged the world's Ransom; you were His body's scales; you carried off the booty of Tartarus.

From your bark you give off spice; in taste you surpass nectar. You are delightful with abundant fruit; you clap your hands in noble triumph.

Hail altar, hail sacrificial Victim from the glory of that Passion, where life submitted to death and through death was reborn.

B.2. Venantius Fortunatus, *Sing, Tongue*

Text: *MGH, Auctores Antiquissimi,* 4, 1 (Berlin, 1881), 27-8.

Sing, tongue, the course of the glorious battle; tell of the noble triumph on the trophy of the Cross, how the world's Redeemer was victorious after His sacrifice.

The Maker, grieving over the deception of our first-created parent when he tumbled into death at the bite of a fatal apple, then chose a tree Himself to redeem the injuries caused by a tree.

The order of our salvation required this miracle, so He might artfully outwit the art of the ever-crafty deceiver, and produce a cure from the very tree the enemy had used to inflict pain.

Therefore, when the fullness of the sacred time had come, the Son, the world's Creator, was sent from His Father's citadel, and incarnated in a Virgin's womb and born.

The infant cries, hidden in a little manger. The Virgin Mother binds His limbs and wraps them in swaddling clothes; a snug band adorns His feet and hands and legs.

After He had lived thirty years and fulfilled His body's time, the Lamb surrenders voluntarily to His Passion and is raised on the trunk of the Cross to be sacrificed; He had been born for this reason.

Vinegar is here, gall, a reed, spitting, nails and the spear. His soft body is pierced; blood and water issue from it—the earth, sea, stars and the world are washed by this river.

Faithful Cross, among all trees the only noble tree, no forest produces a tree like you in flower, leaf or seed: sweet wood sustaining a sweet weight with a sweet nail.

Bend your boughs, tall tree, loosen your tense muscles; let your native hardness become pliant, so you can stretch the limbs of heaven's King on a soft trunk.

Only you were worthy to carry the world's Ransom; to bring, like a sailor, the shipwrecked world to the port which sacred blood anointed when it poured from the Lamb's body.

C. Antiphon of the *Magnificat* for the Feast of the Invention of the Cross (First Vespers)

Text: Stephen Willoughby Lawley, ed., *Breviarium ad usum insignis ecclesie Eboracensis,* Surtees Society, No. 75 (Edinburgh, 1882), p. 275.

O Cross, more radiant than all the stars, celebrated throughout the world, worthy of great love from men, holier than all. You alone were worthy to carry the wealth of the world, sweet wood, sweet nails, bearing a sweet weight. Save this present company gathered today in your praise.

D.1. Eusebius (Hwaetberht), Riddle 17

Text: *CC,* 133, 1.277.

Cross

Men acquire death and grasp the good life through me. Many flee me and many others worship me often. Bad men ought to fear me, but I am not terrible to good men. [One] man I condemned and so I released many from prison.

D.2. Tatwine, Riddle 9

Text: *CC,* 133, 1.176.

Christ's Cross

Now I appear iridescent; my form is shining now. Once, because of the law, I was a spectral terror to all slaves; but now the whole earth joyfully worships and adorns me. Whoever enjoys my fruit will immediately be well, for I was given the power to bring health to the unhealthy. Thus a wise man chooses to keep me on his forehead.

E. *The Passion of Saint Andrew the Apostle*

Text: Maximilian Bonnet, ed., *Acta Apostolorum Apocrypha,* II, 1 (Leipzig, 1898), 23-31.

10. Then in his rage Aegeas ordered Andrew to be fixed to a cross. He told the executioners to stretch him by his bound feet and hands as if he were on the rack; in this way he would not die quickly—as he would if he were pierced with nails—but rather be tortured by a long execution. When the executioners led him out, a crowd of people gathered, crying out and saying, "What has this just man, this friend of God, done that he should be led to the cross?" But Andrew asked the people not to hinder his passion, for he went with joy and exultation, steadfast in [Christ's] teaching. When he arrived at the place where they had prepared the cross, he saw it a long way off and cried out with a loud voice, "Hail, Cross! You were consecrated by Christ's body and adorned with the pearls of His limbs. Before the Lord ascended you, you caused earthly fear; but now that you have acquired divine love, you are received as a gift. For believers know how many joys you have within you, and how many rewards you have ready. So I come to you safe and rejoicing that you may joyfully receive me, a disciple of Him who hanged upon you. I have always been your lover and always yearned to embrace you. O good Cross, you received glory and beauty from the Lord's limbs; you have been desired for a long time, loved anxiously, sought without ceasing, and now you are at last

prepared for a soul that covets you. Take me from men and return me to my Master, so that He who redeemed me through you may receive me through you." Having said this, Andrew stripped himself and handed his clothes over to the executioners, who set upon him and lifted him onto the cross. When they had stretched out his whole body with ropes, they hanged him as ordered.

[11-12. The people demand that Andrew be taken down from the cross.]

13. Then Aegeas became afraid of the people and promised he would set off at once to get Andrew down. When Saint Andrew saw him, he said, "Why have you come to me, Aegeas? If you will believe in Christ, the way of forgiveness will be opened to you, as I promised. But if you have only come here to set me free, [know that] I can never be taken down from this cross while my body is alive. For I see my King now; I adore Him now; I stand now in His sight, where there are choirs of angels, and where He alone reigns as Emperor; where there is light without darkness, and flowers never wither, and grief is never known, nor the name of sadness heard; where happiness and exultation have no end. O blessed Cross, without your love no one reaches that land, no one enters it."

F. Ambrose, *An Exposition of the Gospel according to Luke*

Text: *CC,* 14.376-7.

108. [Christ] was about to ascend the Cross and nobly laid aside His royal clothes, so you may know He suffered as a man, not as God the King. Although Christ was both, yet He was fixed to the Cross as a man, not as God. But [Roman] soldiers, not the Jews, know the occasion when Christ should have royal clothes. He stands like a victor at the trial; He comes humbly, like a man condemned, to His Passion.

109. Now because we have already seen the monument of victory, the Conqueror may ascend His triumphal car. He may hang the booty seized from His mortal enemy, not on tree-trunks or four-horsed chariots: he may hang these spoils captured from

the world on the triumphal gibbet. Here we do not see people with arms tied behind their backs, nor images of devastated cities, nor models of captured towns; we do not marvel at the submissive necks of captured kings—such are the usual forms of human triumphs—nor do we have outlines of the boundaries of conquered countries. Instead we see the peoples of the nations rejoicing—chosen not for punishment, but reward; kings worshipping with unfettered love; cities surrendered voluntarily out of good will; and models of towns reconstructed for the better, models which have not been painted with garish hues, but colored by faith's devotion. We see the might and laws of Christ's victories coursing through the whole world; the prince of the world captive; his wicked demons in the sky obedient to the command of the human voice; tyrants subdued and various powers shining in morality rather than silk. Chastity glows and faith is radiant; devotion which was clothed in the garments of death rises again in the garments of strength. The Cross of the Lord, God's one triumph, has now made nearly all men triumph.

110. It is important to consider how He ascends. I see Him naked. So must He who is prepared to conquer the world ascend, for He cannot seek the world's help. Adam who looked for clothes was conquered; He who laid aside His clothes conquered. The Christ who ascends is like us, formed by God the Creator and nature. Just as the first man lived in paradise, so the Second Man entered paradise. He extends His hands to conquer for all, not only for Himself, so He might draw all things to Himself. Having stripped those men who formerly belonged to the earth from death's knot and made them hang on the Cross of faith, He might thus unite them with the heavenly ones.

VI

ELENE

Syria provided fertile ground for the creation of the legends surrounding the Invention of the Cross; however, it was not long before Greek and Latin imitations became the means of their propagation in the western world. A large number of Latin texts containing the various narrative details still survive and, for a number of reasons, Cynewulf's source was undoubtedly based on the stem of that tradition (see P. O. E. Gradon, ed., *Cynewulf's "Elene"* [London, 1958], pp. 15-8). As F. Holthausen remarks, the source of *Elene* must have closely resembled three Latin versions (*Cynewulfs Elene*, 4th ed. [Heidelberg, 1936], p. xii): 1. *Acta Quiriaci* in the *Acta Sanctorum*; 2. *Inventio Sanctae Crucis*, ed. Alfred Holder [Leipzig, 1889], pp. 1-13; and 3. the legend in the *Sanctuarium seu Vitae Sanctorum*, ed. B. Mombritius [Paris, 1910], I, 376-9). Though John Gardner has recently argued that Cynewulf did not depend on a single text but "manipulated diverse sources for an original purpose" ("Cynewulf's *Elene*: Sources and Structure," *Neophil*, 54 [1970], 65), scholars usually hold that the *Elene* is most similar to the *Acta Quiriaci*.

The originality of the "autobiographical" epilogues to Cynewulf's poems has often been overstated. Gradon uncovered a precedent, at least for the "combination of an epilogue with a narrative" (p. 21), in the ending to the *Vita Sanctae Mariae Meretricis* (*PL*, 73.659-60). This work forms a part of the *Vita Sancti Abrahae*, itself an item in the immensely popular *Vitae Patrum*. Dom André Wilmart has demonstrated, however, that the Migne text improperly separates the lives of Mary and Abraham and also contains many post-medieval additions ("Les Rédactions Latines de la Vie d'Abraham Ermite," *RB*, 50 [1938], 222-45). Contemporary scholarship no longer attributes the *Vita Sanctae Abrahae* to Ephraem Syrus, but assigns it to the sixth century (see Marcel Viller, SJ, F. Cavallera and J. de Guibert, SJ, in *Dictionnaire de Spiritualité Ascétique et Mystique, Doctrine et Histoire*, 4, 1 [Paris, 1960], 803, 818). Wilmart prints a text which includes the life of Mary from a lectionary, "copied in the Roman style of the eleventh century" (p. 234); he believes, nonetheless, that this text goes back to the end of the antique period (p. 235). The selection printed below would thus serve as an analogue for all Cynewulf's poems (see Entries III, VIII, and XII).

A. *The Acts of Saint Cyriacus*

Text: Godefridus Henschenius and
Daniel Papebrochius, eds.,
Acta Sanctorum, Maius, Tom. I (Antwerp, 1680), 445-8.

After the Lord's Cross was revealed to Saint Helena, Saint Cyriacus is said to have replaced Saint Macarius on his death in Jerusalem, and been ordained by the Pope Saint Eusebius.

1. In the two hundred and thirty-third year after the Passion of our Lord Jesus Christ, in the sixth year of the reign of Constantine (a great man and reverent worshipper of God), a large barbarian host gathered beyond the Danube, prepared to wage war against the Roman Empire. When this was announced to King Constantine, he too mustered a great army and set out against the enemy. He found they had laid claim to and had occupied parts of Roman territory on the Danube. Seeing their countless numbers, he was sad and mortally afraid. During the night a man surrounded by radiance came and woke him and said, "Constantine, do not be frightened, but look up to heaven and see." When he cast his eyes towards heaven, he saw the sign of Christ's Cross fashioned out of pure light; over it was written

in letters the title: *Conquer through this.* Having beheld the sign, King Constantine made a replica of the Cross he had seen in the heavens; and marching off, he attacked the barbarians with the sign of the Cross before him. He and his army came upon the barbarians, and directly it was dawn, he began to massacre them. The barbarians were terrified and fled along the banks of the Danube; not a few of them died. On that day God gave victory to King Constantine through the power of the Holy Cross.

2. When King Constantine returned to his city, he called together all the priests of every god and idol and asked them to whom this sign of the Cross belonged or what it meant. They could not tell him. But certain of them replied, "This is the sign of the God of heaven." When the few Christians who were present at the time heard this, they came to the king and preached the mystery of the Trinity and the Advent of God's Son—how He was born, crucified and rose again on the third day. King Constantine sent to Eusebius, the bishop of the city of Rome, and ordered him to come to him. Eusebius instructed Constantine in the Christian faith and all its rites. He baptized him in the Name of our Lord Jesus Christ, and confirmed him in Christ's faith. Constantine ordered churches to be built everywhere, but the idols' temples to be destroyed. Blessed Constantine, perfect in his faith and fervent with the Holy Spirit, studied Christ's Holy Gospels. When he learned from them where the Lord had been crucified, he sent Helena, his mother, to seek the holy wood of the Lord's Cross and to build a church in the same place. The grace of the Holy Spirit reposed in the Emperor Constantine's most blessed mother, Helena. She studied all the Scriptures, had exceeding love for our Lord Jesus Christ and afterwards sought for the life-giving wood of the Holy Cross. When she had read attentively about the coming of our [Lord] Jesus Christ, the Saviour of mankind, His Crucifixion on the Cross, and Resurrection from the dead, she lost no time till she found the wood of Christ's victory, upon which the Lord's holy body had been nailed. This is how she found it.

3. On the twenty-eighth day of the second month, Helena entered the holy city of Jerusalem with a mighty army and gathered there a large assembly of the wicked Jewish race. She ordered not only those present in the city to be assembled, but also those from the surrounding area [who lived] in castles,

estates and towns. However, Jerusalem was deserted at the time, so scarcely three thousand Jews in all could be found. Helena proceeded into Jerusalem and diligently asked the natives about the place where the holy body of our Lord and Saviour, Jesus Christ, had hung, fixed to the Cross. It was difficult to find for this reason. Long ago during the reign of the Emperor Hadrian, a persecutor of Christians, a statue of Venus had been erected in that place, so that any Christian who wished to worship Christ there would appear to be worshipping Venus. Consequently, the place had been nearly forgotten. But when someone remembered the temple, which had been entirely demolished, and also the idol, the faithful queen discovered ancient ruins under the mounds of rubbish. Using a crowd of soldiers and peasants, she had the whole place emptied of everything brought there by the envious Jews since the time of the Lord's Passion.

4. After this she gathered a great assembly of the wicked Jewish race, and, summoning them, blessed Helena said, "I have learned from the prophets' holy books that you were God's chosen ones. Rejecting all wisdom, however, you cursed Him who wanted to redeem you from the curse; you wronged Him who with His spit brought light to your eyes, spitting filthily instead on Him; you betrayed into death the man who brought life to your dead; you assumed the light was darkness and the truth a lie; accordingly, the curse which is written in your law has come upon you. Now from among yourselves choose men who know your law well, so they can answer the questions I shall ask them." When they had departed full of fear and had argued much among themselves, they found a thousand doctors of the law whom they led to Helena. They vouched that [these doctors] had great knowledge of the law. Helena said to them, "Listen to my words; give an ear to my speech. For neither you nor your fathers have understood how the prophets' sayings foretold Christ's coming. It was prophesied before, 'A child will be born and his mother will not know man.' And Isaiah told you, 'I have begotten and raised children, but they have spurned me. The ox knew his owner and the ass his master's stable, but Israel did not know me nor my people understand me' (Isaiah 1.3). All Scripture has spoken about Him. You, who knew the law, have erred. Now from among yourselves choose those who have earnestly acquired a knowledge of the law, so they may reply to

my questions." And she ordered the soldiers to guard them with great care.

5. When the council had assembled, they chose from among themselves fifty of the best doctors of the law, who came and stood before Helena. She said, "Who are these men?" They said to her, "They are the men who know the law best." She said to them again, "According to the Scriptures, you are the sons of Israel; yet how stupid you are! You have followed your fathers' blindness in saying that Jesus is not God's Son; you have read the law and the prophets and not understood them." But they said, "We have read the Scriptures and we do understand them. Lady, explain why you are saying this to us, so we too may know and reply to what you ask." Once more she said to them, "Go away again and choose better doctors of the law." As they departed, they said among themselves, "Why do you think the queen puts us to this trouble?" One of them called Judas said, "I know. She wants to question us about the wood on which our fathers hanged Christ. Therefore, see that no one confesses to her. For truly our ancestral traditions will be destroyed and the law reduced to nothing. Zachaeus, my grandfather, warned my father, and my father, as he was dying, informed me.

6. "He said, 'Son, when someone asks about the wood on which our fathers hanged Christ, tell them about it before you are tortured. For then the Hebrew race will reign no more; but they who worship the Crucified [Christ] will reign, and He will reign forever and ever.' I said to him, 'Father, if our ancestors knew that this man was the Christ, why did they lay their hands on Him?' He said, 'Listen to me, son, and know [by] His ineffable Name that I never gave them advice or agreed with them, but I contradicted them many times. Yet because [Christ] challenged our elders and high priests, they condemned Him to be crucified—thinking to bring death to Him who is deathless. They took Him down from the Cross and buried Him. But the third day after He was buried, He rose again and showed Himself to His disciples. For these reasons, Stephen, your brother, believed [in Him] and began to teach in His Name. When the Pharisees and Saducees had assembled in council, they condemned Stephen to be stoned, and the multitude took him away and stoned him. As he was giving up his soul, blessed Stephen spread his hands towards heaven and prayed, "Lord,

do not hold this sin against them." Listen, son, and I will teach you about Christ and His mercy. Paul, who sat in front of the temple carrying out his job as a scribe, had persecuted those who believed in Christ. He incited the people against your [*tuum*] brother, Stephen; and the Lord, taking pity on Stephen, made him one of His saints. On this account my parents and I believed in Him, that He is truly the Son of God. Now, son, neither blaspheme Him nor those who believe in Him, and you will have eternal life.'

7. "Simon, my father, bore me witness of these things. Lo, you have heard all. If she questions us about the wood of the Cross, what do you wish to do?" The others said, "We have never heard such things as you have told us today. So if there is an inquiry about this, make sure you reveal nothing. Since you tell us this, you obviously know the place." After they had said this, lo, soldiers came to them and said, "Come, the queen calls you." When they arrived, they were interrogated by her; but they did not wish to answer her questions truthfully. Then blessed Helena ordered them all to be cast into the fire. Because they were afraid, they delivered Judas to her and said, "Here is the son of a just man and a prophet; he knows the law and its statutes. Lady, he will carefully show you all your heart desires." After everyone had vouched for him, she dismissed them and kept only Judas. Then she called him and said, "Life and death are set before you. Choose which you want: life or death." Judas said, "When someone in solitary confinement has loaves set before him, will he eat stones?" Blessed Helena said, "If you want to live in heaven and on earth, tell me where the wood of the precious Cross is hidden."

8. Judas said, "How can I attest to something which happened two hundred years ago, more or less? Since we are much younger [than that], how can we know this?" Blessed Helena said, "History records that many generations ago there was a war in Ilium and in the Troad and [yet] all who died there are now remembered; history also records their localities and monuments." Judas said, "True, lady, but it is because those happenings were written down. However, we do not have these events preserved in writing." Blessed Helena said, "Why did you yourself acknowledge a little while ago that something happened?" Judas said, "I spoke in doubt." Blessed Helena said, "I

have the blessed voice of the Gospels [to tell me] where the Lord was crucified. Just show me the place called Calvary and I will have it purified. Perhaps I shall find there my [heart's] desire." Judas said, "I do not know the place since I was not there at the time." Blessed Helena said, "By Him who was crucified, I will kill you with hunger, unless you tell me the truth." When she had said this, she ordered him to be cast into a dry pit, and guarded by jailors for seven days. After seven days had elapsed, Judas cried out from the pit, "I implore you, take me out and I will show you Christ's Cross."

9. When Judas had come out of the pit, he hurried to the place, not knowing for certain where Christ's Cross lay buried. Speaking in Hebrew, he raised his voice to the Lord and said, "God, God, you who made heaven and earth; you who measured heaven with the palm of your hand and earth with your fist; you who sit upon the chariot of the Cherubim—Cherubim fly through the courses of the air in endless light where human nature cannot go, and you made them for your ministry. (There are six creatures with six wings: four of these flying beings are called Cherubim and are your ministrants; they cry with unceasing voice, 'Holy, Holy, Holy.' Two of them you have put in paradise to guard the Tree of Life, and they are called Seraphim.)—you have dominion over all things, for we are of your making. You cast the unbelieving angels into deep Tartarus and they dwell in the bottom of the abyss, tortured by the dragon's stench, unable to contradict your command. Now, Lord, if it is your will that Mary's Son, who was sent by you, shall reign—unless He came from you, He would not have performed such great miracles; unless He was your Son, you would not have raised Him from the dead—give us a sign, Lord. Just as you listened to your servant, Moses, and showed him the bones of our father, Joseph, so now, if it is your will, show us the hidden treasure. Make a smoke full of the fragrant sweetness of spices rise from the place, and I also will believe that Christ Crucified is the King of Israel, both now and forever."

10. When Judas had prayed thus, immediately the place was in turmoil and a smoke dense with the sweet aroma of spices rose so that Judas clapped both his hands in wonder and said, "In truth, Christ, you are the world's Saviour. Thank you, Lord. Although I am unworthy, you have not deprived me of the gift

of your grace. I beseech you, Lord Jesus Christ, remember me and wipe away my sins; number me with my brother, Stephen, who has been written about in the Acts of your twelve apostles." After he had said this, he took a spade, girded himself manfully and began to dig. When he had dug twenty paces, he found three hidden crosses which he lifted out and carried into the city. Blessed Helena asked which was Christ's Cross—for we know that the other two were the thieves' crosses who were crucified with Him. They laid them down in the middle of the city and waited for the glory of Christ. Around the ninth hour a dead boy was carried in on a litter. Full of joy, Judas said, "Lady, now you will recognize the beloved Tree and its power." Judas took hold of the litter and ordered the dead man to be set down. He put the crosses on him one by one and he did not rise. But when he had put the third, the Lord's Cross, on him, the young man, who was dead, rose at once. All those present glorified the Lord.

11. However, the devil, always envious of everything good, shouted furiously into the air, "Who is this who once again will not allow me to receive my own souls? Jesus, Nazarene, you have drawn all men to you; lo, you have uncovered your Cross in order to harm me. Judas, why did you do this? Wasn't it through a Judas that I first effected [Jesus'] betrayal and incited the people to act wickedly? Lo, now it is through a Judas that I am cast out of here. I will see what I can do against you. I will raise up another king who will forsake [Christ] Crucified and follow my counsels; he will inflict grievous torments on you. When you have been tortured, you will deny [Christ] Crucified." But Judas, crying aloud with the Holy Spirit, said, "May Christ who raised the dead damn you to the abyss of everlasting fire." Hearing this, blessed Helena marvelled at Judas' faith. And when she had placed the precious Cross among gold and precious stones with great care, she made a silver coffer and put Christ's Cross in it. She also built a church on Calvary. Judas received the baptism of incorruptibility in Christ Jesus; for his previous actions attested to his faith. Helena commended him to the bishop who was still in Jerusalem at the time, and he baptized him in Christ. While blessed Helena lingered in Jerusalem, it happened that the blessed bishop fell asleep in Christ. Blessed Helena summoned Eusebius, Bishop of the city of Rome, and he consecrated Judas

Bishop of Christ's church in Jerusalem. Judas changed his name and was called Cyriacus.

12. Blessed Helena was filled with God's faith and understood the Scriptures, both the Old and New Testaments. Instructed and filled by the Holy Spirit, she began again to inquire zealously for the nails which had been fixed in the Cross and with which the wicked Jews had crucified the Saviour. When she had summoned Judas, surnamed Cyriacus, she said to him, "My wish concerning the Cross has been granted, but I am very sad about the nails which were fixed in it. I shall not rest in this matter until the Lord grants my desire. Come here and pray to the Lord about it." Holy Bishop Cyriacus came to Calvary with the many brothers who believed in Jesus Christ because of the discovery of the Holy Cross and the miracle wrought upon the dead man. Raising his eyes to heaven and striking his breast with his hands at the same time, he cried to the Lord with his whole heart, and, confessing his former ignorance, blessed all those who believed in Christ or who would believe in the future. For a long time he prayed that some sign be shown him and that God would do for the nails what He had done for the Cross. When he said "Amen" at the end of his prayer, such a sign did occur, which we all saw who were present. A great radiance shone from the place where the Holy Cross had been found, brighter than the sun's light. And at once appeared the nails which had been fixed in the Lord's body, blazing like gold in the earth. As a result, everyone believed without any doubt and said, "Now we know in whom we believe." With great fear Cyriacus received the nails and took them to blessed Helena, who knelt down, bowed her head and worshipped them.

14. Full of wisdom and much knowledge, Helena wondered what to do with the nails. When she had been able to examine in herself every way to the truth, the grace of the Holy Spirit inspired her to do something which would remind future generations of what the prophets had foretold many ages before. She summoned a man, faithful and learned, whom many people vouched for, and said to him, "Keep the king's commands; carry out the royal pledge. Take these nails and make them into bits for the bridle of what will be the king's horse. They will be invincible arms against all his adversaries. Victory and peace from war will be the king's, so that the words

of the prophet may be fulfilled, 'On that day what is in the horse's bridle will be called sacred to the Lord'" (Zac. 14.20). After blessed Helena had encouraged all those in Jerusalem who had the faith of Jesus Christ and had completed all [her work], she persecuted the Jews, because they had not believed, and frightened them out of Judea. Such grace attended Saint Cyriacus, the bishop, that he cast out demons through his prayers and healed all the infirmities of men. When blessed Helena had left many gifts with the holy Bishop Cyriacus to minister to the poor, she died in peace on the seventeenth day before the Kalends of May [April 15]; and charged everyone who loved Christ, both men and women, to commemorate the day when the Holy Cross had been discovered, that is the fifth day before the Nones of May [May 3]. Whoever remembers the Holy Cross, may he join with God's mother, Holy Mary, and with our Lord Jesus Christ, who with the Father and the Holy Spirit lives and reigns forever, world without end.

B. *The Life of Abraham the Hermit*

(formerly ascribed to Ephraem of Edessa)

Text: André Wilmart, "Les Rédactions Latines de la Vie d'Abraham Ermite," *RB*, 50 (1938), 238-9.

(XI-XIII.) Blessed Abraham lived for ten years after he had converted blessed Mary, his niece, to penitence. When he had seen her excellent repentance and had glorified God, he rested in peace with Christ. He was sixty years old when he passed to the Lord. The presbyters and deacons came and buried him with great honor in the church. The whole city congregated there as well and everyone hurried to his venerable body to receive a blessing from his clothes; for his touch used to cure all those who were ailing instantly.

(XIV.) Christ's handmaiden, Mary, lived five more years after Abraham's death. She was exceedingly zealous and besought God with her tears day and night. Many men who passed by the place heard her weeping; and they too stood there lamenting and glorifying God because of her great penitence. At the hour of her death all those who were present and saw her face gave glory to God for the great beauty which came over her.

(XV.) Beloved, they sleep in the Lord whose understanding is not tied to the things of this world or to worldly lusts, but to love of the Lord alone. Yet I have remained unprepared [for death, and acted] according to my own will. Now endless winter has seized me and I am naked and unprepared.

(XVI.) I am amazed at myself, beloved, that I daily sin and daily repent. Every hour I build up and every hour I pull down. In the evening I say, "Tomorrow I will repent." But when the morning comes, I wander around all day in my pride. Again at midday, I say, "Tonight I will stay sober and beseech the Lord with my tears to be kind to me." But when night falls, I am weighed down with sleep out of weakness. I received a talent from God and I should try to do business with it night and day, so that I may deserve His praise and He may place me over the ten cities. But, because I am lazy, I hide it under the ground. When my Lord comes to ask me for the talent, doubled in value, what shall I do? What shall I say to Him?

(XVII.) Have pity on me, you who alone are without sin. Save me, you who alone are kind and good. Blessed Father, except for you and your only-begotten Son who was incarnated for us and the Holy Spirit who gives life to all, I know no other; there is no other God I believe in. Now in your great mercy, remember me and lead me from the prison [*carcere*] of my iniquities. Both are yours, Lord: my entry into this world and my departure from it. Remember me who can say nothing, and save me, a sinner. May your grace come upon me now, that grace which is my support and refuge, glory and praise. May it shelter me under its wings on that fearful, terrible day. For you are the one who gazes into my heart and thoughts and [knows] that I have rested by many a wicked way full of sin. I beseech you, holy Lord, bring my soul safely into your kingdom. Make me worthy to join blessed Abraham (whose story I have written) where the choir of saints abides. Through the mediation of our Lord Jesus Christ, who lives and reigns with you and the Holy Spirit, now and forever, world without end. Amen.

VII

CHRIST I

Evidently two scholars at the same time discovered the major sources for *Christ I* (now often called, depending on one's critical point of view, the *Advent* or the *Advent Lyrics*). Albert S. Cook in his first edition (Boston, 1900), and Johannes Bourauel in his article, "Zur Quellen-und-Verfasserfrage von Andreas Crist und Fata," *Bonner Beiträge*, 11 (1901), 65-132, both call attention to the clear relationship between the Old English "lyrics" and the Advent antiphons which were chanted at the hour of Vespers, usually once before and once after the *Magnificat*. Their use normally commences on December 17 and runs through December 23, on days called the Greater Ferias (see Jackson J. Campbell, ed., *The Advent Lyrics of the Exeter Book* [Princeton, 1959], p. 6). Originally there were seven such antiphons, the "Great O's" or the *antiphonae majores*. Early in the medieval period other antiphons were patterned on the "Great O's," and are referred to as either the "Monastic" or "Additional O's." The Old English poet bases nine of the twelve extant lyrics directly on one or the other of the antiphons from these two series.

I—*O Rex gentium* (Great O).
II—*O Clavis David* (Great O).
III—*O Hierusalem* (Monastic O).
IV—*O Virgo virginum* (Monastic O).
V—*O Oriens* (Great O).
VI—*O Emmanuel* (Great O).

VII—Thomas D. Hill has discovered the antiphonal source for this lyric in a "text compiled by Alcuin about 790 AD, the *Libri IV de laudi Dei et de confessione orationibusque sanctorum collecti ab Alchonio levita*" (private correspondence). There seems little question that the antiphon, which begins *O Joseph*, is a source for this lyric, although the full "development of the dialogue no doubt owes something to the quasi-dramatic texts which A. S. Cook has cited as analogues to the poem" (Hill).

Lyric VII plainly reflects the ancient iconological motif known as "The Doubting of Mary" (see Robert B. Burlin, *The Old English "Advent": A Typological Commentary* [New Haven and London, 1968], p. 116). This motif derives from Matthew 1.18-21, undergoes further development in the apocryphal *Protoevangelium*, and finally becomes a common subject in the early sermon literature. Cook calls particular attention to Pseudo-Augustinian *Sermon 195* ("A Remote Analogue to the Miracle Play," *JEGP*, 4 [1902], 446-7). Some patristic scholars believe this sermon was written by Ambrosius Autpertus, who died in 781 (see *PLS*, 2.854).

VIII—*O Rex pacifice* (Monastic O).

IX—*O mundi Domina* (Monastic O).

X—Though previous attempts to identify the general liturgical analogues here had met with some success, it was not until 1970 that Fr. Simon Tugwell found the specific antiphon in "an Additional 'O' so far known only from an eleventh century antiphonar from Ivrea" ("Advent Lyrics 348-77 (Lyric No. X)," *MÆ*, 39 [1970], 34): it begins *O coelorum Domine.*

XI—Though the discovery of an antiphonal source for Lyric X increases the possibility that Lyric XI may also be dependent on a single antiphon, it has yet to be identified. However, three particular analogues, all closely related, have been proposed. For the first half of the lyric Campbell suggests the Common Preface to the *Sanctus* (p. 99). Dom Edward Burgert believes "the unifying element for the whole division appears to have been furnished by another Antiphon which is now used in the Votive Office of the Angels" (*The Dependence of Part I of Cynewulf's Christ upon the Antiphonary* [Washington, D.C., 1921], pp. 44-5): it begins *Laudemus Dominum.* The second half of Lyric XI obviously derives from the *Sanctus* and *Benedictus* of the Mass.

XII—The twelfth and last lyric in the *Advent* sequence uses an antiphon sung at the Vespers of the Vigil of the Octave which closes the celebration of the Nativity (Burlin, p. 170). Samuel Moore first connected this Christmas antiphon to the *Christ* poem ("The Source of *Christ* 416ff.," *MLN*, 29 [1914], 226-7): it begins *O admirabile commercium.*

Texts: Robert B. Burlin, *The Old English "Advent": A Typological Commentary* (New Haven and London, 1968), pp. 41-3 (I-VI, VIII-IX); 162 (XIA); 170 (XII).

Radu Constantinescu, "Alcuin et les 'Libelli Precum' de l'époque carolingienne," *RHS*, 50 (1974), 41 (VIIA).

PL, 39.2108-9 (VIIB).

Simon Tugwell, OP, "Advent Lyrics 348-77 (Lyric No. X)," *MÆ*, 39 (1970), 34.

Jean Deshusses, OSB, ed., *Le sacramentaire grégorien: ses principales formes d'après les plus anciens manuscrits,* Spicilegium Friburgense, 16 (Fribourg, 1971), I, 86 (XIB).

Lyric I

O King of the Nations and the One they long for and the cornerstone; you who make both things one, come and save man whom you fashioned out of clay.

Lyric II

O Key of David and Scepter of the house of Israel; you who open and no one closes; you who close and no one opens, come and lead out the prisoner from the prison-house, where he sits in darkness and the shadow of death.

Lyric III

O Jerusalem, city of the highest God, lift up your eyes around and see your Lord, for now He is about to come and loose you from your chains.

Lyric IV

O Virgin of virgins, how shall this come about? For one like you has never been seen before, nor will there be a successor. Daughters of Jerusalem, why do you gaze at me in wonder? Divine is the mystery which you perceive.

Lyric V

O Orient, Splendor of eternal Light and the Sun of Justice, come and shine on those who sit in darkness and the shadow of death.

Lyric VI

O Emmanuel, our King and Lawgiver, hope of the nations and their Saviour, come to save us, our Lord God.

Lyric VII

A. O Joseph, why did you believe what before you feared? Why indeed? The One whom Gabriel announced would be the coming Christ is begotten in her by the Holy Spirit.

B. Pseudo-Augustine, *Sermon 195*

(2) Listen, brothers, listen to Mary when she speaks to us. She is absent in the flesh, but present in spirit. With a virgin's modesty she looks away from the person to whom she speaks. She tells us how she was made pregnant by the Creator. "I was," Mary said, "a Jewish girl at home, born from King David's seed. I grew up and was betrothed to my spouse, and yet someone else found me pleasing. It was not a case of adultery, but of the Holy Spirit's coming between us. I was betrothed to a Jewish man, and yet I was pleasing to a man who was God; a Jewish man betrothed me, but God as Christ fell in love with me. My spouse, Joseph, was unaware that my God had fallen in love with me, and thought that my womb had been impregnated in adultery. For unknown to Joseph, my spouse, a great friend of my bridegroom, Christ, came to me: it was not the first patriarch or a famous prophet, but the archangel Gabriel. His face was radiant, his raiment shone, his approach was wonderful, his aspect terrifying. He visited me and frightened me. He greeted me, made me pregnant and said, '*Hail, full of grace. The Lord is with you.*' He said, '*The Lord is with you,* but more than He is with me; *The Lord is with you*, but not as He is with me. Although the Lord is in me—the Lord created me—yet He will be born through you. For it is thus, Mary, that *the Lord is with you*. For Him to be in your heart, let Him be in your womb. Let Him fill your soul; let Him fill your womb. Let Him proceed from your womb as handsome as the bridegroom from his bridal chamber; let the King come from your inmost womb as a king from his bedchamber. Let the Prince proceed from his royal court in such a way that your virginity is not violated.'"

3. (*On the same theme*) She said to Gabriel, "*How can it happen* that I shall become pregnant when my womb is chaste and my husband has not touched me, *since I do not know a man sexually?* I am betrothed to an upright man: if I have not had intercourse with him, what will make me give birth? However, if it is possible for me to conceive while I am still a virgin, and to give birth when no man has entered me, show me the way and you will find my soul prepared. For I long to obey my God in every way, to have a child and yet not lose my chastity." The angel Gabriel tells her about the manner of conception, how it will be accomplished

by the Saviour's word. "Mary," he said, "Virgin of God, God's bride, God's beloved, God's daughter, God's mother, if you want me to tell you the way you will conceive as a virgin, give birth as a virgin, and remain a virgin after the birth; and also how He who made you will be made in you, listen to me and do not become inwardly alarmed. *The Holy Spirit will come upon you, and the power of the Highest will come over you like a shadow* (Luke 1.34-5). The power of the Most High will so shadow you that you will not suffer the heat of lust and you will be the Mother of the Creator."

4. (*Joseph is disturbed*) Meanwhile Joseph, Mary's bridegroom, did not know what the angel had discussed with her. Joseph suddenly looked at his betrothed with the intimate glance permitted to a husband. He saw the swollen veins in her throat and her drawn face, and the heavy way she walked. He knew Mary's womb was pregnant. As an upright man Joseph was disturbed when he saw that Mary, whom he had accepted at the Lord's temple and still did not know sexually, was heavy with child. The woman he had not yet honorably possessed in marriage he was now to have in shame. Raging and debating with himself for a long time, he said, "How did this occur? What happened? I did not know her or touch her. If I have not touched her, I have not violated her; and if I have not violated her, I have not made her pregnant. Alas, alas. What has happened? What do you suppose has occurred? What man has made her succumb like this? Whom did she find to flatter her more than I? Although I may have had the right as her husband, I did not force her maiden chastity before the marriage bed. I was afraid to: I was extremely frightened of the judgment set down in Moses' book of law. There it says that any virgin who pollutes her father's house by committing adultery will suffer death by stoning. Likewise, the man who does not bear the bridal sheet to the father, unfold it in the presence of witnesses and produce the stain of [blood proving her] chastity, must be killed along with the girl. Moses wanted both lustful partners to suffer death by this law and he ordered adulterers to die together. The law reads: *You will remove disgrace from the house of Israel, and every man who hears this will be afraid and not act wickedly* (Deut. 22.21,22). I heeded this judgment of Moses and curbed my body's lust, because I knew very well beforehand that she was a daughter of David and that I

was acting as a royal priest. . . . So what shall I do? How shall I act? I am worried. I sigh and suffer. I run about and seek advice, but find none satisfactory. Shall I speak up or stay silent? I really don't know what to do. Shall I report the adultery or keep quiet because of the shame? If I speak up, I shall not be consenting to adultery, it's true, but I shall be committing the sin of cruelty, since I know from the book of Moses that she has to be stoned. If I keep quiet, I am consenting to sin and casting my lot with adulterers. So, since it is bad to stay silent, but worse to report the adultery, I shall quietly forsake the marriage, lest there be a murder on my account." *Joseph thought*, as the Gospel says, *that he would put his wife, Mary, secretly away* (Matt. 1.19).

Lyric VIII

O King of peace, you who were born before the ages, come forth through the golden gate; visit those you have redeemed, and lead them back to the place from which they fell through sin.

Lyric IX

O Lady of the world, born from a kingly seed, Christ has now come forth from your womb like the groom from the bridal chamber; He lies in a manger who also rules the stars.

Lyric X

O Lord of the heavens, you who are eternal with the Father, and one with the Holy Spirit, hear your servants; come to save them now; do not delay.

Lyric XI

A. Let us praise the Lord, whom the angels praise, whom the cherubim and seraphim proclaim Holy, Holy, Holy.

B. Common Preface to the *Sanctus;* the *Sanctus* and *Benedictus*

It is truly meet and just, right and beneficial for salvation that we should at all times and in all places give thanks to you, O holy Lord, Father almighty, eternal God, through Christ our Lord.

Because of Him the angels praise your majesty, the dominations worship you, the powers tremble before you: the heavens and powers of heaven and the blessed company of seraphim celebrate you with exultation. With them we also pray that you will grant our voices to be heard in humble confession, saying, "Holy, Holy, Holy, Lord God of Hosts. Heaven and earth are full of your glory. Hosannah in the Highest; Blessed is he who comes in the Name of the Lord. Hosannah in the Highest."

Lyric XII

O wonderful exchange: the Creator of the human race, assuming a living body, deigned to be born from a Virgin; and, becoming man without seed, bestowed on us His divinity.

VIII

CHRIST II

Recent scholarship has illustrated how broadly and deeply Cynewulf drew upon the vast literature and iconography of the Ascension (see especially George Brown, "The Descent-Ascent Motif in *Christ II* of Cynewulf," *JEGP*, 73 [1974], 1-12; and Peter Clemoes, "Cynewulf's Image of the Ascension," in *England before the Conquest: Studies in Primary Sources presented to Dorothy Whitelock*, ed. Peter Clemoes and Kathleen Hughes [Cambridge, 1971], pp. 293-304). Nevertheless, the two main sources were identified long ago.

In 1853 F. Dietrich proved that Cynewulf used Gregory the Great's "Ascension Homily," *Homily 29* in the *Forty Homilies on the Gospels* ("Cynevulfs Crist," *ZDA*, 9 [1853], 204). At the beginning of this century Albert S. Cook noted the similarities between parts of *Christ II* and Bede's hymn *On the Lord's Ascension* (see his edition, pp. xliii-xlv and 116-8); lately John Pope has further reinforced this view ("The Lacuna in the Text of Cynewulf's *Ascension* [*Christ II*, 556b]," in *Studies in Language, Literature and Culture of the Middle Ages and Later*, ed. E. Bagby Atwood and Archibald A. Hill [Austin, Texas, 1969], pp. 214-9).

The ultimate origin of the narrative is, of course, the Bible; and Cynewulf employs several texts in his expansion of Gregory: Psalm 23, Matthew 28.16-20, Mark 16.14-20, Luke 24.36-53 and Acts 1.1-14 (see Clemoes, p. 294). These should be consulted along with the Gregorian homily and Bede's hymn. For an analogue to lines 664-85, see Entry XIV.

A. Gregory, *Forty Homilies on the Gospels: Homily 29*

Text: *PL*, 76.1218-9.

9. This is the first question we must ask: the angels appeared at the Lord's birth and yet we do not read that they appeared in white garments; however, we do read that the angels appeared in white garments when they were sent at the time the Lord ascended. Why is this? For it is written, "He was raised up while the [disciples] looked on and a cloud took Him away from their sight. And as they looked at Him ascending into heaven, behold, two men stood near them in white garments" (Acts 1.9-10). "In white garments" signifies the soul's joy and celebration. Thus why is it that at the Lord's birth the angels did not appear in white garments, but when the Lord ascended they did, unless it is because there was a great celebration among the angels when God entered into heaven as a man? When the Lord was born, divinity seemed humiliated; but when the Lord ascended, humanity was exalted. And indeed, white garments are more in keeping with exaltation than with humiliation. So at His assumption it was proper for the angels to be seen in white garments, since He who appeared in His Nativity as God humbled, was shown in His Ascension as man uplifted.

10. Dearest brothers, in this celebration we must consider especially that it was on this very day that the certificate of our damnation was destroyed, the sentence of our corruption commuted. For our nature, of which it was said, "You are earth and into the earth you will return" (Gen. 3.19), on this day went into heaven. Blessed Job figuratively called the Lord a bird on account of this "lightening" of the flesh. And because he perceived that Judea would not understand the mystery of His Ascension, he set forth his judgment concerning their want of faith: "It does not know the path of the bird" (Job 28.7). The Lord has rightly been called a bird, since He launched His fleshly body into the ether. Whoever did not know the path of this bird did not believe that He ascended into heaven. The Psalmist says about this solemnity, "Your glory has been raised above the heavens" (Ps. 8.2). Again he says about this, "God ascended with a shout and the Lord with the voice of a trumpet"

(Ps. 46.6). Again he says about this, "Ascending on high, He led captivity captive; He gave gifts to men" (Ps. 67.19). For "ascending on high, He led captivity captive," because He swallowed our corruption by the power of His incorruption. But "He gave gifts to men," because, when the Holy Spirit was sent from above, it allotted the word of wisdom to one, to another the word of knowledge, to another the grace of virtues, to another the grace of healings, to another the various kinds of tongues, to another the interpretation of tongues (I Cor. 12.8). So He gave gifts to men. Habacuc also says about the glory of His Ascension, "The sun was raised up and the moon stood in its course" (Hab. 3.11). Who can be called the Sun except the Lord, and what the Moon except the Church? Until the Lord ascended into heaven, His holy Church feared the adversities of the world in every way; but after she was strengthened by His Ascension, she preached openly what she secretly believed. So "the sun was raised up and the moon stood in its course," because when the Lord sought heaven, His holy Church grew in the authority of her preaching. Hence Solomon speaks concerning the voice of this same Church, "Behold, He comes leaping upon the mountains and springing across the hills" (Cant. 2.8). For Solomon was referring to the high points of [the Lord's] great works when he said, "Behold, He comes leaping upon the mountains." For coming to our redemption, the Lord gave, as it were, certain leaps. Dearest brothers, do you want to understand His "leaps"? He came from heaven into the womb; from the womb He came into the manger; from the manger He came onto the Cross; from the Cross He came into the sepulchre; from the sepulchre He returned into heaven. Behold, so that we would run after Him, the Truth, manifested in flesh, gave certain leaps for us, because "He rejoiced like a giant to run his race" (Ps. 18.6); and so we might say to Him from the heart, "Draw us after you: we will run in the perfume of your ointments" (Cant. 1.3).

11. Therefore, dearest brothers, we should follow Him there with our hearts where we believe He ascended with His body. Let us flee from earthly desires. Let nothing delight us now below, we who have a Father in heaven. And especially we must consider that He who ascended in peace will return with terror; and whatever He commanded us with gentleness, He will exact from us with severity. So let no one undervalue the time given

for repentance. Let no one neglect to do his task while he can, because our Redeemer will come to judge us the more strictly in that He was so patient with us before the Judgment. Make sure you do these things among yourselves, brothers; turn them over in your minds carefully. Although your soul may have floated hither and thither with the confusion of things so far, now fasten the anchor of your hope in the eternal homeland; fix the aim of your mind on the true light. Behold, we have heard that the Lord ascended into heaven; what we believe, therefore, let us keep safe in meditation. Although we are still held here by the body's infirmity, let us follow Him with the footsteps of love. For He who gave us our desire does not abandon us: Jesus Christ, our Lord, who lives and reigns with God the Father in the unity of the Holy Spirit, God forever and ever. Amen.

B. Bede, *On the Lord's Ascension*

Text: *CC*, 122.419-23.

1. Let us sing hymns of glory; let new hymns now resound. Christ ascends to the Father's throne by a new way.
2. In noble triumph and with power, He crosses the heights of heaven; mocked by men, He has conquered death in death.
3. He has lit the thresholds of terrible death and hell's blind shadows; He has bound death's prince with His power.
4. From the ferocious jaws of Avernus He has saved all those He knew were His chosen ones in deed and faith.
5. The Redeemer has opened life's blessed gateway to all the good men deprived of life by the bitter law of mortality.
6. O wonderful brightness of things, marvellous power of the Saviour! Brightness and power [constitute] the twin grace which destroyed death's kingdom.
7. For He has led many from hell's gates in spirit, and rescued many from death's jaws in body.
8. The paschal joys of Christ rising from the dead resound through the double choruses of those rejoicing in their new life.
9. So the two troops following Christ ascended the skies and possessed everlasting thrones among the angels in heaven.

10. Let us all celebrate this day, therefore, with harmonious praises, this day when Jesus the Victor seeks the doors of bright Olympus.

11. This is the day when Jesus, heaven's Creator, led the way and prepared blessed thrones and many mansions with His Father for us.

12. This is the day when the whole company of the world's faithful went ahead and entered heaven's kingdom which Christ opened to them.

13. In the King's marvellous processional triumph marched the high thrones with troops of the celestial host seeking heaven.

14. Standing on the mystical mountain of Olivet, the apostles and the Virgin Mother saw the bright glory of Jesus.

15. Having followed Him as He sought the stars in blessed light, the [angels] led the King of the world through the air with happy hearts.

16. Addressing [Mary and the Apostles], the angels said, "Why do you stand looking at the stars? The Saviour, Jesus, is here. In noble triumph

17. "He has been taken from you to the heavenly kingdoms; thence He will come at the world's end as the Judge of all."

[17A. They proclaimed that Jesus will come to open the splendid arching heights of heaven just as they had seen Him do it then.]

18. Having said this, the angels joined the happy choirs without delay, and came to the gates of bright Olympus with the King of kings.

19. Then an angel's voice came and said, "Now open the gates and the Lord of everlasting peace, the King of glory, will enter in."

20. A voice from the inner ramparts of the bountiful city replied, "Who is this King of glory who can enter heaven's gates?

21. "We are always accustomed to seeing Christ among those who dwell in heaven; we are blessed by Him and His Father in equal glory."

22. But a herald of the great Judge said, "This is the powerful and mighty Lord who triumphantly overthrew the world's black prince in battle.

23. "Wherefore, be lifted up, you gates of eternal heaven, so the King of glory may enter, the King of virtue and grace."

24. Still amazed, the court of celestial citizens asks, "Who is the King of glory, this King who is so praiseworthy?"

25. Straight-away the Master's herald replied, "He is the highest Author of all virtues; He shines forth as the King of glory."

26. At these words the King of glory, together with the shining host, entered into highest heaven, into His kingdom of glory.

27. There in His bounty He gave mansions to each soul He had led from hell's depths because of its good deeds.

28. When He had crossed all the heights of blazing heaven, He sat down on the Father's right hand as the Son co-eternal.

29. From there the Almighty will come in glory to judge the living and the dead in a just trial of their deeds.

30. We pray, Jesus, only Redeemer, in your kindness, join us at that time to your servants in heaven!

31. Grant us to strive with ardent devotion for the place where we believe you sit in the kingdom's height with the Father!

32. Show the Father then to our hearts filled with your spirit, and this one vision will suffice for us.

IX

CHRIST III

Charles W. Kennedy aptly describes *Christ III*, which depicts the Last Judgment, as "a mosaic of borrowings" (*Early English Christian Poetry* [New York, 1963], p. 255): parts of the poem come from specific sources, parts seem to reflect certain patristic writings generally, and parts seem to stand alone. The subject matter itself accounts for this diversity, for the Christian eschatological vision had already become so elaborate that any poet could draw on a vast number of details.

In his edition, Albert S. Cook offers the most thorough examination of the poem's background (*The Christ of Cynewulf*, 2nd ed. [Boston, 1909]); yet several of Cook's attributions must be reconsidered in the light of later patristic scholarship. G. Grau's monograph supplements Cook's work by placing special emphasis on the importance of Ephraem Syrus ("Quellen und Verwandtschaften der älteren germanischen Darstellungen des Jüngsten Gerichtes," *Studien zur Englischen Philologie*, 31 [Halle, 1908]). More recent investigations have been undertaken by Edward B. Irving, Jr., and Thomas D. Hill: Irving finds a new source in Caesarius of Arles' *Sermon 58*; and Hill has contributed several items to the list of sources and analogues for *Christ III* (see below).

Besides the main biblical sources—Revelations, Isaiah 13.9-11, Matthew 24.29-31, Mark 13.24-7, and Luke 21.5-35—all commentators add the apocryphal IV Esdras 5.5, which explains details in lines 1174-76a. These biblical texts must not be undervalued. Rudolph Willard cautions that much of the material in *Christ III* and in *Vercelli Homily 8* is "common to all sermons on the Day of Judgment, and while it appears here and there in the writings of the Fathers, it is ultimately of Biblical derivation" ("Vercelli Homily VIII and the *Christ*," *PMLA*, 42 [1927], 318).

For convenience, the patristic material is categorized as general or specific. Ephraem Syrus' *The Day of Judgment* and the alphabetic hymn quoted in Bede's *De Arte Metrica* are general sources, because they illuminate larger aspects of the poem than the specific ones, which are either sources in the precise sense or illustrative examples of various sections. Obviously, the materials do not all contribute to the poem in the same way. Once or twice where Cook offers alternative analogues in his notes, we have made a choice and briefly given our reasons.

Though the vision of the Last Judgment permeates all medieval literature, we consider the present selections of special interest for the following: *Bede's Death Song, Christ I* and *II* (Entries VII and VIII), *Christ and Satan, The Dream of the Rood* (Entry V), *Elene* (Entry VI), *An Exhortation to Christian Living, Guthlac A* and *B* (Entry X), *Judgment Day I* and *II* (Entry XXI), *Juliana* (Entry XII), *The Phoenix* (Entry XI), *The Seafarer* (Entry XIII), *Solomon and Saturn, Soul and Body I* and *II* (Entry IV), *The Wanderer* (Entry XIII).

A. General Sources and Analogues

1. Cook first singled out Ephraem Syrus' *De Judicio et Compunctione* as a general source for *Christ III* (p. 210). But the sermon has a complicated history. While the Greek version falls within the accepted canon of Ephraem's works (see *VL*, p. 251), the facing-column Latin text to which Cook refers is a Renaissance rendering, as Joseph Assemani, the eighteenth-century editor of Ephraem, duly acknowledged (*Opera* 4 [1 *Graece et Latine*], c). This rendering was in fact done by Gerardus Vossius van Borgloon (see *Biographie Nationale de Belgique*, 5, 850-1), often

confused with his younger relative, the great Gerardus Joannes Vossius (see C. S. M. Rademaker, *Gerardus Joannes Vossius* [Zwolle, 1967], p. 2). Obviously it could not have been used by the Anglo-Saxon poet.

There is another Latin text in Assemani's edition which is older and of some authority (*Opera* 4 [1 *Graece et Latine*], lxxxi; and *Opera* 6 [3 *Graece et Latine*], 579-81; see *CPL*, 1143 and *VL*, p. 251); but it is a shortened and altered version of the Greek. The most authoritative Latin translation is ancient, and in the corpus of the so-called "Ephraem Latinus." It exists only in incunabula (Hain 6598: copies can be found in the Harvard College Library, the Henry E. Huntington Library, the Newberry Library, the University of Pennsylvania Library, the Yale University Library, the Cambridge University Library and the British Library).

Ephraem Syrus, *The Day of Judgment*

(A part of this work also seems to be the ultimate source for lines 1379-1523; see B.7.)

Text: *Libri Sancti Effrem De Compunctione cordis* (Freiburg im Breisgau, Kilianus Piscator, ca. 1491-2), sig. L6r-L7v.

I. Dearest brothers, come and take my advice; always remember the counsel of sinful, ignorant Ephraem. Behold, that great and terrible Day of Judgment is at hand, and we are puffed up and swollen with pride, unwilling to understand and hasten in the brief time we have, and to insure that God be gracious to us. For our days and months and years pass away like sleep or the evening shadows, and the fearful, glorious coming of the Lord will be here in a moment. The world's sinners who refused to do God's will for their own salvation will find that a truly fearful day. I beseech you, dearest brothers, come let us cast off all care for earthly activities, lest our minds be mortgaged to earthly business. For all earthly things are transitory, all perish, all vanish. Nothing can avail us on that Day of Judgment except our holy life and the good deeds we take away with us from here. For the day will come when each of us will carry his deeds and thoughts before the tribunal of that fearful judgment. My heart trembles and my loins melt whenever I consider that our thoughts and words and deeds must be revealed on Judgment Day. For there will be great fear, dearest brothers, and great trembling, my friends. For who will not be afraid; who will not shudder and lament and grieve over this revelation, since everything which has been done here in secret and in darkness will be made public there. Understand, my brothers, what I tell you and consider the example I will give you to help you understand. In their due season fruit trees first conceive fruit internally, and by divine will they later bring forth leaves and fruit externally according to their nature. Thus on that terrible day all men will bear before the Lord's tribunal, as it were in their due season, whatever they have done in this world, secretly, internally: there they will bring their good or bad deeds as their own fruit. Then the just will bring good and pleasant fruit; the saints will likewise bring sweet fruit, adorned with all the flowers of the graces. The martyrs will bring the glorious fruits of their patience in torture and punishment; the monks will bring the imperishable fruits of their holy lives, that is, of continence, humility, of vigils and prayers and obedience. But impious, profane sinners will bring their cursed, rotten fruits, full of the confusion and disgrace of wailing, grief, undying worms and the inextinguishable fire with its lamentation. Dearest brothers, that will be a fearful judgment where all things are brought to light without [the aid of] witnesses. Stationed there are the thousand thousands and the ten ten thousands of angels, cherubim and seraphim; and the choirs of the just stand round, and the choirs of the patriarchs, prophets, apostles, martyrs and of all the countless saints.

II. Then why are we negligent, dearest brothers? Lo, the time is now over, the day approaches when all our hidden deeds will be brought to light. If we knew, brothers, what is impending or hanging over us, we would mourn forever, and beseech God day and night without ceasing to free us from eternal confusion and eternal darkness. For every sinner's mouth will be stopped with great fear and trembling [when he stands] before the judgment seat of God's glory. And every creature will quake and the hosts of the holy angels themselves will be afraid in the day of His coming. What shall we say then, if we have lived negligently and slothfully in this brief life? For He patiently awaits us and invites us all into His kingdom. He will ask us for the reasons for our negligence, and say to us, "For you I was made flesh. I lived openly on earth for you. I was whipped for you. I was spat upon for you. I was slapped in the face for you. I was crucified for you. I was hanged on the Cross for you. I ate gall and drank vinegar to make you holy and celestial. I gave you my kingdom. I opened my paradise to you. I called all of you 'brothers' to my Father. I brought you the Holy Spirit. I sent you all of these things in abundance. What should I have done for you that I did not do? Yet for you to be saved, I asked only that you humble your will. I have not forced you, lest the occasion of your salvation be attributed to necessity. You mortal sinners, subject naturally to suffering [*passibiles*], tell me what you have suffered for me, your Lord, when I, who am not subject to suffering, have suffered for you! Behold, a kingdom is ready and life in tranquil happiness and eternal light. Death is also ready, punishment and grief and darkness. Let each man choose as his own will desires; let him enter on the right path."

III. Come, dearest brothers, let us adore Him and fall down before Him and cry out in the presence of the Lord who made us and say to Him, "O Lord almighty, as God you suffered all these things for us. But we sinners have always angered you and been ungrateful for your kindnesses. God, you are without beginning and incomprehensible by nature, merciful and kind; in your grace you were pleased to save sinners, who did not know you, through the Passion of the Cross, giving them the light of your knowledge after the forgiveness of sins. What shall mankind give you in return, invisible and kindest Lord? For as the kind lover of men, you saved us when we were wicked, not because of our nature, but our own will. Thus we have fallen into sin again through our negligence, but you are always one and the same, merciful, compassionate, terrible and glorious, the Creator of the world, patiently sustaining our perversity from the beginning and giving us time for repentance and remission of sins. Ineffable are the mercies you have shown to the sons of men. Lord, our God, you have been conquered by your love and holy mercies to save the whole world through your Cross. For unless you had been conquered by love, merciful Christ, you would never have offered yourself as a living, spotless sacrifice for sinners. Almighty Lord, your grace has taught me that your servant's mind has been filled by the abundance of your love. Your sweetness forever delights and strengthens me, and yet I am always embittered. I lead myself into bitterness, forever wishing to enjoy your sweetness, only-begotten Jesus, Splendor of the eternal Father, inaccessible Light dwelling in incomprehensible light. You who have illumined the whole world with your grace, illumine what is dark in me, my eyes—for they are veiled and blind. Illumine them with your mercies too, so they are not utterly obscured and darkened by the devil. Lord, our mind in its infirmity has been compared to a transplanted tree which always needs the firmness and illumination of your grace. Lord, your word opened the eyes of the man born blind from the womb who was sent at once to [the pool of] Siloam. After the restitution of his bodily eyes, his spiritual and inner eyes were illumined so he could preach and believe in you, highest Saviour and Doctor, God and God's Son, without any fear. Illumine also our inner eyes, almighty Lord, so we may love you forever and acknowledge you more out of love than necessity, and be able to perform your every will. For though we are far from Siloam where the blind man was sent, yet we are close to the precious cup of your blood, which is full of life and light: the purer the man who approaches this cup, the nearer it is. Thus, merciful Christ, we ought to approach your cup, filled with the grace and illumination of your knowledge and with faith and holiness, so it may bring us to remission of our sins and not to confusion on Judgment Day. For whoever approaches your mysteries and is unworthy, damns his own soul and does not purify himself to receive the heavenly King and immortal Bridegroom in his heart's purest chamber." Our soul is the bride of the immortal Bridegroom and the marriage bonds are the heavenly sacraments. When we eat His body and drink His blood, He is in us and we in Him. Look to yourself, brother; hasten to adorn the bridal bed of your heart with virtues forever, so He and His blessed Father may make their mansion in you. Then there will be praise and great glory for you in the presence of the angels and archangels, and you will enter paradise with great exultation and joy.

IV. O man, what does God seek from you except your salvation? But if you have been negligent and not wished to be saved, and have not walked on God's upright paths nor kept His commands, you are killing yourself and banishing yourself from the heavenly marriage bed. God the Holy Spirit, who alone is without sin, did not spare His own Son for your sake, and you, unhappy man, have not had pity on yourself. Therefore, rouse yourself a little while from your sleep. O miserable man, open your mouth, beseech Him, cast off the burden of your sins. Pray frequently, pour out your tears without ceasing; flee from the soul's weakness; curse negligence; do not love malice. But love gentleness; cherish continence; meditate on psalm-singing. Hurry and pray, brother, while you have been given time. Cherish the Lord with your whole soul, just as He has cherished you. Be God's temple, and God in His eminence will dwell in you. For the soul which has God in itself is God's temple and the Divine Mysteries are celebrated in it. The angels and archangels rejoice in it and hurry to visit it frequently: when God lives in the soul angels hurry to honor it, since it has been made into God's temple. Blessed is the man who has cherished God with his whole heart, and who hates this world and everything in it with all his might, so he may possess you alone in your holiness, the precious pearl and treasure of his life. Whoever sincerely loves God has not made his dwelling on earth, but always on high where his soul longs [to be] and his mind is; and whence he feels sweetness, receives light and enjoys God's love. For truly, the love of God is full of grace and sweetness. Blessed is the man who has tasted it and is not sated by it. For who is there, do you think, who can talk worthily about the sweetness of God's love? The apostle Paul, who tasted it and was filled by it, exclaims, saying, "Neither the height, nor the depth, nor life itself, nor death, nor the future, nor angels, nor principalities, nor powers nor any other created thing can separate us from God's love which is in Christ Jesus, our Lord." God's love is the fire of immortality and is always at work in the soul. The man who has cherished that illumination, grace and virtue raises his sense from earthly things to heaven so that it hates all which is earthly and contemplates and cherishes only God, the Author of its life. By their example the souls of the saints may teach us that they have tasted this love no less than the apostles. God's love is a soft chain, but the two-edged sword cannot cut through it. Tyrants always severed the holy martyrs' limbs, but they could not sever the love of God which abounded in them. O sweetest chain of God's love, full of amazement and wonder, which [the tyrant] was unable to sever and which could not be melted! The two-edged sword did not sever it nor the burning fire melt it. Limbs were severed, but love was not severed; entrails were burnt, but love's chains were not melted. Again, the saints' bodies were drowned in the deep, but God's love could not be drowned at all.

Who do you think is not amazed at this chain of love? So whoever has cherished [God] with a pure and sincere heart is proved to possess such love. God gave this love to His church so it might always be adorned and strong. This love exists in our souls as God's pledge. This love is the base of the column for those who cherish God. This love drew God's only-begotten Son down to us from heaven. Because of this love, God was made man. Because of this love, the soul was made into Christ's bride. Because of it, He who was not subject to suffering suffered. Because of this love, paradise was opened. Because of this love, the fleshless one was made flesh. Because of this love, the invisible one was made visible. If the soul does not have this love, God will take no pleasure in it nor delight over it. Who do you think is properly able or sufficient to praise and glorify God the Saviour who has given us so much grace from His ineffable goodness?

V. Dearest brothers, listen to the good advice I have to give you in my faintheartedness. Let us always hurry while we have time to live chastely, soberly and in a way worthy of the Lord, so the Holy Spirit may dwell in us, Christ's love fill us and His will be perfected in us in all things. Let us have no other care, dearest brothers, except this alone: how our soul may be discovered in that light with all the saints. Let us not tie or bind it to earthly affairs or the troubles of possessions and money. Rather, let us adorn the soul with prayers, fasts, vigils and tears, so it may find faith, however small, in that terrible, fearful hour when all the souls stand by with fear and trembling and the elect are separated from the sinners, and the sheep are stationed on the right hand and the goats on the left. Believe me, my brothers, the Lord's coming is at hand when each man will be rewarded according to his works. The saints and His elect will be rewarded with peace and happiness, but sinners and those who have angered Him, with punishments and torments. Blessed is the man who finds faith in that hour and who hears that blessed voice saying, "Come, blessed of my Father, receive the kingdom prepared for you from the beginning of the world." Then the just, when they see themselves in the light, in that indescribable glory, will be amazed and each will say, "Do you think that I have been chosen? How have I been found worthy of this glory?" When the angels have approached the saints with great joy, they tell them about their spotless life, their continence, vigils, prayers, voluntary poverty and the land they have purchased. Dearest brothers, the work we put into our preparation is little and great is the repose. The affliction of continence lasts for a short time, but its reward, that is, the delights of paradise and exultation and happiness, lasts world without end. Whoever is himself aware that he has sinned against the Lord through his own negligence and will, let him pour forth tears from his heart while there is time; let him lament continually. May he find happiness of heart and remission of sins through tears. May he possess remorse of heart and bathe his body's bed each night with tears. Dearest brothers, do you think you have the experience of tears? Do you think any of you is illumined by that grace of remorse which is according to God? Believe me, brothers, there is nothing on earth sweeter than the grace of tears. Whoever has contemplated God in his prayer and desires Him always is filled with the sweetness of tears, and thus raised above earthly things: he is completely outside the body in heaven. What I call outside the body is wholly of heaven, although a man is found living his life on earth. Such a one speaks with God, is illumined in Christ and is sanctified in the Holy Spirit. It is a great miracle that man, who is earth and ashes, may converse with the Lord in his purest prayer. Blessed is the man who has eternal remorse according to God. Remorse, brothers, is the soul's health and the mind's illumination. Remorse, brothers, requires of us remission of sins. Remorse, brothers, makes the only-begotten Jesus dwell in us when we desire Him and seek Him. Brothers, I wish to tell you about the power of tears. Through tears Anna received the prophet Samuel from the Lord to the elevation and glory of her soul. The debts of the sinful woman in Simon's house were absolved by the Lord Christ: she wet His feet with tears and wiped them with her hair.

Great is the power of tears; tears according to God often prevail. Tears always acquire the Lord's faith; they expel sordid thoughts and do not allow them to approach the soul which has remorse of heart. What can be more sublime than this blessedness when the soul contemplates God Himself in its own prayer? For when it desires Him and is always enslaved to Him, remorse of heart is a never-failing treasure. The soul which has remorse of heart exults with ineffable joy. But I am not talking about the remorse which lasts one day, but about the remorse which overflows and abounds from the soul's purity like a fountain for days and nights. Remorse of heart is a pure fountain, always watering the soul's fruitful young trees. I call the soul's virtues fruitful young trees—the grace of penitence and the good works which are watered assiduously with tears and which bear good and useful fruit. Therefore, may your holy saplings always be watered by you through blessing in the Lord's grace; when this is done, they will grow daily and produce fruit in their season.

VI. Therefore, do not live imitating my sin and idleness, always talking and never acting; for I am full of weakness and overwhelmed by negligence, having no remorse of heart and no purity of prayer. I always recognize myself as a sinner, always afraid of the future Judgment, and having no excuse at all for my negligence. I beseech you, my dear brothers, you who fear God and who always do things that please Him, to pray for me in my frailty and weakness that heavenly grace may come upon me and my soul be saved; and that I may find mercy on that terrible day when the Lord will come to render to each man according to his works.

Glory be to our merciful and immortal Lord who has opened our lips through grace to meditate on the words of His Judgment; and on the words of delight and remorse which are the soul's edifices, the heart's foundation, the mind's illumination. Thus every soul which meditates on them may be drawn to eternal life. Amen.

2. In a prior article (*MLN*, 4 [1889], 341-52), and then again in his edition (p. 171), Cook suggested that an alphabetic hymn quoted by Bede was a source for *Christ III*. Although this has not met with complete acceptance, the hymn certainly helps to illuminate the poem.

The Day of Judgment

(The Alphabetic Hymn quoted by Bede in *De Arte Metrica*)

Text: *MGH, Poetae Latini Aevi Carolini*, 4, 2 (Berlin, 1914), 507-10.

1. Suddenly the Lord's great day will appear, like a thief attacking the unready on a dark night: on the fearful Day of Judgment.

2. Then all the old world's luxury will seem brief, when the whole world has clearly perished with it: on the fearful Day of Judgment.

3. The trumpet's blast resounding through the four corners of the earth will rouse the living and the dead to meet with Christ: on the fearful Day of Judgment.

4. The Judge will come from heaven's heights, blazing in majesty, accompanied by bright angelic choirs: on the fearful Day of Judgment.

5. The moon's disk will turn red and the sun will grow dark; the fading stars will fall and the world's circumference tremble: on the fearful Day of Judgment.

6. Before the face of the just Judge will go the fire's flame, devouring the sky, the earth and the waves of the deep sea: on the fearful Day of Judgment.

7. The glorious King will sit on the high throne; the trembling troops of angels will stand around Him: on the fearful Day of Judgment.

8. All His chosen ones will be gathered on His right hand; wicked men, like stinking goats, will be quaking on His left: on the fearful Day of Judgment.

9. "Go," the King will say to those on the right, "receive the kingdom of heaven, which the Father has prepared for you before all ages": on the fearful Day of Judgment.

10. "You who came to my aid with brotherly love when I was poor, now as rich men bear away your love's reward": on the fearful Day of Judgment.

11. The blessed will say, "O Christ, when did we see you as a pauper, or when did we have pity on you and help you in need, great King?": on the fearful Day of Judgment.

12. The great Judge will say to them, "When you helped the poor and gave them bread, shelter and clothes, you helped me as a pauper": on the fearful Day of Judgment.

13. Nor will the just Judge hesitate to address those on His left, "Accursed men, away; descend into Gehenna's flames": on the fearful Day of Judgment.

14. "When I was a beggar asking for alms, you scorned to hear me; when I was naked, you did not give me clothes; when I was weak, you neglected me": on the fearful Day of Judgment.

15. The sinners will say, "O Christ, when did we spurn you in your poverty; great King, when did we despise you in your sickness?": on the fearful Day of Judgment.

16. The high Judge will counter them, "As long as you refused to aid the beggar, you were spurning me, wicked men": on the fearful Day of Judgment.

17. Then the unjust will fall backwards into everlasting fires. The worm that eats them never dies and the flame is never quenched: on the fearful Day of Judgment.

18. That dark prison holds Satan and his ministers; wailing and groaning are there and everywhere is gnashing of teeth: on the fearful Day of Judgment.

19. Then the faithful will be raised to their heavenly home; they will seek the kingdom's joys among the angelic choirs: on the fearful Day of Judgment.

20. They will enter into the glory of the highest city, Jerusalem, where shines the true vision of light and peace: on the fearful Day of Judgment.

21. Now they contemplate Christ the King, splendid in His Father's brightness, with the high hosts of the blessed: on the fearful Day of Judgment.

22. So beware the serpent's guiles, succor the sick, despise gold, flee from luxury, if you wish to seek the stars: on the fearful Day of Judgment.

23. Wrap your loins now with chastity's bright girdle; bring burning lamps to meet the mighty King: on the fearful Day of Judgment.

B. Specific Sources and Analogues

1. lines 905-25.

Recently Thomas D. Hill has revived the idea that lines 905-25 parallel a part of Gregory's *Moralia* ("Notes on the Eschatology of the Old English *Christ III*," *NM*, 70 [1969], 672-5; see also Cook, p. 297).

Gregory, *Moralia or an Exposition of Job*

Text: *PL*, 76.640-1.

(But you, Lord, are calm when you judge [Sap. 12.18].)

(9.) Therefore at the Last Judgment He Himself will remain immutable, not subject at all to vicissitude or change. Yet He will not appear to the saved in the same immutable form as to the damned, since He will seem calm to the just, but angry to the unjust. With their conscience as witness they will each visualize Him differently. Accordingly, their minds may see one and the same [Judge], but not think of Him in the same way: to the just, their former righteousness will make Him seem benign, but to the unjust, sin will make Him seem terrible. Who can describe the dread when the time comes for the wretched to acknowledge their inner sins and to see the righteous Judge before them? Indeed, in the course of this present life men's hearts are taught daily about the nature of the coming Judge. For when two men go to trial, one conscious of his innocence, the other of his guilt, they both look at the silent judge before he passes sentence; but the one in debt to sin suspects that the judge's silence betokens heavy wrath. It is not the judge's outward emotion which indicates this anger to him, but the memory of his own depravity: although he has not yet been publicly acclaimed guilty, his inner conscience harshly accuses him. By contrast, the man who is the lover of righteousness sees the judge's face, but inwardly rejoices—the memory of his own goodness is there as testimony. The more he lacks within what causes fear, the more he sees the judge opposite him as wholly kind. Thus this text says that the Lord's anger is not the troubling of the divine substance, but the sinners' examination of their due punishment when conscious of their guilt. Although they may see the Judge is calm when He gives sentence, yet they think He is inwardly troubled, since they are certain He will punish them.

2. lines 1084-1102.

Cook writes that lines 1084-1102 depend on "a passage in Ephraim Syrus, or one doubtfully attributed to Augustine" (p. xlv). Actually, Cook's "passage" is a pastiche of quotations which he has excerpted from several of Ephraem's supposed works. As the alternative, we print part of Pseudo-Augustinian *Sermon 155*. This sermon is an early Latin translation of one of Saint John Chrysostom's homilies on *The Cross and the Thief* (see *PLS*, 2.850; and André Wilmart, "La Collection des 38 Homélies Latines de Saint Jean Chrysostome," *JTS*, 19 [1918], 314). Both the Ephraem and the Pseudo-Augustine, however, must be consideŕed remote analogues.

Pseudo-Augustine, *Sermon 155*

Text: *PL*, 39.2051-2.

(10.) Listen to the following: Matthew says, "At the moment He comes, the sun will grow dark and the moon will not give out its light" (24.29-30). Christ's splendor will be so overpowering that even the brightest luminaries of the sky will be invisible beside the brilliance of the divine light; and "the stars will fall when the sign of the Son of Man appears in the heavens." Think of how much power there is in this sign, that is, the sign of the Cross. "The sun will grow dark and the moon will not give out its light," but the Cross will be ablaze: when the luminaries of the sky grow dark and the stars have fallen, it alone will be radiant. The Cross, you must understand, will be brighter than the moon and more radiant than the sun, whose splendor it will eclipse with the divine light's brilliant glory. Just as an army precedes the king when he enters a city, bearing on its shoulders the regal signs and standards, and announcing the king's entrance with parade of clashing arms, so the army of angels will precede the Lord when He descends from heaven; it will bear the sign, that is, the standard of triumph, high upon its shoulders, and announce the divine entrance of the heavenly King to the trembling worlds. "Then," Matthew says, "the powers of heaven will be shaken" (24.29)—he refers to the angels, for they will be seized with trembling and great fear. Tell me, therefore, why is this? It is because the judgment will be so terrible that even the angels will be terrified; for the whole human race will be brought to judgment and stand before the fearful Judge. This is why the angels will be afraid. But why do they tremble, for they do not have to be judged? When a king holds court, it is not only the accused, but also the innocent officials who are seized with terror and trembling, because they fear the judge. In the same way the celestial ministers will be frightened when humanity is judged; when they witness the Judge's awful magnificence, they will quake with fearful dread.

11. *Why the Cross will appear at the Judgment.* But why will the Cross appear then, and why will the Lord come with [the Cross] preceding Him? The reason is clear: it is so they who crucified the Lord of majesty may recognize the measure of their iniquity. Thus the shameless impiety of the Jews is rebuked through this sign. Hear the Lord Himself declare in the Gospel how He will come bearing the Cross: "then all the tribes of the earth will wail," when they see their accuser, that is, the Cross itself. And when it accuses them, they will recognize their sin too late and confess their wicked blindness in vain. But why are you surprised if He comes bearing the Cross, when He will also be showing His wounds: "Then they will look," John says, "on Him they have pierced" (19.37). For just as He did with Thomas when He wished to correct the disciple's disbelief and error for the faith of many—He brought the signs of the nails and the wounds themselves to show Him—and said, "Put in your hand and see; for a spirit does not have bones and flesh, as you see I have" (John 20.27; Luke 24.39); so at that time He will show His wounds and reveal the Cross to demonstrate that it is He Himself who was crucified.

3. lines 1127b-98.

Homily 10 of Gregory's *Forty Homilies on the Gospels* seems to be a direct source for these lines and was first noticed by Dietrich and then by Cook (p. 195). For lines 1174-76a, see IV Esdras 5.5.

Gregory, *Forty Homilies on the Gospels: Homily 10*

Text: PL, 76.1111.

2. Among all the miraculous signs appearing at the Lord's nativity and death, we must particularly remark the hardness in the hearts of certain Jews; it was so great that they did not recognize Him through the prophecies or the various signs given them. In fact, all the elements testified that their Creator had come. Let me say something about them by way of personification. The heavens knew He was God, for they sent a star immediately; the sea knew, for it offered itself for His feet to tread on; the earth knew, for it trembled when He died; the sun knew, for it hid the rays of its light; the walls and stones knew, for they were rent at the time of His death; and hell knew, for it surrendered the dead in its possession. And yet this [Jesus], whom all the inanimate elements recognized as the Lord, is still not recognized as God by the hearts of the faithless Jews. Harder than stones, they do not want to be rent apart for the sake of repentance. They refuse to acknowledge Him, whom the elements, as we said, acclaimed as God by signs and rendings.

4. lines 1204-18.

A passage in Augustine's *De Trinitate* parallels lines 1204-18 (see Thomas D. Hill, "Vision and Judgment in the Old English *Christ III*," *SP*, 70 [1973], 233-6).

Augustine, *On the Trinity*

Text: *CC*, 50.70.

It is meet that the Jews who persist in wickedness should be punished at the Last Judgment, as it is written elsewhere, *They will look on Him whom they pierced* (Zach. 12.10).

When the good and bad go to see the *Judge of the living and the dead* (Acts 10.42), there is no doubt the bad will be unable to see Him except in the guise of the *Son of Man* (Matt. 9.6); but it will be *in the glory* (Matt. 16.27) in which *He will come to judge* (Hebr. 10.30), not *in the humility* (Acts 8.33) in which He was judged. Moreover, there is no doubt the wicked will not see Christ *in the form of God* (III John 11) where *He is equal to the Father* (Phil. 2.6): they are not *pure in heart.* For *blessed are the pure in heart for they shall see God* (Matt. 5.8). This vision is *face to face* (I Cor. 13.12) and is the highest reward promised the righteous.

5. lines 1247-59.

As Cook notes (p. 202), Gregory's *Homily 40* serves only to illustrate the ideas in lines 1247-59; it is not a source.

Gregory, *Forty Homilies on the Gospels: Homily 40*

Text: PL, 76.1308-9.

(8.) So that sinners in torment may be punished the more, they see the glory of those they despised and are punished grievously for the things they uselessly loved. But we must believe that, before the retribution of the Last Judgment, the wicked see some of the righteous in peace; so that, seeing them in bliss, they are afflicted both by their own torment and by the good the righteous enjoy. But the righteous always gaze upon the wicked in torment so their joy can thus increase (because they see the evil they mercifully escaped). They will render greater thanks to their Saviour insofar as they see others suffer what they themselves would have suffered had they been left behind. Watching the reprobate being punished does not darken the brightness of the great blessedness in the souls of the righteous. Since the blessed will not pity this misery, it will certainly be unable to diminish their happiness. But what a marvellous thing if, when the righteous gaze on the torments of the wicked, it should serve to bring them joy. For when black is used as the ground in a painting, white or red are seen more clearly. As the saying goes, the joys of the good will increase insofar as the evils of the damned which they escaped lie before their eyes. Though their joys are enough for them to be completely happy, yet without question they will always see the evils of the wicked. For nothing happens in creation which those who see their Creator's brilliance cannot see.

6. (lines 1261-1311); lines 1312-31.

Irving first identified a sermon by Caesarius of Arles as the source for lines 1312-31. Caesarius' sermon may also have influenced lines 1262-1311 (see Edward B. Irving, Jr., "Latin Prose Sources for Old English Verse," *JEGP*, 56 [1957], 588-95).

Caesarius of Arles, *Sermon 58*

Text: *CC*, 103.254-8.

Saint Faustus' noble warning for us always to think about our sins and about the Judgment Day or eternal blessedness.

Now, dearest brothers, during the course of the divine reading, we heard the blessed apostle warning us in a frightening, yet beneficial, way. He said, "We must all appear before Christ's judgment seat, so each of us can account for whatever his body is responsible for doing—good or bad" (II Cor. 5.10). The Lord also stated this in the Gospel, "The Son of Man will come with His angels in His glory and then He will repay each man according to his deeds" (Matt. 16.27). Listen to this carefully, please, dearest brothers, and become as afraid as I. For the Lord did not say He would repay according to His own mercy, but "according to each man's deeds." For here He is merciful, but there He is just. That He does not punish sinners instantly is patience, not negligence: He has not lost His omnipotence, but saved us for penitence. Therefore, what we must truly fear is not how much longer He will wait for us to improve, but how much more harshly He will punish us if we do not wish to improve. Since such is the case, dearest brothers, we ought to know and understand that nothing is more beneficial for us than this: having condemned the pleasure of all present things, we should think rather about the time when we will be transported from this world, and lay aside the tabernacle of our body as our last day comes upon us; and we should think about the time when we will get the same body back again at the resurrection, so that in it we can receive deserts according to our good or bad deeds.

2. Thus I ask you, brothers, let us think daily about the sort of people we will be on Judgment Day, when we are offered to the pure gaze of the angels and render an account to the eternal Judge from the books of conscience. Now all the probationary trials are over; it is certain that man must be set before himself on that day and his soul be revealed in his own heart's mirror. Witnesses will be brought forward to testify against the soul, witnesses that do not come from outside, but from within, from the soul itself. No other external testimony will have to be called, but rather the testimony that is known too well—the soul's own deeds. Its sins and crimes will be arranged before the unhappy soul, and the trial will convict it; its own recognition [of those crimes] will confound it, according as it is written, "I will accuse you; I will put the evidence in front of your eyes" (Ps. 49.21). Whoever neglected to correct himself while he could will first receive punishment before the heavenly host from the shame; and the soul which only pretends to repent and cure its wickedness by an abbreviated catalogue of its sins will stand before that fearful tribunal forever wounded and beyond all remedy.

3. Since such is the case, it would be to our benefit if we repented of our bad deeds now, even as we will repent of them then without any remedy. If we are going to see our foulness and confusion then, we should be able to see and be horrified at them now. If only the body's eyes could see the face of the sinful soul now; if only we were allowed to lead the face of our conscience into the presence of our eyes! If we were permitted this, it would be impossible to describe the degree of zeal and fear which would drive us to dispose of our filthiness, wipe away our stains and cure our wounds. Therefore, since we cannot see with the body's eyes, let us examine ourselves, insofar as we can, with the heart's eyes: let each one of us place his conscience before the sight of the inner man. Let us castigate ourselves; let us make ourselves probe into our daily conduct. Let each soul address itself in the secrets of its heart and say, "Let me see if I

have lived through this day without sin, without jealousy, disparagement or complaint. Let me see if I have done today things which profited my soul. Upon reflection, I have lied today; I have been overwhelmed by anger or desire; I have not done anyone any good; I have not groaned for fear of eternal death. Who will restore this day to me which I have squandered on vanities, which I have consumed with harmful, evil thoughts?" Thus, brothers, let us feel compunction about the things we have not done "in our cells" (Ps. 4.5), that is, in our hearts. Let us blame ourselves; let us accuse ourselves daily to our Judge. While we exist in the flesh, with God helping, let us struggle daily against that flesh. Let us suppress our wishes and purposes until the time comes—the longed-for and blessed time—for us to make the happy change to eternal life, when these sayings of the Lord will be fulfilled, "Men will be like the angels" (Matt. 22.30); and again, "Then the just will shine like the sun in their Father's kingdom" (Matt. 13.43).

4. Can you imagine how brilliant our souls will be when our bodies shine with the sun's brightness? For when we reach this beatitude, there will be no sadness, no fear, no infirmity, no death. To serve our God we shall no longer be opposed by any infirmity or have physical adversity as our enemy; and there will be no need to fight any more. The day is coming, I repeat, when we shall not long for food or sleep to refresh us, or feel the tiredness of hunger, or fear being upset by the flesh or tempted by the enemy. Rather, with the enemy driven into hell's depths, we will enjoy this felicity for the first time; that is, we will neither wish to sin further nor be able to. Now that all iniquity, misery and grief have stopped, innocence, happiness and felicity will possess all of us totally. The humble man will feel no misery and the more fortunate man will feel no envy, since the angels' love will cross into men's breasts when all malignity has been voided and utterly extinguished. Having mingled with the angels, men will now shine like celestial beings: they will have received flesh without the flesh's infirmity. They will no longer feel disdain for the Lord's eternal power, nor cease from the everlasting exultation of praising Him. Among all the immense blessings of our God, we will be filled with such happiness that we will never tire of thanking Him; we will have been made the co-heirs of Him

who said, "Come, blessed ones, see the kingdom which has been prepared for you from the beginning of the world" (Matt. 25.34).

5. Behold, what blessedness that man will lose who does not want to correct himself while there is time for repentance, who will not release himself from his [worldly] things while they are his, who rejects medicines for his wounds and bows his miserable neck to avarice and lust. With God helping, brothers, let us scorn to serve sin, since we have this great happiness prepared for us in heaven. Therefore, while we can, while it is within our power, let us expel false, transitory things, so we may be worthy to receive those things which are truly good. Let us empty ourselves of vices and fill ourselves with virtues; for no one can receive good things if he does not wish to liberate himself from the bad. Vessels full of mud cannot receive or contain a completely pure liquid, and a thorny field—unless it has been cleared by a hardworking farmer—does not nourish seeds thrown upon it; rather, it chokes them, as it is written, "the benign and Holy Spirit will not inhabit a body enslaved to sins" (Sap. 1.4). We sail in this world as if we were on a stormy sea. To reach the homeland of paradise, let us hurry to remove the bilge of vices, so that our soul, adorned with good works like a boat full of various wares, may be worthy to drop anchor in the port of eternal beatitude and enter the society of angels. There, freed "from hearing evil things" (Ps. 111.7), we may be worthy to hear that happy, longed-for voice, saying, "Well done, my good and faithful servant. Because you have been faithful over a few things, I will set you over many. Enter into the joy of your Lord" (Matt. 25.21). For our Lord Jesus Christ gave us this promise, and to Him be honor and dominion, world without end. Amen.

7. (lines 1362-78); lines 1379-1523.

Cook points to Ephraem Syrus' *The Day of Judgment* as the ultimate source for lines 1379-1523 (see above, p. 86), but notes that the direct source is another sermon by Caesarius of Arles (p. 210). Irving suggests that the sermon may also have influenced lines 1362-78 (p. 594).

Caesarius of Arles, *Sermon 57*

Text: *CC*, 103.252-4.

4. Beloved brothers, what shall we do on that fearful Day of Judgment when the Lord, the world trembling before Him and in the blare of the angels' trumpets, will sit on His throne of majesty surrounded by the light of the heavenly host? After humanity has been wakened from the earth's bosom out of ancient dust and each man's conscience stands ready for testimony; after the punishments of the sinners and the rewards of the just have been publicly laid down, the Lord will summon each man to give an account of his life. Now He will be more just than merciful: with the severity of a judge who has rejected mercy, He will begin to accuse the damned, saying, "Man, with my hands I fashioned you from clay. I imparted a spirit into your earthly limbs. I deigned to confer my image and likeness on you; I placed you among the delights of paradise. You spurned my life-giving commands and preferred to follow the deceiver rather than the Lord. But I will pass over the events of long ago. After you were thrown out of paradise according to the law and were bound by the chains of sin and death, moved by mercy, I entered a Virgin's womb to be born (and she did not lose her virginity). I lay placed in a manger, wrapped in swaddling clothes; I suffered an infant's annoyances and a man's griefs: in them I became like you, so I could make you like me. I endured the blows and spit of those who mocked me; I drank vinegar mixed with gall; I was beaten with whips and crowned with thorns; I was fixed to a cross and wounded through the side. In order for you to snatch yourself from death, I abandoned my soul to torments. See, here are the marks left by the nails which fixed me as I hanged; look, here are the wounds in my side. To give you my glory, I sustained your griefs. So you might live eternally, I endured your death. So you might reign in heaven, I lay buried in the tomb. Why have you lost what I suffered for you? Ungrateful man, why have you renounced the rewards of your redemption? I do not complain to you about my

death. Give me back your life, the life for which I gave mine. Give me back your life, the life you kill incessantly with sins' wounds. Why have you polluted the soul's dwelling-place with the filth of luxury? I had consecrated it in you for myself. Why have you defiled my body with the foulness of illicit pleasures? Why have you afflicted me on the cross of your crimes, which is heavier than the one on which I once hanged? For I hang upon the cross of your sins against my will; it is heavier for me than the Cross I willingly ascended out of pity for you to kill your death. Although I was immutable, I was made man for you; although I was invulnerable, I deigned to suffer for you. But you despised the God in man, the health in sickness, the return home at the journey's end, the mercy in the Judge, the life on the Cross, the medicine in the sufferings. Since, after all your wickednesses, you did not want to take refuge in the medicines of penitence, you do not deserve to escape the voice of condemnation. You and those like you will hear the words, 'Depart from me, accursed ones, into the eternal fire prepared for the devil and his angels' (Matt. 25.41). And you will descend with the devil into hell's eternal fire, [because], captured by sweet snares and false goods, you have preferred the fire to me, your life."

8. lines 1530 ff.

Cook proffers Prudentius' *A Hymn Before Sleep* as an illustrative analogue (p. 216).

Prudentius, *Liber Cathemerinon, 6: A Hymn before Sleep*

Text: *CSEL*, 61.35.

(Lines 85-100)

A two-edged sword is the weapon held by His mighty hand. Flashing on both sides, it threatens a double blow.

He alone is the Judge of soul and body. Twice fearful, the sword is the first and second death (Hebr. 4.12).

Yet the same avenger benignly checks His anger and does not allow the few good men to perish for eternity.

The glorious Father has given Him the judgment seat forever. He has ordered Him to take the Name above all names. (John 5.22; Acts 17.31).

9. lines 1649-64.

Cook remarks that these concluding lines, which dwell on the joys of the blessed, depend on Gregory and a passage from Augustine (pp. xlv and 222). But patristic scholars now reject Gregory's authorship of *The Exposition of Seven Penitential Psalms*, ascribing it to the late eleventh century (see *PLS*, 4.1583; and *CPL*, 1721). In addition, Cook's "passage" from Augustine is neither a passage nor by Augustine (see *PLS*, 2.1371). The tradition of the joys of the blessed goes so directly to the heart of Christianity that it would be difficult to locate a precise source. However, Thomas D. Hill suggests an eighth-century Irish-Latin sapiential, the *Collectaneum Bedae,* as a close analogue ("The Seven Joys of Heaven in *Christ III* and Old English Homiletic Texts," *N&Q*, 214 [1969], 165; see also *CPL*, 1129).

Pseudo-Bede, *A Collection*

Text: *PL*, 94.545.

There are twelve abuses in this world: the wise man without good works, the old man without religion, the young man without obedience, the rich man who gives no alms, the woman without modesty, the master without authority, the quarrelsome Christian, the arrogant pauper, the unjust king, the negligent bishop, workers without discipline, a people without law. God's justice is upheld through such [virtues]. Seven things are not found in this world: life without death, youth without age, light without darkness, joy without sorrow, peace without discord, desire without injury, a kingdom which never changes. But these seven are found in the kingdom of heaven. Do not be slothful and lazy, but work with your hands so you may have something to give to the poor and needy. For demand is made of you in proportion to the loan intrusted to you.

X

GUTHLAC

The two poems which comprise the quite separate parts of *Guthlac* have different relationships with the Latin hagiographical tradition. For *Guthlac B* (lines 819a-1379b) the source is *Chapter 50* of Felix of Crowland's *Vita Sancti Guthlaci*, a work "written at the request of King Ælfwald of the East Angles" sometime between 730 and 740 (Bertram Colgrave, ed., *Felix's Life of Saint Guthlac* [Cambridge, 1956], pp. 15 and 19).

Arguments on the relationship of *Guthlac A* (lines 1a-818b) to Felix are long and complex. Most contemporary scholars do not believe that this poem depends on Felix at all, but that the poet relied mainly on oral traditions (see Claes Schaar, *Critical Studies in the Cynewulf Group* [Lund, 1949], pp. 39-41; and Frances Randall Lipp, "*Guthlac A:* an Interpretation," *MS*, 33 [1971], 51n). As Lipp notes, however, the problem is not settled and several scholars have asserted that *Guthlac A* was influenced by Felix, Gordon Hall Gerould being the most convincing ("The Old English Poems on St. Guthlac and their Latin Source," *MLN*, 32 [1917], 77-89).

Since Felix's *Life* is rather lengthy, we have chosen to translate the one chapter that is a demonstrable source for the Old English. Complete translations of Felix are available in three modern versions: 1. Colgrave's edition; 2. Clinton Albertson, SJ, *Anglo-Saxon Saints and Heroes* (New York, 1967), pp. 167-212; and 3. Charles W. Jones, *Saints' Lives and Chronicles in Early England* (Ithaca, N. Y., 1947), pp. 125-60.

Felix of Crowland, *The Life of Saint Guthlac*

Text: Bertram Colgrave, ed., *Felix's Life of Saint Guthlac* (Cambridge, 1956), pp. 150-60.

CHAPTER 50

The many temptations Guthlac endured in his sickness and the instructions he gave for his burial; the last orders he sent his sister and how he gave up the ghost while praying.

Since mankind daily passes from the beginning to the end of mortal misery, and generations and kingdoms change with the passing of years, so master and servant, learned and ignorant, young and old, are all brought to the same conclusion and reduced to the same state. Although our merits, punishments and rewards may be different, still the same death awaits us all. For as death was given to rule over Adam, so it will rule over all men. Whoever has savored this life cannot escape death's bitterness. Thus it happened that after God's beloved servant, Guthlac, had led a solitary life for fifteen long years in devout service to the King of heaven, the Lord Jesus desired to call His servant from the laborious servitude of this life to the repose of eternal blessedness.

One day, while Guthlac was devoting himself to prayer in his oratory, a sudden spasm gripped his insides. When the holy man perceived that he had been seized by a spell of terrible dizziness, he knew at once that the Lord's hand had come upon him. With buoyant spirit he started to prepare himself for the joys of the everlasting kingdom. He was ravaged by the dreadful sickness for seven days, and on the eighth he reached his end. Since he had fallen sick on the Wednesday before Easter, he was also sick on the next Wednesday, the eighth day, which was the fourth day in the Easter octave; his illness then came to an end and he passed over to the Lord.

At that time one brother, named Beccel, was dwelling with him. We have followed his account of the death of Guthlac, that man of God. On the day Guthlac's sickness began, Beccel came and started to ask the man of God about various things, as he was accustomed to do. Guthlac was slow to reply and eventually fetched a sigh as he did so. The brother said, "My lord, what strange thing has happened to you? Has some sickness struck you ill during the night?" Guthlac replied, "Yes, I was struck ill during the night." Again Beccel asked him, "Do you know the cause of your illness, father, or how the wretched sickness will end?" The man of God replied, "My son, I am faint because my spirit is being separated from these limbs. But my sickness will end in eight days, and, with my life's span completed, I must be let free and be with Christ. For once I have cast aside the burden of flesh, it is fitting that I should follow the Lamb of God." When he heard this, brother Beccel wept and sighed and moistened his sorrowful cheeks with streams of copious tears. Consoling him, the man of God said, "My son, don't be sad; it is no hardship for me to go to the Lord whom I have served, and enter everlasting peace." His faith was so steadfast that he looked on death (which everyone seems to fear and dread) as if it were the repose and reward of his labor.

Meanwhile each moment of the four days hurried past and Easter Day arrived. Despite his waning strength, the man of God arose. Having offered up the Sacrifice of the Lord's body and tasted the libation of Christ's blood, Guthlac began to preach God's word to the brother. Beccel testifies that he has never heard before or since such profound wisdom from the lips of any man. At last, when the seventh day of Guthlac's sickness dawned, the brother visited him about the sixth hour and discovered him lying in a corner facing the altar. Guthlac did not speak to him, however, as the weight of his sickness made it impossible. Finally, when Beccel begged him to say some last words before he died, the man of God raised his weary shoulders away from the wall for a brief moment and sighed, "My son, since the time is at hand, mark my last instructions. When my spirit has left this poor body, go to my sister, Pega, and tell her I have avoided seeing her in this world so we may see each other forever in the presence of our Father and in everlasting joy. Tell her also to lay my body in a coffin and wrap it in the cloth Ecgburh sent me. While I was living I had no wish to cover my body in linen of any kind, but out of love for the beloved virgin of Christ who sent me these gifts, I have kept it carefully to wrap my corpse in." Hearing this, brother Beccel began, "My father, I beg you, since I know you are ill and dying even as I hear you speak, tell me one thing which has disturbed me for some time and which I have never dared to ask about. My lord, from the time I began living with you, I have heard you talking morning and evening with someone I don't know. I beg you not to let me worry about this after you have gone."

After a pause, the man of God drew a deep breath and said, "My son, do not be disturbed; for I will now reveal to you what I did not wish to tell any man while I was living. From the second year I began to dwell in this wild spot, every morning and evening the Lord has sent an angel to converse with me for my consolation. The angel showed me mysteries which I am not permitted to tell; he lightened the hardness of my labor with heavenly oracles and made absent things visible to me as though they were present. My son, preserve my last words and tell them to no one else, except Pega or the anchorite Ecgberht, if you should ever happen to speak with him; he alone will understand that these events befell me." When he had spoken, he leaned his head against the wall and drew long breaths from the depths of his lungs; and his spirit was revived. After he had panted for a short time, there seemed to issue from his lips the sweet fragrance of a flower, so the house where he dwelt was pervaded by the scent of nectar.

That night while Beccel devoted himself to his nightly vigils, he saw the whole house surrounded and ablaze with incandescent light from midnight till dawn. But at sunrise, the man of God briefly stirred his limbs, as if he were getting up, and began to speak to the brother: "My son, get ready for your journey, for time now compels me to be divided from my limbs and I have reached the limits of this life; my spirit longs to be transported to endless joys." Saying this, he reached out his hands towards the altar and strengthened himself by receiving Christ's body and blood in communion. He raised his eyes to heaven and lifted his hands on high and released his soul to the joys of eternal bliss. As this happened, Beccel suddenly saw the house resplendent with celestial light and something like a tower of fire rising from earth to heaven. Compared to its splendor, even the sun standing in mid sky seemed to grow pale, like a lantern in daylight. The angels' song resounded through the vast spaces of the air and the island seemed redolent with the wafting scents of different spices.

Then brother Beccel was struck with great dread; his eyes

could not stand the brightness of this extraordinary splendor. He took a boat, left the haven and started on the journey, as the man of God had ordered him. Coming to Pega, Christ's holy virgin, he told her one by one all her brother's instructions. When she heard them, she fell straight to the ground. Prostrate on the earth, she wasted away to the very marrow with the burden of her great grief: her tongue was silent, her lips mute. All her vital energy drained away as if she were dead. But after a while, she roused herself as from sleep, drew long sighs from the depths of her heart and gave thanks to the will of almighty God.

The next day she and Beccel arrived at the island according to blessed Guthlac's instructions, and they found the whole place and all the dwellings filled with a scent like ambrosia. God's handmaiden spent three days commending her brother's spirit to heaven with divine praises; and on the third day she buried his blessed limbs in his own oratory as he had ordered, and covered them with earth.

XI

THE PHOENIX

Variations on the phoenix legend abound in oriental, classical and early Christian literatures, and scholars have traced the complex development from its beginnings in Egyptian sun worship to its full-blown Christian elaborations in the Middle Ages (see, for example, Albert S. Cook, ed., *The Old English Elene, Phoenix, and Physiologus* [New Haven, 1919], pp. xxxviii-lvi; and R. van den Broek, *The Myth of the Phoenix according to Classical and Early Christian Traditions,* trans. I. Seeger [Leiden, 1972]).

Three texts are of critical importance for the Old English poem, though the poet may have made use of others; he appears to be acquainted generally with the tradition and specifically with several patristic commentaries on the subject. However, Lactantius' *De Ave Phoenice*, Ambrose's commentary in the *Hexameron*, and the description in the *Physiologus* are certain sources. The link between Lactantius and the *Phoenix* is of long standing: J. J. Conybeare noted it early in the nineteenth century ("Account of an Anglo-Saxon Paraphrase of the Phoenix attributed to Lactantius," *Archaeologia*, 17 [1814], 193-7). H. Gaebler first remarked on the parallels with Ambrose's *Hexameron* ("Über die Autorschaft des angelsächsischen Gedichtes vom Phönix," *Anglia*, 3 [1880], 517-9). And Joseph B. Trahern, Jr., has made a convincing case for the connection with the *Physiologus* ("*The Phoenix:* A Critical Edition," unpublished Princeton Univ. Ph.D. dissertation [Princeton, 1963], pp. 26-7).

As a group, these texts show that by Anglo-Saxon times the different strands of the phoenix myth had come together: a late classical poem that may or may not be Christian in spirit has yielded easily to formal Christian exegesis, and then the details have been merged with another entirely separate tradition. It is this conflation which underlies the Old English poem.

A. Lactantius, *The Phoenix*

Text: Mary Cletus Fitzpatrick, ed., *Lactanti De Ave Phoenice* (Philadelphia, 1933).

There is a blessed far-off place in the distant east where the great door of the everlasting heavens lies open. Far from the summer or winter sunrises, it is close to where the sun pours out the day from skies of spring. A plain spreads its open fields there: no mound swells up, no hollow valley yawns. But it surpasses our mountains—whose peaks men think lofty—by twice six fathoms. The sun's grove is here and, planted with many trees, the sacred wood is green in the beauty of perpetual leaves. This spot was not violated by Phaethon's flames when he set the sky ablaze with fires; and when the flood immersed the earth in waves, it rose above Deucalion's waters. Wan diseases do not come here, nor feeble old age, nor cruel death, nor desperate fear, nor unspeakable crime, nor the mad desire for wealth, nor frenzy burning with love of slaughter. Bitter grief, want covered with rags, sleepless cares and violent hunger—all are absent. The tempest and the wind's fearful force do not rage, and the hoarfrost does not cover the ground with its icy dew; no cloud spreads its fleeces over the fields, nor does the dark drenching of rain fall from the sky. A fountain is situated in the middle, which they call *the living fountain*—clear, gentle and full of sweet waters. It gushes forth once in the course of every month and irrigates the whole grove with its streams twelve times [a year]. A species of tree rises upwards here with a lofty trunk and bears ripe fruit which never falls to the ground. In this grove, in these thickets, lives a unique bird, the phoenix. She is unique, but she lives as a result of being recreated by her own death. She obeys and attends Phoebus as his celebrated servant—an office Mother Nature granted to her. As soon as saffron-yellow Aurora ascends and reddens, as soon as Aurora scatters the stars with her rosy light, the phoenix dips her body thrice four times in the holy waves; and thrice four times she sips water from the living flood. She rises and settles on the tall tree's crown, the only one to look down on the whole grove. Having turned to where Phoebus will rise and be born anew, she waits for his beams and coming radiance. When the sun has struck the threshold of the shining door, and the first light's pale gleam has broken through, she begins to pour forth melodies of sacred song and to greet the new light with her wonderful voice. The nightingale's calls and the musical flute with its Cirrhaean measures cannot imitate this voice; and no one imagines that the dying swan or the Cyllenean lyre's melodious strings can copy it. After Phoebus has driven his horses into the open Olympian spaces and his entire disk is revealed as it moves onwards, the Phoenix applauds him with three repeated beatings of her wings; and, when she has worshipped his fiery head three times, she falls silent. It is she, too, who divides the fleeting hours by night and day with her ineffable notes. Priestess of the sacred wood and awful guardian of the groves, she alone is privy to your mysteries, Phoebus. After she has completed her thousand years of life and longevity has weighed her down, she flees from the grove's sweet, familiar bed to renew her lost youth as the ages pass away. Abandoning the holy places in her desire for rebirth, she seeks this world where death is ruler. The bird steers her swift flight to Syria; she herself of old gave it the name *Phoenicia*. She looks for secret groves through the desert wildernesses and wherever an unfrequented wood is hidden in the ravines. She chooses a tall palm with its top high in the air: it is called the phoenix-palm in Greek, after the bird. No harmful creature can crawl into it, neither a slippery snake nor bird of prey. Then Aeolus shuts the winds in hanging caverns lest they violate the clear air with their blasts, or a cloud, condensed by the south wind in heaven's spaces, withholds the sunbeams and hinders the bird. The phoenix then builds herself a nest, or [rather] a tomb; for she dies in order to live, though it is she who begets herself. She gathers from the rich forest such juices and perfumes here as the Assyrian or the wealthy Arab selects, or the Pygmies cull, or India, or the land of Sheba produces in its soft bosom. In the nest she heaps up cinnamon and amomum's far-breathing scent and balsam mixed with spikenard leaf; she is not without a twig of delicate cassia or odoriferous acanthus, nor the thick drop of the frankincense's tear. To these she adds the soft ears of ripening nard and joins your pungency, O panacea, with myrrh. Straight-away she lays her mutable body in the nest she has built; on the life-giving bier she lays her quiet limbs. With her beak she sprinkles juices around and over her wings; she will die [performing] her own exequies. Among the various perfumes she then commends her soul, and is not afraid to entrust this precious deposit [to death]. Her body meanwhile is destroyed in a creative death: it grows warm, and the heat gives birth to flame. Taking fire from the sky's distant light, the body blazes up, is consumed and dissolved into ashes. Creating in death, the phoenix collects the ashes into a heap, as it were, and kindles them; and the result is like a seed. Men say the first thing to come from the heap is a limbless creature, a worm; and they say its color is milky. It grows larger, but after a certain time has elapsed, it is lulled to sleep and takes on the shape of a smooth egg. Just as the country chrysalids, while they are fastened by a thread to stones, usually change into a butterfly, so in the same way the bird resumes her former shape: bursting her shell, the phoenix hatches. She is not given any food from our world, and nobody has the task of feeding the fledgling. From heaven's nectar she sips the soft ambrosial dews, which fall from the starry sky. Gathering these dews together, the bird feeds on them in the midst of perfumes, until she attains her mature form. But when her first youth begins to blossom, she flies off; now she is to return to her homeland. But whatever remains from her own body—the bones, ashes and pieces of her shell—she first preserves with a balsamic ointment, myrrh and Sabaean incense which she rolls with dutiful beak into the shape of a ball. Clutching this ball in her claws, she hurries toward the sunrise, and, alighting on the altar, she displays it in the sacred temple. She offers and presents herself to be admired and revered—so great is the bird's beauty, so great is her prestige. From the beginning she has the color of pomegranates when, under the sign of the Crab, they cover their purple seeds with golden rind, or of petals borne by the wild poppy when Flora spreads her skirts in the blushing land. With this veil her shoulders and breast glisten radiantly, and her head and neck and dorsal feathers sparkle with it too. Her tail extends, flecked with fulvous gold, blended with spots of sanguine purple. From above, Iris paints her wing-feathers, just as she often paints a cloud with her mark. Her wonderful white beak is pure ivory brushed with iridescent emerald; when it opens, it is set with jewels. Her eyes are large: you would think they were twin sapphires with a bright flame shining from their midst. A radiant high crown has been fitted on her famous head, reflecting the brilliance of Phoebus at his peak. Scales adorned with tawny gold cover her legs, but a lovely rose tints her claws. In appearance she seems to be a blend of the peacock's form and the painted bird of Phasis [the pheasant]. The winged creature, whether bird or beast [the ostrich], which is born in the lands of Arabia, can hardly equal her size. She is not slow, however, like those great-bodied birds moving forward lazily from their heavy weight; she is light and swift in the fullness of her regal splendor. She always appears thus in the sight of men. [All] Egypt comes here for the wonders of this sight and an exultant crowd greets the rare bird. Immediately they carve her form in hallowed marble and mark both the occasion and day with a new inscription. Birds of every species flock together; each of them has forgotten fear or [the desire] for prey. The phoenix flies through the air accompanied by the choir of birds, and the crowd follows, rejoicing in its pious office. After it reaches the realms of pure ether, however, it retires, and the phoenix is [again] ensconced in her own realm. To this most happy and fortunate of birds, the god has granted the power of being self-born. Whether female, male or neuter sexually, she is happy because she has nothing to do with Venus and her unions: her Venus is death; her only pleasure is in death. So that she can be born, she desires first to die. She is her own child, her own father and heir; she is always her own nurse and her own nursling. Indeed, she is herself, but not the same bird; and she is the same bird, but not herself. Through the goodness of death she has obtained everlasting life.

B. Ambrose, *Hexameron*

Text: *CSEL*, 32, 1.197-8.

79. Men think the phoenix lives in the lands of Arabia and leads a long life, to the age of five hundred. When it realizes the end of its life has come, it builds a nest for itself from incense, myrrh and other spices. With its life span completed, it enters the nest and dies. From the moisture of its flesh a worm rises; in a little while, it grows larger, and, when the proper time has elapsed, it puts on "the oarage of wings" [*Aeneid* 1. 301]. It is recreated in the form and species of the earlier bird. By its example, therefore, let the bird teach us to believe in the Resurrection, because, without a model and without reason's perception, it renews the signs of the Resurrection in itself. Birds can certainly represent men, but not the reverse. Let this be an example, therefore, that the Author and Maker of birds does not permit His saints to die forever. God did not let the unique bird perish; He wanted it to rise again from its own seed and be reborn. Who is it, therefore, who announces the day of death to the bird, so it can make itself a nest, fill it with good spices, enter it and die there where pleasant fragrances can overpower the stench of death?

80. O man, make yourself a nest too. Having thrown off the old man along with his deeds, put on the new man. Your nest, your sheath is Christ, who can protect and hide you in the evil day. Do you want proof that your nest protects you? "With my quiver," the Lord said, "I have protected him" (Isaiah 49.2). Therefore, faith is your nest. Fill it with the good fragrances of your virtues, that is, of chastity, pity and justice. Enter faith's inner sanctuaries which are redolent with the sweet fragrance of excellent deeds. May departure from this life find you clothed in faith, so your bones may put on flesh again and be like a watered garden whose greenery is quickly awakened. Recognize the day of your death, like Paul, who said, "I have fought a good fight; I

have finished the race; I have kept the faith. There is a crown of righteousness in store for me" (II Tim. 4.7, 8). Like the good phoenix he entered his nest and filled it with the excellent fragrance of martyrdom.

C. Physiologus, *The Phoenix*

Text: Francis J. Carmody, ed., *Physiologus Latinus* (Paris, 1939), pp. 20-1.

There is another bird which is called the phoenix. Our Lord Jesus Christ has the same character as it does: He says in His Gospel, "I have the power to lay down my soul and to take it up again" (John 10.18). The Jews were angry because of these words and wanted to stone Him.

Thus in the regions of India there is a bird called the phoenix. Physiologus says that after the phoenix has completed the five hundred years of its life, it enters the woods of Lebanon and fills both its wings with various spices. Certain signs make this fact known to the priest of the city of Heliopolis in the ninth month, Nisan or Adar, that is, Sarmath or Famenoth, which is either the month of March or April. When the priest has seen the sign, he goes in and heaps wood and twigs on the altar; when the phoenix arrives, it enters the city of Heliopolis with both wings full of spices. Seeing the heap of twigs on the altar, the phoenix ascends it at once. Rolling itself in the spices, it lights its own flame and burns itself up. On the next day, when the priest comes, he sees the charred remains of the wood he had put on the altar. Searching around in it, he finds there a little worm fragrant with the sweetest aroma. On the second day, he finds that a small bird has now formed. Returning on the third day, the priest finds that the phoenix is now a fully grown, perfect bird. The phoenix says "farewell" to the priest, flies off and heads for its original home.

So if this bird has the power to kill itself and bring itself back to life, how is it that stupid men grow angry at the word of our Lord Jesus Christ? As true Man and as true Son of God, He had the power to lay down His soul and to take it up again (John 10.18). Therefore, as we have already said above, the phoenix plays the part of our Saviour, who descended from heaven and filled both His wings with the sweetest fragrances, that is, with the words of the New and Old Testaments, saying, "I did not come to destroy the law, but to fulfill it" (Matt. 5.17); and again, "Every scribe instructed in the kingdom of heaven will resemble the man who brings forth both new and old things from his treasure" (Matt. 13.52).

XII

JULIANA

Medieval Christians were especially attracted to the life of Saint Juliana, the Virgin Martyr beheaded on February 16 at Nicomedia sometime between 305 and 311 A. D. Accounts of her martyrdom exist in many versions and attest to the stability and popularity of the legend, but the earliest vernacular adaptation appears to be Cynewulf's Old English poem. His source was a Latin text that presumably resembled the *Acta auctore anonymo ex xi veteribus MSS*, printed by the Bollandists in the seventeenth century. Despite Professor Woolf's later statement that "none of the surviving texts represents that followed by Cynewulf" ("Saints' Lives," in *Continuations and Beginnings: Studies in Old English Literature*, ed. E. G. Stanley [London, 1966], p. 44), most scholars still subscribe to her earlier claim that the similarities in the progress of the action and the numerous identical phrasings suggest Cynewulf's original was closely related to the *Acta* version (see her edition of the poem [London, 1955], p. 13). The likeness was first noted by the great German editor C. W. M. Grein (*Bibliothek der angelsächsischen Poesie*, II [Göttingen, 1858], 409).

The *Martyrology* ascribed to Bede contains an epitome of

Juliana's life, which parallels almost exactly the events chronicled in both the *Acta* and the poem (*PL*, 94.843; see also Entry III). In this connection S. R. T. O. d'Ardenne, the editor of a Middle English life of Juliana, asserts, "It is plain that Bede had access to a detailed Latin version of the life of St. Juliana, one MS. of which was probably the principal source used by Cynewulf" (*þe Liflade ant Te Passiun of Seinte Iulienne*, EETS, no. 248 [London, 1961], p. xx). D'Ardenne's genealogical table showing the relations of the several versions should also be consulted (pp. xxiii-xxiv).

The Acts [of Saint Juliana] by an anonymous author

Text: Johannes Bollandus and Godefridus Henschenius, eds., *Acta Sanctorum, Februarius, Tom. II* (Antwerp, 1658), 873-7.

CHAPTER I

Saint Juliana, having rejected marriage with a pagan prefect, is harshly tortured by him and her father.

Our Saviour's mercy (to which the martyrs' perseverance has testified) crowned the friends of the faith in the end, and dispelled their enemies from the very gates of hell.

In the days of the Emperor Maximianus, a persecutor of the Christian religion, there was a senator in the city of Nicomedia named Eleusius. He was a friend of the emperor and was betrothed to a girl from a noble family named Juliana. Her father was called Africanus; he was a persecutor of Christians also. His wife, while she was inwardly horrified at the sacrileges committed in Mars's name, did not associate with either Christians or pagans. Juliana, who was intelligent, had good sense, dignified conversation and was full of virtue, pondered the fact that He who made heaven and earth is the true God. Devoting herself to prayers, she used to attend God's church every day so she might understand the divine readings. But Eleusius, her fiancé, made haste to celebrate the wedding. She said to him, "Unless you attain the rank of prefect, there is no way I can marry you." When he heard this, Eleusius gave the Emperor Maximianus gifts and replaced another prefect in the administration. Eleusius sat in the coach of state and performed his official duties. When a few days had passed, he sent again to her. Juliana studied [the proposal] with good sense and said to his messengers, "When you return, say to Eleusius, 'If you believe in my God and worship the Father, the Son and the Holy Spirit, I will accept you as a husband; if not, look for another wife.' "

2. When the prefect heard this, he called her father and told him word for word what Juliana had sent him. Upon hearing it, her father said, "By men's merciful and loving gods, if these words are true, I will hand her over to you." Having said this, he rushed to his daughter in a great rage and exclaimed, "My sweetest daughter, Juliana, light of my eyes, why don't you want to take the prefect as your husband? I wish to make your marriage to this man final." Trusting in Christ, blessed Juliana said, "If he will worship the Father, the Son and the Holy Spirit, I will marry him; if not, he cannot receive me in marriage." Hearing this, her father said, "By the merciful gods, Apollo and Diana, if you persist in speaking like this, I will hand you over to wild beasts." Juliana replied, "Father, don't believe I'm afraid of you. By the Son of the living God, I will never give in to you, even if I have to be burnt alive." A second time her father asked her to give in to him so she shouldn't lose the great honor. Juliana replied, "Ah, father, you don't understand what I am saying to you. I speak the truth and do not lie when I say I will suffer every trial and judgment joyfully. I will not abandon the teaching of my Lord Jesus Christ." At once her father ordered her to be stripped and beaten, and said to her, "Why won't you worship the gods?" She cried out, "I do not believe in, I do not worship, I do not sacrifice to deaf and dumb idols. But I worship the Lord Jesus Christ who lives forever and reigns in heaven." After she had been tortured, her father handed her over to the prefect, her fiancé.

3. The prefect ordered her to be led before his tribunal at dawn. When he saw her beauty, he addressed her with the

gentlest words, "Tell me, my sweetest Juliana, why have you mocked me for so long? Who persuaded you to worship a strange god? Turn back to me and escape all the torments prepared for you if you refuse to sacrifice." Blessed Juliana replied, "If you agree with me to worship God the Father, the Son and the Holy Spirit, I will give in to you. But if you refuse, you will not be my lord." The prefect said, "My lady Juliana, give in to me and I will believe in your God." Blessed Juliana replied, "Receive the Spirit of God and I will marry you." The prefect said, "I can't, my lady, because, if I do, the emperor will hear about it; and when he has appointed a successor to me, he will behead me with a sword." Saint Juliana replied, "If you fear this mortal emperor, who sits on a dunghill, how can you compel me to deny the immortal Emperor? So you can't deceive me with all this coaxing. Inflict on me whatever torments you like. I trust in Him, whom Abraham, Isaac and Jacob trusted in, and they were not confounded; for He is powerful enough to free me from your torments."

4. When he heard this, the prefect grew very angry and ordered her to be beaten. After Saint Juliana had been stretched out on the ground, he ordered her to be scourged naked with four switches in such a way that three soldiers alternated beating her in turn. Then the prefect told them to stop and said to her, "Look, this was just the beginning of the test. Give in; sacrifice to the great Diana and you will be freed from torment. But if you refuse, by the great god Apollo, I won't spare you." Saint Juliana replied, "Don't think you can recall me from my Lord Jesus Christ with your threats." Then the prefect ordered her to be suspended by the hair. When she had been hanging for six hours, she cried out, "Christ, Son of God, come and help me." The prefect then ordered her to be taken down and said to her, "Give in, Juliana, and sacrifice so you won't die in torment. For the One whom you think you worship as God will not be able to free you." Juliana replied, "Wretched man, you won't be able to conquer me through your torments. In the Name of my Lord Jesus Christ I shall overcome your savage spirit and make your father, Satan, redden with shame. I will find courage in the sight of my Lord Jesus Christ." Moved with anger, the prefect commanded them to heat metal pots. When Juliana had been

stripped, he ordered her to be plunged in and scalded from head to toe. This was done, but she suffered no harm. Next he ordered her to be bound by the legs and thus taken to prison.

5. Afterwards, when Juliana had been put into prison, she said, "My Lord, almighty God, my soul is at the point of death; strengthen me, hear me, pity me and pity those who stand around me grieving. Give me your mercy, just as you gave it to all who pleased you. Also, I beseech you, Lord, don't forsake me because my father and mother have abandoned me; but receive me, O Lord my God, and do not cast me from your countenance. Don't desert me in this time of trouble, but keep me safe among these tortures. As you saved Daniel in the lions' den and freed Hananiah, Azariah and Mishael from the fiery furnace, so protect me in the brevity of this life. Lead me into the harbor of your will, as you led Israel's sons through the sea, when they fled from Egypt; the sea became land as it were [for them], but buried their enemies. So think me worth listening to, Lord. Drown the threats of the tyrant who has risen against me. Destroy his power and spirit; because you, Lord, who know human nature, know it cannot endure captivity. God, be a ready helper and aid in the torments which Eleusius (who does not obey your express commands) is about to heap upon me. Make this prefect, who is the demons' companion, the object of my scorn. Have him grievously tormented and consumed by worms, so that your power may be revealed through me, your handmaiden. For you alone are God and we proclaim your glory forever and ever. Amen."

CHAPTER II

When he urges wicked things upon her, a demon is beaten by Juliana and dragged away captive.

6. When she had finished the prayer, a demon called Belial appeared to her in an angel's form, and said to her, "My dear Juliana, the prefect is preparing the most evil and terrible torments for you. Only listen to me and you will be saved. When he orders you to leave the prison, give in and sacrifice and you will escape the torments." Saint Juliana thought he was an angel

of God and said to him, "Who are you?" The devil said to her, "I am the Lord's angel. He sent me to you so you would sacrifice and not die." Sighing most bitterly, Juliana cried out to the Lord; raising her eyes to heaven, she said with tears, "O Lord, God of heaven and earth, do not desert me or let your handmaiden perish. Strengthen my heart in your might and show me, as one who trusts in your Name, who it is that speaks such things and urges me to worship idols." Immediately a voice came to her from heaven, saying, "Have faith, Juliana; I who speak to you am with you. Seize the person talking to you so you may know who he is."

7. Rising from the ground, Saint Juliana made the sign of Christ and seized the demon Belial. She said to him, "Tell me, who are you; where do you come from and who sent you to me?" The demon replied, "Let me go and I will tell you." Blessed Juliana said, "You tell me first and then I will let you go." Then the demon began to speak, "I am the demon Belial, whom some call Jopher the Black. I have been entertained by men's wickednesses. I rejoice in murders. I love luxury. I embrace war. I destroy peace. It is I who made Adam and Eve transgress in paradise; I who made Cain kill his brother Abel; I who made all Job's fortune waste away; I who made the people of Israel worship idols in the desert; I who had the prophet Isaiah cut like wood by a saw; I who made King Nabuchodonosor set up an idol; I who had the three boys sent into the fiery furnace; I who caused Jerusalem to be burned; I who had the infants killed by Herod; I who made Judas betray the Son of God (I took possession of Judas so that he finished his life with a noose). It is I who goaded the soldier to pierce the side of God's Son with a lance; I who had John beheaded by Herod; I who said, through Simon, that Peter and Paul were sorcerers; I who entered into the Emperor Nero so that he crucified Peter and beheaded Paul; I who had Andrew betrayed in the region of Patras. I and my brothers have done all these things and worse."

8. Blessed Juliana said, "Who sent you to me?" The demon replied, "Satan, my father." Saint Juliana said, "What do they call your father?" The demon replied, "Beelzebub." Saint Juliana said, "What does he do?" The demon replied, "He is the inventor of all evil. For the moment we are in his presence, he directs us to tempt the souls of the faithful." Saint Juliana said,

"What does the demon rejected by a Christian suffer?" The demon replied, "He suffers the most evil and terrible torments. If we have been sent against a just man to ruin him, and if we cannot do it, we hide from Satan who sent us. For when he has looked for us and doesn't find us, he charges the other demons: once they find the demon he sent, they must torment him cruelly. Then the demon flees so he cannot be found. We have therefore to do what Satan commands and obey him as the most gracious of parents." Saint Juliana said, "Tell me, against what just works do you proceed?" The demon replied, "Listen, my lady, so I may tell you everything and you may know the truth from me. The way in which I have come here to you in my wickedness, thinking to persuade you to sacrifice and deny your God, is the way I and my brothers enter into all men.

9. "When we find a wise man holding fast to God's work, we fill him with many lusts. We turn his soul toward those objects we place near him; we introduce error into his thoughts; and we do not allow him to persevere either in prayer or any good work. Again, if we see people attending church, sorry for their sins, and desiring to hear the Divine Scriptures in order to keep some part of them, we immediately enter their homes. We do not allow them to do anything good and we introduce many thoughts into their hearts. But if one of them can overcome us, and withdraws from his idle thoughts, begins to pray, to listen to the Holy Scriptures and to receive the Divine Mystery, headlong we flee from him. For when Christians receive the Divine Mystery, at that very hour we retreat from them. We care only about the ruination of men who live well. And if we see them do anything good, we afflict them with bitter thoughts so they may follow our wishes."

10. Saint Juliana said, "Impure spirit, how do you presume to meddle with Christians?" The demon replied, "You tell me! How do you dare seize me, unless it is because you trust in Christ? So I too trust my father, since he is the author of wicked deeds; and I do what he wants. For I have tried to carry through a number of evil schemes and several times my plans have turned out successfully. But how miserable I am, now that I have been sent to you! If only I hadn't seen you! Alas, what I suffer in my misery! Why didn't my father see what would happen to me? Let me go, so I can cross over to the other place. For I will

denounce you to my father and it will go badly with you." Saint Juliana then bound his hands behind his back and threw him to the ground. Taking one of the ropes with which she herself was bound, she struck the demon. The demon cried out imploringly, "My lady Juliana, companion of the apostles, associate of the martyrs, partner of the patriarchs, consort of the angels, I entreat you through the Passion of the Lord Jesus Christ, have pity on my wretchedness."

11. Saint Juliana said, "Confess to me, impure spirit, which men have you injured?" The demon replied, "I have blinded the eyes of many men; broken the feet of others; sent others into the fire; hanged others; caused others to vomit blood; drowned others in the sea; made others end their lives violently; made others tear themselves in fury with their own hands. And, to put it briefly, all the evils which exist in this world are executed on my advice, and I myself perform them. Others, whom I have found without the sign of Christ, I have killed. While I did all these evils, nobody dared to torture me as much as you. None of the apostles even gripped my hand, but you have bound me. None of the martyrs beat me. None of the prophets inflicted on me the injuries I have received from you. None of the patriarchs laid a hand upon me. For I undertook the temptation of the Son of God Himself in the desert; I made Him climb a high mountain, but He did nothing to me. And you destroy me with torments like this? Virginity, why are you armed against us? John, why did you reveal your virginity to oppose us?"

12. While the demon was saying this, the prefect ordered Juliana to be brought to him from prison. Saint Juliana dragged the demon with her as she was being led out. The demon pleaded with her, "My lady Juliana, let me go. Don't make me even more ridiculous now to men, for afterwards I'll be unable to conquer them. You have conquered my father; you have bound me. What more do you want? The unbelievers say the Christians are merciful, but you seem ferocious to me." As the demon said this, Saint Juliana dragged him through the market-place; and although he pleaded with her a long time, she threw him into a place full of dung.

CHAPTER III

Saint Juliana is beheaded after various tortures, and one hundred and thirty are converted by her. The translation of her body.

13. As Juliana came into the palace, her face seemed full of glory to everyone. When the prefect had looked at her, he said admiringly, "Tell me, Juliana, who taught you such things? How have you overcome torments as great as these with incantations?" Saint Juliana replied, "Listen to me, most irreverent prefect, and I will tell you. My Lord Jesus Christ taught me to worship the Father, the Son and the Holy Spirit. It was He who conquered your father, Satan, and his demons; it was He who sent His angel from His holy dwelling-place to help and comfort me. But you, wretch, do not know that eternal torments are prepared for you. You will endure unending tortures there, the devouring worm that never stops, and eternal darkness. Unhappy man, repent. For the Lord Jesus Christ is merciful and loving, and He wishes to save all men. He gives repentance for salvation and remission of sins."

14. Then the prefect ordered an iron wheel to be brought in and pointed swords fixed on it; and he ordered the virgin to be placed over the wheel so it would stand between two columns with four soldiers on one side and four on the other. The soldiers drew up the wheel and had Juliana set upon it. After they had drawn it up, they spun the machine, and the noble body of Christ's virgin was split apart in all its members. Marrow came out of her bones and the whole wheel was bathed in it. Flames raged from the fire. Blessed Juliana, however, stood resolute in Christ's faith—her body broken, but her faith firm. And the angel of the Lord came down from heaven and put out the flame; and the chains were melted by the fire.

15. Saint Juliana stood without pain and glorified God; she stretched her hand toward heaven and began to speak with tears and sighs, "Lord God almighty, you who alone possess immortality, Giver of life, Creator of all ages; you who extended the heavens with your hands and established the earth's founda-

tions; you who fashioned man with your hands, Planter of paradise and Governor of the living tree of humanity; you who freed Lot from Sodom because of his hospitality; you who blessed Jacob and freed Joseph from the envy of his brothers (when he was sold into Egypt) and bestowed on him the honor of princes; you who sent your servant Moses into Egypt, saved him from Pharaoh's hand, and led your people through the Red Sea as if it were land; you who subjugated the foreign race, cast down the giant Goliath by the hands of your holy youth, David, and raised him to royal power; you who assumed flesh from the Virgin and were seen by the shepherds; you who are worshipped by angels and were adored by the Magi; you who revived the dead, gathered the apostles together, and commanded them to announce your kingdom; you who were betrayed by Judas, crucified in the flesh, buried in the earth, seen by the disciples after the Resurrection, and ascended into heaven; you who gave knowledge of yourself to all who believe, when you sent your apostles throughout the world; you who are the salvation of the dead, the way for those who err, the refuge for the weak: you are the one, the almighty and only true God; none can praise you for the wrong reason, but only for the right reason. I give thanks to you, God of all, you who have deigned to lead me, unworthy and sinful as I am, into your protection. And I beg, O Lord, that you deign to free me from this tyrant's malice so that he may be totally disgraced, along with his father, Satan. And I will always give glory to you forever and ever."

16. When she had said, "Amen," the tormentors of the city of Nicomedia cried out, "There is one God omnipotent, the God of the holy maiden Juliana and there is no other God but Him. Prefect, we repent that till now we have been led into error." And with one voice they all said, "We flee to you, O Lord. Let it suffice that we have erred thus far; henceforth we will believe in the God whom Juliana worships." Having been converted, they said to the ruler, "May all the pagan gods perish; may all who worship idols be struck down. Irreverent prefect, punish us so that we may expiate our sins, we who have worshipped idols till now. Light the fire. Think of your father's works. For henceforth we choose to have the Lord Jesus Christ as our Father, since we have been afflicted too long by your father, the devil." The prefect, filled with anger, reported everything to the

Emperor Maximianus. The Emperor Maximianus passed sentence against them, and ordered all their heads cut off; but the prefect himself ordered everybody to be struck down by the sword at the same time, and one hundred and thirty men and women were beheaded.

17. The prefect ordered Saint Juliana, however, to be burnt alive. When Saint Juliana heard this, she stretched her hands toward heaven and said with tears, "O Lord God almighty, do not desert me, nor depart from me, nor banish me from your countenance; but be the one who helps me. Deliver me from this punishment and blot out my sins—those I may have committed in word or thought. O Lord, my kind and merciful God, have mercy on me so that my enemy, the tyrant Eleusius, may not say, 'Where is her God?' For you are a God blessed forever." While she was saying this, behold, the angel of the Lord came suddenly, parted the fire and put out the flame. Saint Juliana stood there unharmed, glorifying God in the fire.

18. The prefect roared at her like an evil beast and wondered what punishment to inflict upon her. He commanded a pot to be brought in, filled with lead, and placed over a raging fire [*ignem*]. When Juliana had been set over the pot, it became like a warm bath for her. But the pot itself recoiled from her and burned seventy-five of the men who were standing nearby. When the prefect saw this, he tore his clothes in a rage and berated the gods with a groan, because they could not hurt her, and also because, though she had injured them, they could not harm her at all. He sentenced her at once to be punished by the sword.

19. When Saint Juliana heard this, she was filled with great joy because the end of her struggle had come. After she had been dragged to the place where she was to be beheaded, the demon she had tormented suddenly came running up to the ruler and said, "Don't spare her. She has blasphemed the gods and injured men. I too have endured many evils from her. So give her what she deserves." Saint Juliana opened her eyes slightly to see who was saying such things. Then the timid demon cried out, "Alas for me, miserable wretch; now perhaps she wants to seize me again." He vanished immediately and stopped talking, as he fled.

20. When she had been led to the place where she was to be beheaded, Juliana began to speak to those who had been

converted to the faith and the other Christians there present, "My fathers and mothers, listen to me. Repent that you have sacrificed to demons. Build your houses on firm rock, so you will not be shattered by the coming fierce winds. Always pray constantly in Holy Church, pay attention to the Holy Scriptures, love each other, and the Lord will grant that you find mercy in the sight of His saints. It is good to keep the vigil for God. It is good to sing psalms frequently. It is good to pray without ceasing, because you do not know when you may end this life. I ask you to pray for me, so that my Lord Jesus Christ will find me worthy and will deign to lead me, His humble handmaiden, into His holy court, and watch over the course of my trial so the enemy may not vanquish me." When she had given the peace to all, she prayed again to the Lord, "O Lord God, Father of all, Lover of faith, you who do not betray your image into enemies' hands, have mercy on me, help me and receive my spirit with peace, Lord." As she said this prayer, she was beheaded.

21. After a short time, a certain Sephonia, the wife of a senator, was going through the city of Nicomedia on her way to the city of Rome. She took blessed Juliana's body and embalmed it with aromatics and precious linens. While she was travelling to the city [of Rome], a mighty tempest arose and the boat turned aside to the land of Campania. Juliana was buried near the territory of Puteoli, where she has a mausoleum, a mile from the sea.

22. While the prefect Eleusius, however, was sailing to his estate, a mighty tempest came and swamped his boat. Twenty-four men died and when the water had cast them up in a desert place, their bodies were devoured by beasts and birds. Blessed Juliana suffered on the fourteenth day before the Kalends of March [February 16], at the hands of the prefect Eleusius in the reign of our Lord Jesus Christ, to whom is glory forever and ever. Amen.

XIII

THE ELEGIES

A fragile bond unites the nine poems in *The Exeter Book*, "generally though not unanimously referred to as *elegies*": the *Ruin, Wanderer, Seafarer, Resignation, Riming Poem, Wulf and Eadwacer, Wife's Lament, Husband's Message* and *Deor* (Stanley B. Greenfield, *A Critical History of Old English Literature* [New York, 1965], pp. 213-4). The term begs many questions and we can only point to Greenfield's rather persuasive attempt to define it in a way which is both comprehensive and sensitive to the individual poems: it has obviously come to stay (see "The Old English Elegies," in *Continuations and Beginnings*, ed., E. G. Stanley [London, 1966], p. 143). Along with the problem of the genre, critics have always been drawn to the related problem of the background. Having viewed the elegies first in terms of the melancholy Germanic spirit, they next turned to the Celtic laments and especially to the Welsh lyrics. Most recently, they have stressed the primacy of Latin Christianity, though most acknowledge that all three traditions played a part.

Several interesting Latin parallels have been unearthed for short passages in some of these works. Peter Clemoes, for example, writes convincingly that a portion of Alcuin's *De Animae ratione liber* must have influenced lines 58-64a of *The Seafarer* ("*Mens absentia cogitans* in *The Seafarer* and *The Wanderer*," in *Medieval Literature and Civilization: Studies in Memory of G. N. Garmonsway*, ed. D. A. Pearsall and R. A. Waldron [London, 1969], pp. 62-77). J. E. Cross has done important work on the backgrounds of the "*ubi sunt* motifs" and the "*sum* catalogues" ("*Ubi Sunt* passages in Old English—Sources and Relationships," *Vetenskaps-Societetens i Lund Årsbok* [1956], 25-41; and "On *The Wanderer* Lines 80-84: A Study of a Figure and a Theme," *Vetenskaps-Societetens i Lund Årsbok* [1958-9], 75-110). Yet none of the nine poems considered as a whole has a specific source or a precise analogue; they contain the kind of ruminations on mortality which are universal.

Our selection is therefore arbitrary. Over sixty early sermons have been cited as possible analogues (or sources) to one or another of the elegies; and a similar situation pertains with Latin poetry. In both cases we have included those suggestions encountered most frequently (see I. L. Gordon, ed., *The Seafarer* [London, 1960], pp. 14, 22-3; R. F. Leslie, ed., *The Wanderer* [Manchester, 1966], pp. 25-37; P. L. Henry, *The Early English and Celtic Lyric* [London, 1966], passim; and G. V. Smithers, "The Meaning of *The Seafarer* and *The Wanderer*," *MÆ*, 26 [1957], 137-53; 28 [1959], 1-22, 99-104). Other analogues can be found under Entries IV, IX and XXI.

A. Christian Latin Poems

1. Columbanus, *Verses to Hunaldus*

Text: G. S. M. Walker, ed., *Sancti Columbani Opera* (Dublin, 1957), pp. 184-6.

The seasons of life run on with numberless misfortunes. All things pass away; the months roll by year after year. Life sinks into decay with every moment. Now scorn the soft enticements of fallen life, so you can grasp eternal life. Noble virtue is overcome by the lure of luxury; the breast is aflame with avarice and blind desire. Devoted to empty cares, the mind knows no moderation. Silver is baser than gold, gold baser than the virtues. Best of all is peace: to want nothing beyond what necessity requires.

I have sent you these little verses for you to read often. I beg you to let my words enter your ears. Do not let an empty, perishable pleasure deceive you; see how brief is the power of kings and princes. The deceitful glory of mortal life passes quickly. Forgive me my words; perhaps we have talked too much. Always remember to shun everything excessive.

2. Columbanus, *A Poem on the World's Mutability*

Text: Walker, pp. 182-4.

This world will pass away; daily it wanes. No one will stay alive; no one has stayed alive.

The whole human race is born in the same manner, and, having lived the same life, is subject to the same end.

Uncertain death steals life from those who try to put it off; and death's sorrow seizes all who proudly roam [over the earth].

What greedy men do not want to give away for Christ's sake, they all lose when least they want; others gather it up after them.

When they are alive they hardly venture to give God [one] little thing; but they leave all to death. They keep nothing they possessed.

The present life they love fades daily; the punishment they prepare for themselves will never fail.

The slippery thing they try to amass slips away; and they are not afraid to believe in what seduces them.

They loved the hideous darkness more than the light; they scorned to imitate the Lord and Leader of life.

They rule as if in dreams; for one hour they are happy, but everlasting torments are prepared for them already.

In their blindness they do not see what awaits them after death, and what wickedness bestows on wicked sinners.

Friend, it becomes you to think about all this; keep aloof from loving this life's beauty.

See, all flesh is grass: although it blooms, it is burning. All its glory is like the flowering grass.

The grass withers when the sun comes up and the flower perishes; all youth does the same when virtue departs.

Men's beauty disappears as it grows old; all former dignity is painfully stripped away.

You must love Christ's radiant face, lovely beyond all things, more than the frail blossom of the flesh.

Child, beware of women's beauty, through which death, no small disaster, enters.

Many men have suffered the fires of punishment because they did not want to lose a wayward affection.

Never drink from a wicked woman's cup; you often see many men, happy and laughing there.

For know that the men you see laughing foolishly will be weeping bitterly on the Last Day.

My dear son, realize that lust is like [Adam's] death-bringing bite that destroys sweetness.

Do not rush forward on the road men take, where you can see many have been shipwrecked.

Walk on tiptoe between the snares, which have caught the rest unprepared, as we have learned.

Lift the eyes of your heart from earthly things and love the most loving hosts of angels.

The family which dwells above is blessed; no old man groans there, no infant wails.

There no voice is kept from praising the Lord; no one hungers there, no one ever thirsts.

The heavenly race is fed on celestial food; and no one dies because no one is born.

There is a royal palace . . . in which no unharmonious voice is ever heard.

Life will be youthful and true; neither death nor fear of sorrow will waste it away.

Having passed through death, the joyful will see their joyful King: they will reign with their Ruler; they will rejoice with Him as He rejoices.

Then sorrow, weariness and labor will be abolished; then the King of kings, the immaculate King, will be seen by those who are themselves immaculate.

3. Venantius Fortunatus, *The Destruction of Thuringia*

Text: *MGH, Auctores Antiquissimi*, 4, 1 (Berlin, 1881), 271-5.

Sad condition brought on by war, life's evil fate! How suddenly proud kingdoms fall to their ruin! Roofs which happily stood for ages lie wasted and burnt in the vast destruction. The palace which once flourished with courtly elegance is now roofed with gloomy embers instead of arches. A pale ash has smothered the lofty buildings which used to gleam and shine, adorned with gold. [Thuringia's] royalty has been forced into captivity under an enemy lord; its proud glory has fallen and been humbled. The crowd of glittering attendants which stood there in better days is covered with dust; they have met their fatal day. The famous throng of mighty ministers has no tombs and lacks the honor due to death. A woman, white as milk, lies prostrate on the ground; in her beloved's hair glows the raging, conquering gold of flames. Alas, unburied corpses hideously cover the battlefield: an entire people thus lies in one grave. Troy is no longer alone in lamenting her ruins; the land of Thuringia has suffered the same calamity. The mother with torn hair is bound and taken away: she could not say a sad farewell to her household gods, nor plant kisses on the captured doorpost, nor look at places she will never see again. The [wife's] naked foot has trodden on her husband's blood. The gentle sister passed by her brother as he was lying there. Snatched from his mother's embrace, the boy has been hanged by the neck and no one cried or lamented at his funeral. For the boy to lose his life this way is a milder fate: his sobbing mother has wasted her loving tears.

A foreign woman, I am not equal to the grief; in my overwhelming sorrow I cannot swim in a lake of tears. Each person has had his own grief, but I alone have all. This sorrow is both private and public for me. Fortune took care of those whom the enemy destroyed; I alone survive them all to weep. Not only must I mourn those close to me who died, but also weep for those whom kind life detains. My eyes often press tears down my wet face; and though my murmurs are secret, my care does not stay silent. Gladly I watch to see if the wind will announce that one of my kinsmen is safe, but none of their shadows appears. You whose sight comforted me with its tender love, hostile fate has taken from my embrace; or, since you are gone and my sorrow does not vex you, is it that the bitterness of slaughter carried away your sweet love? Amalfrid, from your earliest years remember what I, your Radegunde, meant to you: son of my father's brother, my kind cousin, remember how much you loved me when you were a sweet child. You alone stood for my dead father and mother, my sister and brother. As a baby, I was held in your loving hands; I hung, alas, upon your soft kisses and was caressed with your gentle words. Scarcely an hour passed when you did not return to me; now centuries flee by and I do not hear your words. Cousin, in my stricken heart, I used to wonder frantically how or when or whence you could be recalled. If your father or mother or affairs of state kept you, to me you were still late, although you hurried. That lot was a sign, dearest, that I would soon be without you. Impassioned love cannot possess for long. I used to be anxious and troubled if one house did not cover us both; if you went outside, I imagined you had gone far away. Now East darkens you and West darkens me; I am held by the Ocean's waves and you by the waves of the East. And the whole earth lies between us lovers. Those whom no place ever kept apart before, the world now separates. However far the earth extends is the distance which has divorced me from my love; if the plains stretched further, you would have gone on an even longer journey. Dwell now where kinsmen's better prayers hold onto you; and be more prosperous than the land of Thuringia permitted.

I am tortured the more, weighed down by heavy sorrows, wondering why you have not wanted to send me some sign of yourself. I do not see you whom I desire. A letter might have depicted your face, a portrait restored the man whom distance keeps from me. By the flattering power of a portrait one may bring back ancestors and those close to one, just as your father's ruddy complexion plays [again] in your handsome face. Believe me, cousin, if only you wrote something, you would not be completely absent; if you sent a page, a part of my brother would speak to me. Everyone has some solace, but I have no consolation for my tears. It is unjust that the more I love, the less I have. If some search for their servants out of a sense of duty, why, I beg you, am I, a kinswoman joined to you by blood, forgotten? To ransom a family slave, the master himself often struggles through the Alps, through waters frozen by cold and snow. He enters shadowy caves carved in the rocks; no frost can extinguish the burning love he feels. With none to guide him, the lover runs barefoot and seizes his own booty in the teeth of the enemy opposition. Though he is wounded, he crosses the hostile lines to recover the object of his longing: love never spares itself. But waiting in suspense for you through all these hours, my mind scarcely enjoys a moment's rest from care. If the air whispers, I ask it where you live; if the overhanging clouds wing by, I ask them the place. Does warlike Persia or Byzantium choose you; or the wealth of the royal city of Alexandria lead you away? Do you live near Jerusalem's citadel where the Virgin Mother gave birth to Christ God? No letter in your hand has come to tell me; my grief is heavier, therefore, and takes up arms. But if the earth and sea send me no tokens, I wish a bird would come and bring me happy news! If a monastery's sacred cloisters did not keep me, I would have arrived unexpectedly in the region where you dwell. I would have been ready to cross the storm-tossed seas in a boat. Gladly I would be moved on the waves by winter winds; bravely I would float on the risen flood. A lover would not tremble at what a sailor fears. In the menacing storms, if a wave shattered the ship, I would seek you by rowing across the sea carried on a plank. If my luckless fate forbade me to seize hold of it, I would come to you exhausted by simply swimming. When I saw you again, I would deny the journey's dangers—your sweetness would at once remove the burden of shipwreck. Or, if my ultimate fate were to have my sorrowing life snatched away, the sand would give me a grave dug by your hands. I would die before your kind eyes, a lifeless corpse, in order to bring you to my exequies. You, who reject my living tears, would cry then and bury me; you, who refuse to write me now, would then lament.

Cousin, why do I flee from remembering, why do I postpone my mourning? Deep grief, why are you silent about my brother's murder? How could an innocent man have fallen into that dreadful ambush; and was he snatched from the world when there had been a pledge of faith? Alas for me, by referring to the dead, I renew my tears; when I talk of those lamentable events, I suffer again. When my brother hastens longingly to see your faces, [kinsmen,] his love is not fulfilled as long as mine blocks the way. When he shrank from hurting me, he inflicted wounds on himself: that he was afraid to cause pain is the reason for present sorrow. As a young man, his beard soft with down, he was killed. I did not see his grim funeral; his sister, I was not there. Not only did I lose him, I did not even close his loving eyes. I did not say a last farewell, casting myself on top of him. I did not warm his cold heart with my hot tears, nor bear kisses away from the dying [lips] I loved. I did not cling to his neck in a sad embrace and weep. I did not cherish his body in my hapless bosom and cry. Life was being denied him: why couldn't a sister seize the breath [in a last kiss] as it left her brother's mouth? The things I embroidered for him when he was alive, I would have sent for his bier; or isn't my love allowed to adorn a dead brother? Believe me, brother, I am the wicked one; I am the person answerable for your safety. I alone was the cause of your death and I never gave you a grave. I left my homeland once, but twice remained a captive. I endured my enemies again while my brother lay dead. Father, mother, uncle, kinsmen, you whom I would weep for in the grave, this grief restored [him to you]. Since my brother's funeral, no day is empty of tears; he has carried my joys to their ghosts with him. Thus wretchedness has consumed my dear kinsmen; and my royal father's blood, was it the beginning of a succession [of murders]?

[Cousin,] the evils I have suffered I would not tell you now. Wounded like this, I am not heartened by your words. Glad kinsman, please write me a letter quickly, so your loving tongue may lighten my grievous misfortune. My care for you is for your sisters too; I cherish them in my heart with the love that comes from a blood-tie. I am not permitted to embrace the precious limbs of my parents, nor plant a sister's eager kisses on my brother's eyes. If, as I hope, they dwell in heaven, I ask you to greet them for me; and bring them dear kisses according to my prayers. I beg you to commend me to the kings of the Franks who look after me with a mother's love. Breathe and live long: may my salvation bloom out of your honor.

Christ, hear my prayers. May loving [eyes] look upon this page; may a letter come back to me with a pen's sweet strokes. I have had my hopes delayed and tormented for so long. May my prayers succeed and the swift dispatch of a letter comfort me.

4. Alcuin, *On the Sack of the Monastery at Lindisfarne*

Text: *MGH, Poetae Latini Aevi Carolini*, 1 (Berlin, 1881), 229-35.

After the first man had left the gardens of paradise, and entered the earth's desolate regions as a wretched exile, he paid the penalty of grevious banishment along with his offspring. Because mortal life brings with it covert evils and treachery, it encounters various disasters. Each man's days are different. Sad things are mixed with happy in the course of fate, and no one has been firmly assured of happiness. No one's days have all been forever prosperous, and no one has joys which always endure. Under the heavens' high pole nothing remains everlasting, and all things change at various times. One day laughs and on the morrow another bewails its misfortunes. A happy throw of the dice will not make anything permanent for you. Impious chance always troubles prosperity with sorrow; vicissitudes roll in and out like waves of the sea. Day shines kindly now, but black night will come with its shadows. Spring puts forth its buds, and winter bears off their glory. The celestial vault is painted with kind stars and suddenly storm clouds snatch them away. At midday the burning sun itself is hidden, when a surging southwind thunders from heaven's height. Lightning more often strikes lofty mountains; its flame is used to hitting tree-tops. Unexpectedly, yet without cease, the greatest things will come to greater ruin, fall to their utter destruction. The world which is everywhere on the brink of annihilation gives us these examples: the man who blossoms with riches, perishes in the sea. Now you can see the overthrow of the kingdoms, long ago predicted by the voice of the prophets through the earth's four corners. O mighty Babylon and the Chaldean provinces, the kingdom's capital and its kings' chief source of power, you have fallen! Alas, one woman alone with her arrows destroyed you, Persia, though you were famous for war and magnificent triumphs! Look how envious fate carried off Alexander, conqueror of the earth, at the peak of his prosperity! Rome, head of the world, the world's glory, golden Rome, nothing is left for you now but dire ruins! Swords have levelled the pride of the soldier's camp: the shabby threads of mats lying useless is all you can see. What shall I sing of you, holy, glorious city of King David, beyond comparison with all the places in the world? In you dwelt God's temples and worship, praise, glory and power; in you dwelt triumphant the fathers' holy children. Who can restrain his tears when he sees your end: a race hateful to God now occupies your buildings. Alas, Judea, your citizens of old now wander at random and your fame has died completely! The noble temple which Solomon made, and which was venerated through the entire world, the Chaldean flame devours. The Roman power hurled it down again in war, burning its ramparts and roofs together into ashes. Look how the home at Siloam has remained abandoned through the centuries, where stood the sacred ark of almighty God! Thus all the glory that man's hand has made passes away; the world's glory vanishes like a shadow. Just as a thirsty man vainly dreams of flowing waters, so a rich man will possess the world's wealth and still be destitute.

Why should I tell of remote times only in my grief; why bewail the unhappy days of the past with my song, when throughout the world the present age suffers still worse calamities and the earth grieves under the sway of misery? Broad Asia groans, weighed down by pagan chains; a race hateful to God afflicts and despoils her. To one's grief, alas, Africa, the third part of the great world, is wholly enslaved by evil rulers. The people of Spain, a nation once renowned in war, also serve hated scepters. Whatever glory fine lords and temples possessed, the pagan hand has devastated and seized for itself. Yet the evil which is general throughout the world may bring relief to the particular evil each man endures alone, so he may bear it more easily. Now God's bountiful home where Prince Peter rests in body, the first father in the apostolic ark, is said to have been ravaged by perfidious troops; their wicked hands carried off the treasures of that house. All Italy mourned at the time of the Goths: everywhere the enemy ruined God's temples; the blood of saints poured out and swam in the palace where the Almighty was first loved and honored. For thrice three years all Gaul felt the Huns' swords and was robbed of its goods. The voracious fire seized upon churches, cities, villages, forts and sanctuaries and their residents alike. I am not in a position to know, Jesus, why, in your hidden judgment, you permit such disasters to happen in the world. Another life awaits your [chosen] ones in heaven's height, where gentle peace flourishes and no battles are waged. As the flame proves the gold, so temptation purifies good men; and so the purer soul may seek out the heavenly stars. For a good man this entire life is a temptation, as the pages of Scripture have sung in your ears. Lovingly the father embraces the child whom later he will hurt with a hard beating. Thus God omnipotent proved the saints through cruel scourgings and afterwards gave them the rewards of happiness in heaven.

Do not let yourselves be overthrown by inconstancy, holy brothers, nor by the changeable waters of the world. The world's order has been and always will be transient; one can never have certain faith in its gladness. The man who once strove in the fields hunting the stag, now lies in bed because weary old age has arrived. The man who once happily reclined on a purple spread, scarcely covers his cold limbs with an old rag. The long day which used to number the atoms as they wandered in a sunbeam closes the eyes with a black mist. The hand which brandished swords and heavy weapons now trembles and laboriously lifts food to the mouth. Look how the voice that used to be clearer than a trumpet has suddenly stuck in the throat; even for ears brought close, it produces only stifled murmurs.

Why should I sing further? All youth grows feeble and all the body's beauty dies and falls away; the empty skin barely sticks to the bones. The old man does not recognize his own limbs. He will be other than he was and not his former self; at various times he will be his own thief. Thus the day that is to come will change our minds and limbs. Would that a better day might profit those who deserve it. Therefore, let us always love things that last in heaven rather than those that perish on earth. Here time changes; you see nothing that does not change. There, there will always be one day which will ever be. You, my reader, turn your mind, I beg you, thither: behold, you will find whatever your heart longs for. Stranger in this world, as long as your hope never fails you, you will see the homeland your love desires. When you come there, you will discover the blessed goods of eternal life, which you can possess forever. A happy citizen, you will be united to Christ for eternity. He lives forever, and you too will live forever. Why do you sadly bewail the loss of your gold? It is better to win God than gold. Why, my son, do you pursue vanities with your tearful complaints; why do you yearn for things that die? A lover of the world, not a lover of Christ, mourns for such things. I beg you, let Christ be your love, not gold.

O brothers, whom I care for, let me turn to you; let me address you and the Muses now with a few verses. You are a royal breed, the venerable offspring of holy parents who begot you for God. For their heavenly gifts, bring hither your thirsty ears, together with a reverent heart, mind and hand. May prayers always preserve the holy sheepfold, which they established for God with a single heart. Do not let the fearful temptation, which a wicked, ungodly hand has inflicted on you, break your spirits. But rather let it enrich you, so you may learn to live better, and spur your minds to be in God's presence always. God raises those who have been crushed; He wounds and heals; He strikes and makes whole; He grinds down and lifts up. Apply yourselves to holy prayers both night and day, so that merciful Jesus may everywhere preserve you. With a single heart learn what is pleasing [to Christ], and set your hand to what your devout mind longs for. Thus a heavenly shield will descend for you at last, and the Lord's hand protect and guide you. Remember your fathers, to whom kind assistance always came from heaven, from the generous Thunderer. Now Moses, even stronger in his prayers than in arms, extends his palms and wages sacred battles. Many thousands of the wicked are overthrown by death through King Hezekiah's tears—merciful God added fifteen years to Hezekiah's life because of the prayer that poured from his mouth as he was dying.

Brothers, let me sing things known to you, the former deeds of the pontifical head of your church. Once through the prayers of the famous bishop, Aidan, who was some distance away from the city of Bamborough, the flame turned back on itself. Through his prayers Eadbert, your reverend bishop and father, allayed the winds which were threatening death. And our little verses need not say how many things the great father Cuthbert, the glory of your church, bishop, shepherd and priest, himself performed with his reverent prayers through God's generosity. Although the famous master Bede earlier expounded the glorious deeds of Father [Cuthbert] in his heroic verses, the whole of Britain now both celebrates him with countless praises and beseeches him to help them with their pious prayers. If you always maintain their precepts with a firm love of God, these and other fathers instantly favor prayers to guard your sheepfold and ramparts when the enemy has been expelled.

Brothers, you have read that the time which is to come will be better than that which has gone before; this may be true for you as well, if you trust in the Lord with your whole heart. He is accustomed to give greater gifts after great suffering. But you, Bishop [Higbald], successor of holy ancestors, you who feed the people and hold the holy places, I see you are weighed down by a great burden of cares, because such dire calamities have struck in your time. Dearest brother, I weep with you for your misfortunes; tears flow down my face; my sad heart grieves. Frequently, murmuring in silence, I say to myself how all must lament that day, when the pagan troop, coming from the ends of the earth, suddenly sought our shores by boat. Despoiling our fathers' venerable tombs of their splendor, they even disfigured the temples consecrated to God. Sorehc, the purest vineyard of Christ God, was suddenly food for the fox's teeth. The living stones perished around the altars. Thus, behold, my lyre groans the more: it used to bear gifts to the Lord (and I believe it too was a holy gift), but it has now become a victim [to grief]. Though the day has made us sad in heart, it was a happy one for the monks when they thus set out for heaven. They suffered the sword for Christ's sake and were joined by their sacred blood to the saints. Therefore, I do not think we should mourn them; a better life in heaven has seized them for itself.

So cease, bishop, to weep for them with tears; Christ will have them as His companions forever. Rather, furnish yourself with greater strength so there may be no sadness wherever you go. Glorious patience bestows perpetual life, as God's truth-telling voice has told us. Sad priest, bear Christ's burden patiently. Job, the victor, will give you an example; and Paul, powerful in mind, the Church's soldier through a thousand triumphs, did not grieve over his wounds. What warrior may take the palm of victory without a struggle? Heinous wars will give great rewards to their own; the saints seek the blessed kingdoms in martyrdom, through swords, deaths, diseases, weapons, fires. That man already rejoices with the garland of war, who conquers with the garland [of martyrdom]; after earth's battles, he reigns in heaven's heights. Now quickly correct whatever in your conduct has displeased Christ (who sees all things), so the Holy Shepherd may guard the famous sheepfold, lest the wolf surprise it in his raids. God must not be blamed for these punishments, but we must at once live better lives. With our prayers we must acquire His holy mercy, so He may free us from these tribulations and mercifully give comforts to His servants, granting them everlasting prosperity. With a joyful mind, let us sing hymns of praise with all the thrones on high, at all times and in all places. Praise be to Him, worship, honor, virtue, blessing and song; to God be great glory forever and ever.

B. Latin Homilies

1. Pseudo-Augustine, *Sermon 68*

Text: *PL,* 40.1354-5.

How we should resist vices with virtues; and on hell's misery.

Brothers, there are three causes that should make us particularly afraid: gluttony, cupidity and pride; because it was through these three that the devil deceived our father, Adam, when he said, "The day you eat this fruit, your eyes will be opened and you will be like gods" (Gen. 3.5). Let us understand these three evil causes and be afraid of them; otherwise we may be expelled like Adam, naked from paradise. Practise abstinence against gluttony and stuffing the stomach; practise spiritual poverty and almsgiving against cupidity and avarice; practise true humility and total obedience against pride and arrogance. Know that we have God's angel[s] as guardians, as the Saviour Himself said, "Truly I tell you their angels always see the face of my Father who is in heaven" (Matt. 18.10). So we can certainly believe that everything we do by day and night—good or bad—will be announced by them in God's presence. For the good angel encourages us with the counsel of right action to believe that when we do something good he is at our right hand. But when we think about or do something evil—big or small—undoubtedly we have the bad angel encouraging us. He rejoices over this and laughs at us, while the good angel sorrows and grieves. So when we talk idly or do something evil, the counsel is diabolical. But when we lament and sigh over our sins or perform good deeds, then we have God's holy angel helping and counseling us. So let us use expert vigilance to watch for these three causes, which we mentioned above, and which the devil gave to Adam, by urging his bad advice. For these three—gluttony, cupidity and pride—generate an infinite number of evils. The main bad roots of vices, they occasion sacrilege, homicide, fornication, theft, avarice, luxury, false testimony, anger, discord, perjury and so on. Therefore, dearest brothers, against pride and arrogance, let us oppose true humility; against gluttony, abstinence; against cupidity, almsgiving; against sacrilege, perfect penitence; against homicide, the love of God and neighbor; against theft, kindness; against avarice, charity; against luxury, chastity; against false testimony, the truth of heart and tongue; against anger, peace; against discord, true concord and the firm bond of peace; against perjury, fear of the Lord; and above all these let us put firm hope, upright faith and perfect charity. Thus with virtues countering vices and opposites curing opposites, let us live before God and men with justice and equity. For the angelic arms are the corselet and bow of the virtues, the steadfast shield of faith and the helmet of salvation. He who does not hesitate to carry these with him in faith cannot be harmed by the devil in any way. Dearest brothers, we must so arm ourselves against the wicked enemy, that is, mankind's most savage foe, that we can have the strength to overcome him like men; like a thief, he is always ready to steal our good deeds by offering us bad counsel. Many men are certainly deceived by his diabolical audacity, and they are deceived too by their own sense of security which is self-invented; for they say, "I am young; while I have the time and youth blossoms in me, I will enjoy the world. When I reach old age and can no longer do what I want, then I will be abstinent and do penance." The wretched man does not know that not one hour or moment is guaranteed him, nor even power over his own life. Alas, dearest brothers, do not let this wicked security deceive or seduce you; it cannot be called security, but rather danger. So let us always remember the day of death and always stand in the fear of the Lord. Let us do penance; for our crossing, that is, our life in this world, is brief, and the power of this present temporal world is transitory, fragile and wretched. Tell me, where are the emperors and kings, where are the generals, the princes and barons, and where are their treasures, gold and silver? It is written: "Those in power will endure powerful torments" (Sap. 6.7). Woe for such a dark mansion, woe for such a torpid pit, woe for such a shadowy, deep, dim cavern. Dearest brothers, let us consider how such a long-lasting calamity comes from such small comfort; how such long sadness comes from such brief delight; how such great darkness comes from so little light; how such terrible loss comes from such meager wealth; how such dire danger comes from such worthless security; how such long and endlessly enduring torments come from such little power in this life; how such continual and yet bitter tears come from such passing mirth. Let us consider how the dreadful pains of hell come from the pomps of this empty world. The father will not free his son from these pains, nor will the son go bail for his father. There you will not find a friend to redeem you, nor a brother to help you; there people try to die, but cannot obtain death. Slow, bitter penance is done there, but the penitent gains nothing by it. There is no life there, but the dread mansion and eternal death, the dark fire and place of horror, the inextinguishable, infernal flame, vast torments and deep sighs, mournful lamentations and endless weariness. There the wretched dwell with the wretched, the proud with the proud, the murderers with murderers, the adulterers with adulterers, the greedy with the greedy, the thieves with the wicked, the false lords with their false subjects, the dissolute religious with their dissolute associates and lascivious women, and so with each one. All of them will be tortured together indescribably and endlessly tormented in the infernal prison. May almighty God deign to rescue from it those of us who have corrected our vices, God who lives and reigns, world without end. Amen.

2. Caesarius of Arles, *Sermon 151*

Text: *CC,* 104.617-21.

Saint Caesarius' sermon on the earthly pilgrimage of Christians, the pleasant way which leads to death and the rugged way which leads to life, and the fact that our home is paradise where all the saints departed from this world await us with outstretched arms of love.

We are going to preach to you, dearest brothers, about the text in the gospel: "Strait and narrow is the way which leads to life; broad and spacious is the way which leads to death" (Matt. 7, 13-4); that is, our sermon is about the earthly pilgrimage of Christians.

If the exigency of time permitted, dearest brothers, we would like to visit you not just once a year, but two or three times, so we could see enough of each other; which is what both you and I want. But the exigency of time does not allow us to do what we want. Still, it does not really matter to you or me that we see each other in body rather infrequently, when we are always together in love and charity. For, even if we could be in one city, we could not always be together on this pilgrimage through the world. But there is another city where good Christians will never be separated from each other.

2. There are two cities, dearest brothers: one is the city of the world, the other is the city of paradise. In the city of the world

the good Christian is always a pilgrim; in the city of paradise he is an acknowledged citizen. The former is the city of work, the latter of rest; one is wretched, the other blessed; men are always laboring in the one, in the other they rest from labor. Men who live evil lives here can never arrive at the city of paradise. We ought to be pilgrims in this world, so we can deserve to be citizens in heaven. The person who loves this world and wants to be a citizen in it will have no share in heaven. We prove that we are pilgrims in this world if we long for the homeland. Do not let anyone of you deceive himself, dearest brothers; the homeland for Christians is in heaven, not here: the city for Christians, the blessedness for Christians, the true, eternal happiness for Christians, is not here. The man who looks for happiness in this world will not have it in heaven. Our homeland is paradise; our city is the celestial Jerusalem; our fellow citizens are the angels; our fathers are the patriarchs and prophets, the apostles and martyrs; and our King is Christ. Let us live on this earthly pilgrimage so that while we are here we can long for such a homeland; for the person who wants to live an evil life cannot long for that home.

3. A multitude of patriarchs and prophets have gone there before us, the glorious army of apostles and martyrs, the many thousands of confessors and virgins, and the no small number of the faithful. They are already established in blessed repose and they wait for us daily with outstretched arms of love; together they hope and pray that they may receive us as victors with triumph and exultation into the homeland of paradise from this world's arena (where we have to fight against the devil). For if we do good things, if we scorn the sins of the devil in this world and the delights which bring death, we create joy among all those in heaven. But if we despise God and love the world, if we embrace crimes and sins, we bring sorrow, as we said above, to all the angels, apostles and martyrs in heaven, and we prepare eternal fire for ourselves. So I ask you, brothers, if we do not grieve for our own sake, let us grieve for the sake of those we make sad when we do evil.

4. Behold, Christ with His angels waits in heaven to see how we will fight against the devil and his angels. Let us not be afraid, brothers; for Christ not only waits for us, but He also helps us. Do not be afraid; do not despair. The devil rages, but Christ

offers us consolation. He waits for you while you fight; He helps you while you struggle; He crowns you when you are victorious. Do not despair; do not give in. You have such a general over you and you are afraid? Consider what the devil promises you and what Christ will give you: the devil promises false pleasure; Christ, true happiness. The devil offers the vain joys of the world; Christ, the true happiness of paradise. In adultery the devil provides the delight of one lustful hour, so he can kill the immortal soul; Christ recommends that you be chaste in this world for the few days of your life, so He can make you like the angels in heaven. Through the broad and spacious way of self-indulgence the devil tempts you into hell; through the strait and narrow way of chastity and mercy Christ invites you into heaven.

5. Behold, man, you have "water and fire" (Eccl. 15.17); you have "life and death"; "good and evil" (Eccl. 15.18) are before you, hell and heaven, the true King and the cruel tyrant, this world's false pleasure and the true happiness of paradise. Power has been given you through the grace of Christ: "put out your hand and take what you want" (Eccl. 15.17); "choose life in order to live" (Deut. 30.19). Abandon the broad way on the left which leads you to death and take the narrow way on the right which leads you happily to life. Let not the breadth of the way on the left take hold of or please you; it is indeed wide, level and adorned with various flowers, but its flowers quickly wither and poisonous snakes frequently lurk among them, so that when you chase after false joys, you will be struck with deadly poison. That way is broad, but not long. You care about the kind of road you walk on, but you do not care about the sort of home you reach. If you believe me, you will drag yourself away from death; but if you do not believe in Christ, you will perish in hell. For the Lord Himself said in the Gospel, "Broad and spacious is the way which leads to death and there are many who enter it" (Matt. 7.13). Indeed, it is pleasant for a time, but it deceives for eternity. On the other hand, the right way cannot make you sad or frighten you: it is indeed narrow, but it is not long. On the broad way a man will not rejoice for very long; on this narrow way he will not labor for very long. After being broad for a short time, the former leads to everlasting imprisonment; after being narrow for a short time, the latter leads to eternal blessedness.

6. So with God's help, let us try to work hard, dearest

brothers, and repudiate our sins; let us so adorn ourselves with good deeds that Christ, our King, and our fellow citizens, the angels, and our fathers, the patriarchs, prophets, apostles, martyrs, confessors and virgins, who have already gone before us happily into our city, heavenly Jerusalem, may receive us with joy and exultation. Let us do this, brothers, so our good deeds may occasion "joy in heaven for the one sinner who repents" (Luke 15.7), as the Lord Himself once deemed to tell us. If we occasion joy in heaven when we repent, we shall certainly cause sorrow when we return to the pleasures of our sins.

7. And therefore, dearest brothers, in order that we may avoid all sins with God's help, let us take care to preserve perfect charity; to love not only our friends, but also our enemies; to wish everybody well and to pray for all men. For, if you do to all men what you wish them to do to you, you shut the door on your sins completely; if with your whole heart you desire to love not only your friends, but also your enemies, sin will have no way of entering your soul.

8. I beg you, brothers, let us live in this world as if we were strangers and pilgrims. Whatever we acquire by doing some work, or by some legitimate business, or by some upright and considerable effort, let us restore to our everlasting homeland through almsgiving. Leaving aside our daily food and basic clothing, do not let indulgence squander what is left in this exile, in this earthly pilgrimage, but let pity send it to our homeland. Brothers, we journey towards, we aim for, our homeland; on the journey through this life let us not be self-indulgent, let us never be careless. But always vigilant, cautious and careful, let us not prepare pleasures for ourselves along the way; thus we can carry home something better. If we use [*consumus*] whatever we may acquire through work in this [transitory] home for indulgence, gluttony and drunkenness, how shall we reach the eternal home? With what sort of affrontery can we walk in among the angels and archangels when we are naked of good works, covered with the sordid rags of our sins and lacerated by our evil deeds? Whatever gluttony would squander, let almsgiving restore; whatever avarice has hidden in the earth, let pity send to heaven; so when our soul departs from this weak body, it may be adorned with the splendid garments of chastity and mercy, with

the pearls of patience, humility and concord; and so we may deserve to hear these words from the Lord: "Well done, my good and faithful servant; enter into the joy of your Lord" (Matt. 25.21). We ought to long for this voice, brothers, and we ought to be afraid of that other voice which the soul, naked of good works and covered in the filth of its vices, will hear. For the Lord speaks about this kind of soul in the Gospel: "Friend, how is it you entered here without your bridal gown?" (Matt. 22.12). When the soul remains mute, the Lord says to His attendants, "Bind his hands and feet, and throw him into the outer darkness, where there will be wailing and gnashing of teeth" (Matt. 22.13). May God avert this sentence from us. The people who indulge themselves will be the only ones to hear it: those who are clothed with precious ornaments for the sake of worldly vanity and pomp, and who seize other people's possessions, who satiate themselves upon numerous delights to the point of nausea, who ruin themselves with too much wine and restore nothing or very little to heaven through almsgiving. The apostle says about such people, "The soul which dwells in these delights is dead while it is still alive" (cf. I Timothy 5.6). When their souls depart from the body, they are not lifted up by angels into Abraham's bosom along with Lazarus; they are drowned in the depths of hell with Dives in his purple. When we think about these things, insofar as we can, let us be sparing in our food and clothing while we are in this world, so we may deserve to be adorned in heaven after our death with the glorious, priceless garments of our almsgiving, and to hear that longed-for voice saying, "Well done, my good and faithful servant; since you have been faithful over a few things, I will set you over many. Enter into the joy of your Lord." (Matt. 25.21). May the merciful Lord protect us and lead us to this joy, He who lives and reigns [forever].

XIV

THE GIFTS OF MEN

Three Old English poems treat the theme known as "the gifts of men": one poem is so named, while substantial sections of *The Fortunes of Men* (67-98) and *Christ II* (664-85) also contain the theme. A. S. Cook cites classical examples attesting to its universality (*The Christ of Cynewulf* [Boston, 1909], pp. 136-7). In a Christian context, J. E. Cross directs our attention to the Parable of the Talents (Matt. 25.14-30); to the Pauline comments on the Parable (Romans 12.6-8; I Cor. 12.8-10; Eph. 4.8); and to the patristic writings, especially Gregory's *Homily 9* from the *Forty Homilies on the Gospels* (see "The Old English Poetic Theme of 'The Gifts of Men'," *Neophil*, 46 [1962], 66-70). Cross discovers the most interesting analogue to the three Old English texts "in a sermon for the common of saints on confessors" by the ninth-century bishop, Haymo of Halberstadt (p. 68). The work should probably be attributed to Haymo of Auxerre, who flourished at the same time as the Bishop of Halberstadt—so Glorieux claims in his "Tables Rectificatives" to Migne (*PRM*, p. 57). Although the source for Glorieux' note mentions only the works which precede and follow the section under consideration (see P. C. Spicq, *Esquisse d'une histoire de l'exégèse latine au moyen âge* [Paris, 1944], p. 51), none of the items in *PL*, 118 seems to belong to Haymo of Halberstadt, and Glorieux' attribution is therefore reasonable. We print that portion of the sermon which is relevant to all three English versions, while reminding the reader that the biblical sources are more important. (See also Entry VIIIA.)

Haymo of Auxerre, *Several Homilies on the Saints, IX*

Text: *PL*, 118.784-5.

(D) Thus, dearest brothers, following in the footsteps of our most blessed Father, none of us must hide the talent we received from God in the earth, but study with great zeal how to spend it, so we may return it to God doubled. And let each man study how to spend [his own particular talent]—one his skill in reading, another in singing, another in preaching, another in painting, another the talent he received in making those things required to adorn a church, another [in teaching] what he has learned.

Such [talents] exist not only in ecclesiastical occupations, but also among the people, who have various skills by which they support themselves: some are masons, others carpenters, others smiths, others workmen; and for each man the skill by which he earns his living will be considered worth a talent. If he instructs others in what he knows, he will receive a reward in the future.

XV

PHYSIOLOGUS

The origins of the *Physiologus* are obscure, but Alexandrian scholars probably created it in the second or third century by working over the tales of beasts, plants and stones, real and fantastic, that "were the common property of the ancient world" (Florence McCulloch, *Medieval Latin and French Bestiaries*, University of North Carolina Studies in the Romance Languages and Literatures, No. 33 [Chapel Hill, 1960], p. 19). These tales were then made into Christian allegories so that "creatures of nature were to be explored for what they revealed of the hidden power and wisdom of God" (McCulloch, pp. 17-8). While the original *Physiologus* was in Greek (and it has been attributed to several early Church Fathers), translations eventually appeared in nearly all the languages of Europe, Asia Minor and North Africa. During the fourth century there was almost certainly a translation into Latin, for Ambrose quotes material about the Partridge in his *Hexameron* composed between 386 and 388.

Different types of the Latin *Physiologus* exist; but "it is from the complete *Versio B*, which takes its name and part of its substance from MS B (Bern, Lat. 233, f. 1-13, VIII-IX cent.), that the main Latin versions in England and France were to develop in the Middle Ages" (McCulloch, p. 25). The Bern MS is particularly important, since scholars have often compared it with the Old English triptych (see A. Ebert, "Der angelsächsische Physiologus," *Anglia*, 6 [1883], 241-7; and Francesco Cordasco,

"The Old English *Physiologus*: Its Problems," *MLQ*, 10 [1949], 351-5).

Two questions dominate study of the three Anglo-Saxon poems: are they a whole "cycle" or part of a longer series? What bird is described in the third poem (see *ASPR*, III, xlix)? Krapp and Dobbie (p. li) and Cordasco (p. 355) believe that the Old English "cycle" is complete and that the bird is probably the Partridge. We print translations, therefore, of the Panther, the Whale and the Partridge from the Latin of *Versio B*.

Texts: Francis J. Carmody, ed., *Physiologus Latinus* (Paris, 1939), pp. 40-6.

A. *The Panther*

There is an animal called the panther: it is mottled, but very beautiful and exceedingly gentle. Physiologus says it has only one enemy, the dragon. When the panther has eaten and satisfied its hunger on various game, it hides itself in its own cave, lies down and sleeps. After three days it arises from sleep and at once lets out a great roar. Along with this roar a fragrance of such sweetness comes out of its mouth, that it overpowers every spice. When all the beasts from far and near hear its voice, they all gather together and follow the sweet fragrance which comes from its mouth. Only the dragon is stricken with fear when it hears the panther's voice; it shuts itself up in the earth's underground caves, where it will not have to endure the sweet aroma's strength. Curled up in itself, the dragon drowses and stays there without moving, as if dead. But the rest of the animals follow the panther wherever it goes.

So our Lord Jesus Christ, the true Panther, drew the whole human race (which had been captured by the devil and held subject to death) to Himself through His Incarnation. "He led captivity captive" (Eph. 4.8). As the prophet David says, "When you ascended into heaven, you seized captivity and accepted gifts among men" (Ps. 67.19). For when the panther seizes everything, this is the interpretation: He is our Lord God (as we said) and, when He saw the human race in the demons' power, enslaved to idols, and every race and nation made prey to the devil, He descended from heaven, seized us away from the devil's power and joined us to His goodness. With a father's love He carried off His sons and fulfilled what the prophet had previously foretold, "For Ephraem I became like a panther, and for the house of Judah like a lion (Judah was serving idols at that time)" (Hos. 5.14). The prophet meant here the calling of the Gentiles and the Jews.

The panther is a various animal. So Solomon said the same about the Lord Jesus Christ, "He is the Wisdom of God, He is Intelligible Spirit, He is holy, one, multiple, subtle, mobile, fixed, pure, true, sweet, the Lover of good, fit. He never forbids the enactment of good; He is merciful, firm, unmoving, secure, omnipotent, all-seeing, omnificent, the Mover of wisdom, etc." (Sap. 7.22). Paul, the teacher of truth, bears witness that Christ is the Divine Wisdom when he says, "We preach Christ Crucified. This is a stumbling block for the Jews and an absurdity for the Gentiles. But to the Jews and Gentiles who have been called, we preach Christ who is the Power and the Wisdom of God" (I Cor. 1.23).

Since the panther is a beautiful animal, David says of Christ, "His form is more beautiful than the sons of men" (Ps. 44.3). And since the animal is exceedingly gentle, Isaiah says, "Rejoice and be glad, O Zion's daughter; proclaim, O Jerusalem's daughter, because your king comes to you with gentleness and salutation" (Isa. 62.11).

When the panther has eaten and is satisfied, it becomes quiet immediately and goes to sleep. So our Lord Jesus Christ, after He had had His fill of mockery from the Jews—of whippings, blows, injuries, insults, thorns, spittings—was hanged by His hands on the Cross and fixed with nails; He drank gall and vinegar and was pierced by a spear. Therefore, when He had had His fill of these many numerous gifts from the Jews, Christ slept; He rested in the grave and descended into hell and there bound our great enemy, the dragon.

The panther rises on the third day from sleep and lets out a great roar, and a sweet fragrance blazes from its mouth. So our Lord Jesus Christ also rose from the dead on the third day. As the Psalmist says, "The Lord awoke as if from sleep like a strong man intoxicated by wine" (Ps. 77.65). And He immediately cried out with a loud voice so that the sound as it issued forth could be heard all over the earth (Ps. 18.5), and His words to the world's ends, "Rejoice and do not be afraid, for I have conquered the world" (John 16.33); and again, "Holy Father, I have guarded those you gave me, and none of them has perished except the son of perdition" (John 17.12); and again, "I go to my Father and to your Father and to my God and to your God" (John 20.17); and again, "I will return to you. I will not send you away as orphans" (John 14.18); and at the end of the Gospel, He says, "Behold, I am with you always until the end of the world" (Matt. 28.20).

In this way the sweet fragrance issues from the panther's mouth and all who are near or far (that is, the Jews, who at one time reacted like the beasts [that followed the panther] and were near him because they had the law; and the Gentiles, who were far away because they did not have the law) hear His voice.

Filled with and refreshed by the sweetest fragrance of His commands, they follow Him and cry out with the prophet, "How sweet are your words on my palate, O Lord, sweeter than honey or the honey-comb in my mouth" (Ps. 118.103). David says about the fragrances of His commands, "Grace is poured upon your lips; therefore God has blessed you for eternity" (Ps. 44.3). And Solomon in the Canticle of Canticles says about Him, "The fragrance of your ointments is above all spices" (Cant. 4.10). For what else can Christ's ointments be, if not His commands, which are beyond all spices? For just as the presence of any kind of spice gives off a sweet fragrance, so too the Lord's words, which come out of His mouth, make happy the hearts of those men who hear and follow Him: "For your name is an ointment poured forth; therefore the maidens love you" (Cant. 1.3); and "They draw you after themselves; and we run in the fragrance of your ointments" (Cant. 1.4); and then immediately, "The king has led me into his chamber" (Cant. 1.4). We must be as quick as the maidens—those souls that have been renewed in baptism; we must run as quickly as they after the ointments of Christ's commands, and cross over from earthly to heavenly things, so the King may lead us into His palace, that is, into Jerusalem, the city of God, and into the mountain of all the saints. And when we have deserved to enter there, let us say, "Glorious things are said about you, city of God" (Ps. 86.3); "as we have heard, so have we seen in the city of the Lord of hosts" (Ps. 47.9). Physiologus speaks well about the panther.

B. *The Whale*

There is a sea monster which is called the "serpent-tortoise" (*aspidochelone*) in Greek, and the same (*aspido-testudo*) in Latin: it is the whale. The whale is huge and has something like sand on its skin, the sort found on the seashore. The monster lifts its back so high above the sea's waves in mid-ocean that men out sailing think it's nothing but an island, especially when they see the whole place covered with sand like every seashore. Taking it to be an island, they steer their boat alongside, alight, fix in their stakes and tie up their boats. Then, in order to cook themselves a meal after their work, they make fires on the sand, just as they would on the ground. But when the monster feels the fire's heat, it immediately plunges into the water and drags the boat with it into the sea's depths.

All unbelievers and those who are ignorant of the devil's wiles and place their hope in him suffer likewise. When they fasten themselves to his works, they are plunged down with him into the Gehenna of burning fire; such is his cunning.

The beast has a second characteristic: when it is hungry, it opens its mouth and exhales a sort of sweet-smelling fragrance. As soon as the little fish smell this fragrance, they gather together inside the whale's mouth. But when the whale has its mouth stuffed full with various little fish, it suddenly closes it and swallows them.

All those who have little faith and are fattened by pleasures and delights (by certain diabolical fragrances, as it were) suffer in the same way: like little fish, they will be suddenly swallowed by him. For the bigger fish keep themselves away from him and do not go near. So those who have Christ always in their minds are like the bigger fishes with the whale. Although they are perfect, they know about the devil's manifold wiles. They guard themselves from him, resist him totally and he flees away from them (cf. James 4.7). But when men who doubt and have little faith rush after the devil's pleasures and luxuries, they are deceived. For, as the Scriptures say, "They are delighted by the ointments and various fragrances" (Prov. 27.9). Thus the soul is destroyed by its errors.

C. *The Partridge*

There is a very deceitful bird called the partridge, just as the holy prophet Jeremiah says, "The partridge called out and gathered together what it had not laid, acquiring riches for itself unjustly. But in the midst of its days, they will forsake the partridge and in the end it will be left a fool" (Jer. 17.11). Physiologus says that the partridge is clearly cunning: it steals the eggs of another partridge and warms them with its body. But it cannot reap the fruits of its deceit. For after it has hatched the others' pullets, it loses them; because when they hear their mother's voice (the one who had laid the eggs), they fly away at once and join their natural parents. Having acquired a gift and then lost what it loved, the partridge (who expends its labors in vain on what is not its own, and pays the price of its deceit) is left foolish, alone and empty.

The devil, who tries to seize the children of the eternal Creator, imitates this bird. If he is somehow able to gather those who are foolish and lack the strength of common sense, the devil warms them with fleshly delights. But when the children hear Christ's voice, they take on their spiritual wings through faith, fly away and entrust themselves to Christ. Christ receives them immediately under the shadow of His own wings out of His great sense of fatherly duty and love, and gives them to Mother Church to be fed.

XVI

RIDDLES

Benjamin Thorpe was the first to remark on the affinities between the Latin and the Old English riddles in his *editio princeps* of the *Exeter Book* (*Codex Exoniensis: A Collection of Anglo-Saxon Poems* [London, 1842], p. x), but later scholars have reached little agreement about the nature and extent of indebtedness. Some maintain that nearly all the riddles can be traced to Latin sources; others, very few. Latin originals definitely do lie behind some of the Old English examples, and riddles in both languages often share common details or the same solution; yet they cannot invariably be related, for each may derive separately from traditional themes. We have attempted to thread our way through the maze, relying on three modern editions (and the subsequent scholarship): Frederick Tupper, Jr., ed., *The Riddles of the Exeter Book* (Boston, 1910); A. J. Wyatt, ed., *Old English Riddles* (Boston, 1912); and *ASPR, III*.

Four Latin riddlers provide the quarry from which material for the Old English poems may have been drawn: Symphosius, Aldhelm, Tatwine and Eusebius (Hwætberht). With the exception of Symphosius, all were English clerics writing between the middle of the seventh and eighth centuries when most of the English riddles were also being composed. Symphosius, the originator of the art riddle in the Latin West, seems to have flourished in the late fourth or early fifth century (see Raymond

T. Ohl, ed., *The Enigmas of Symphosius* [Philadelphia, 1928], p. 15).

Texts: *CC,* 133

(Riddles of Tatwine, Eusebius and Aldhelm).

CC, 133A

(Riddles of Symphosius and Pseudo-Symphosius).

A. K-D 9

1. Pseudo-Symphosius 1 (analogue)

Cuckoo

I leave when it gets cold; when it gets warm I return again. I desert what I have laid, but another mother brings it up. What else do you want me to say? My voice gives me away.

B. K-D 12, 38 (and perhaps 72)

1. Symphosius 56 (analogue)

Soldier's Boot

Once, while there was still life in me, I was much larger. But I am lifeless now; I have been torn off, cut up and tied. I've been consigned to the ground, but I haven't been hidden away in a tomb.

2. Aldhelm 83 (analogue)

Bullock

When I thirstily sucked my drink from twice two fountains through foaming jaws, I loosened my parched mouth. During my life I break up the earth's fertile clods and the deep roots by laboring with my mighty strength. But when the spirit leaves my cold limbs, I can bind men with fearful thongs.

3. Eusebius 37 (analogue)

Calf

After my mother has given me birth, I am often accustomed to drink twice two streams coming from one spring. And if I live, I begin to plow up hills; or if I die, I bind up many who are alive.

C. K-D 14 (and perhaps 80, 88, 93)

1. Eusebius 30 (remote analogue)

Inkhorn

Once I was used as a weapon: the strong one carried me among his arms, and I was worn on the crest of the warlike bull. But since I have an internal cavity, I now contain a bitter substance inside me; and when I belch, something bright emerges with a good smell.

D. K-D 16

1. Symphosius 61 (source)

Anchor

My twin points are joined by a single bar of iron. I struggle with the wind; I fight with the deep sea. I probe into the middle of the waters; I also bite the earth itself.

E. K-D 22

1. Aldhelm 53 (probable analogue)

Arcturus

(in modern terms, the constellation Boötes or its brightest star, but referring here to the constellation of The Great Bear or Charles' Wain)

I am pressed in by starry hosts at the top of the world. In common speech I bear the nickname "the wain." Continually turning in a circle, I never bend downwards like the rest of heaven's stars which hurry to the sea. I possess a treasure in the fact that I am nearest the polar sky which circles high above the Riphaean mountains of Scythia. I have the same number of stars as the Pleiades in the arch of the sky—the arch's lower part is said to sink down under the swamps of Styx and Lethe and the black ghosts of hell.

F. K-D 26 (and perhaps 67)

1. Aldhelm 32 (analogue)

Writing-Tablets

I was first born from the honey-bearing bees, but the rest of my outer part grew up in the woods, and my hard backs were given me by shoes. An iron point now carves my beautiful face with artful windings and turns the furrows like a plow. But the nourishing seed is brought to this field from heaven; it produces huge bundles of grain a thousandfold. Alas that such a holy stand of corn is destroyed by the grim weapons of war.

2. Aldhelm 59 (analogue)

Quill

The dazzling pelican, whose gaping throat swallows water from the sea, bore me, his white daughter, a short while ago. I go through white fields on a straight path; on the shining road I leave behind deep-blue footprints, and darken the bright plains with my black windings. It is not enough to open up one track through the fields; rather, the way goes forward with a thousand footpaths and it leads those who do not stray to the heights of heaven.

3. Tatwine 5 (analogue)

Parchment

A fierce despoiler stripped me of my fur and also removed the pores that gave me vital breath. But an author turned me into a flat field for a second time. Soon a planter irrigates my fruitful furrows with waves and my meadows return a bountiful harvest of nard. With it I will give the healthy nourishment and the sick a remedy.

4. Tatwine 6 (analogue)

Quill

Alas, I am wholly cheated of my true nature by an enemy: at one time I used to fly swiftly through the upper air; now, bound by three [fingers], I pay tribute on earth. I am forced to plow along the levels of the flat fields and the labor of love always forces me to pour fountains of tears on the dry furrows.

5. Eusebius 32 (analogue)

Parchment

At one time a voice did not speak words through us at all; now without a voice we usually produce words that are quite distinct. Although we are white fields, we are crossed by thousands of black [paths]. Alive, we say nothing; dead, we give an answer.

6. Eusebius 35 (analogue)

Quill

In nature, I am artless; I don't know anything at all. But now every wise man will follow my tracks. I live on earth now, but formerly I wandered through the heights of heaven. To look at, I am white, but I leave black footprints.

G. K-D 28

1. Symphosius 20 (probable source)

Tortoise-Lyre

I was slow, had a lazy walk and was endowed with a beautiful back. Indeed I was studiously learned, but betrayed by a harsh fate. Alive, I said nothing; dead, I sing in this way.

H. K-D 35 and *The Leiden Riddle*

1. Aldhelm 33 (source)

Breastplate

The dewy earth brought me forth from its ice-cold womb. I am not made from the coarse fleece of sheep; I am not drawn out into threads, or bounced to and fro in chattering yarns. The Chinese worms have not woven me from golden filament; and I am not carded with spikes or raked with a hard comb. And yet, look, I will be called "a coat" in common speech. I am not afraid of arrows drawn from long quivers.

I. K-D 36

1. Aldhelm 84, lines 1-5 (remote analogue)

Pregnant Sow

Now inside one body I have twice six eyes and twice three heads; but the other [lower] parts govern them. I walk along with twice twelve feet supporting me, but my body has ninety-six nails. [When I give suck], I will look like two parallel and equal lines of feet.

J. K-D 37, 87

1. Symphosius 73 (analogue)

Bellows

I do not die immediately when the breath leaves, for it returns continually; although it often departs again too.

At one time my soul's power is considerable; at another, it is nothing.

K. K-D 40 (and perhaps 41; in addition, this Aldhelm riddle may be an analogue to 66 and 94.)

1. Aldhelm 100 (source)

Creation

The Creator, who sustains the universe on eternal columns, the Ruler of kingdoms who governs the thunderbolts with law as the hanging roofs of the broad sky turn over, made me diversified when He first formed the world.

I am always awake and on the alert; it will never do me any good to sleep, but my "eyes" are closed in sleep immediately. Just as God governs the world by His own authority, so I embrace everything under the heaven's axis. No one is more hesitant than I, for a tiny ghost terrifies me; yet I am braver than a bristly boar when I make a stand. Except for God, who reigns in His heavenly citadel on high, no one surpasses me in his desire for triumphal banners. I exude a scent of ambrosia that is more intense than the fragrant frankincense; with the full sweetness of blowing nard I can also surpass the thriving lilies of the field mixed with the bright beds of roses; and yet I am decaying now with the rank filth of squalid mire. As long as the Father who rules the heavens permits, I govern by law everything which is under the pole and controlled by its axis. I embrace both the coarse and graceful forms of things. Look, higher than the sky, I search into the Thunderer's secrets; but, lower than the earth, I see foul Tartarus. Older than the world, I came before the earliest times; yet, look, I sprang this year from my mother's womb more beautiful than the gold studs on a shining buckle, but more prickly than buckthorn and viler than the despised seaweed. Look, I appear to be broader than the earth's wide ends, and yet I am contained in the middle of a fist. I am colder than winter and the dazzling hoarfrost, although I can burn with Vulcan's scorching flames. On the palate I am sweeter than a mouthful of syrupy nectar; on the other hand, I am more bitter than the grey wormwood of the field. When I bite into food, I gorge like the gluttonous Cyclops, though I can happily live without food forever. I am swifter than an eagle, quicker than a zephyr's wings, and faster too than a hawk; yet the shrinking earthworm, the snail, the slow marsh turtle and the black grub born from foul dung, all are quicker and beat me if a foot race is called for. I am heavier than lead; I outweigh the heaviest rocks, but I am lighter than a feather which is lighter even than a water spider. I am harder than iron or flint which scatters showers of sparks from its heart; but I am softer than broiled sweetbreads. I don't wear locks on the top of my head to adorn my brow with vanity and my temples with ringlets, though my wavy hair floats round my head with tighter curls than those set by the curling-iron. Look, I grow fatter than greasy breeding-sows when they carry their hulks back from nut-laden beech trees and the swineherds rejoice in their fattened flesh; yet fierce, pale hunger will torment me with thinness when I am in need and deprived of splendid feasts forever. I am fair, I admit, brighter than Titan's orb and whiter than the snow when a cloud lets fall its fleeces; but I am much darker than the prison's dismal gloom or the secret shadows which Tartarus surrounds. I am shaped round and smooth like an astral globe, or a little sphere or the form of a crystal ball; on the other hand, I am stretched out like Chinese silk which is drawn into the graceful thread or fabric for a royal robe. Look, and this is a marvel, I extend much farther than the six zones comprising the world's boundaries. Nothing exists below or above me on earth, except for the Creator of things who governs it with His word. I am larger than the black whale on the gray waves and smaller than the little worm which furrows through corpses or the tiny atom vibrating in Phoebus' rays. I walk with a hundred feet through the country pastures, but when I walk I never step on the earth at all. In this way my wisdom conquers clever professors; but I was not taught by the eloquent letter in books and I never knew what made up a syllable. I am drier than the summer heat of the burning sun, but drenched with dew and wetter than the fountain's stream. I am much saltier than the surface of the swelling sea, but I wind along fresher than the cool streams of the land. I am adorned with all the various shades of color which ornament the fabric of the present world, although at the same time I am pale and cheated of all color.

Listen and believe what I say. They are things a learned teacher could scarcely expound in words. Yet, in rejecting [these paradoxes], the reader still does not consider them frivolous. I ask conceited professors what name I am dealing with.

L. K-D 43

(The solution to this riddle is Soul and Body; see Entry IV for the analogues to the separate poems bearing that title.)

M. K-D 47

1. Symphosius 16 (probable source)

Bookworm

Writing has fed me, but I don't know what writing is. I have lived in books, but I am no more learned because of it. I have consumed the Muses, yet up till now I have not improved myself.

N. K-D 48, 59

1. Aldhelm 55 (analogue)

Chrismal

I am revered as a house of nourishment and filled with a divine gift; but no one unlocks folding doors or opens an entrance, nor does a squared atrium support a roof. Though gems blaze on the outside of my body where a gold knob glistens with lustrous metals, my dull insides are adorned much more richly: Christ's most beautiful form burns there. The radiant glory of holy things shines so. There is no timber in this temple and the roofs do not rise on columns.

O. K-D 49

1. Aldhelm 89 (analogue)

Bookcase

My insides are now full of divine words, and my whole stomach carries sacred volumes. Yet I can never learn a thing from them. I am unfortunate: my destiny is to be cheated of this gift until the harsh Fates carry the lights of books away.

P. K-D 51 (and perhaps 19, 64, 74)

(See under F., Aldhelm 59, Tatwine 6 and Eusebius 35, for analogues to this riddle.)

Q. K-D 53

1. Aldhelm 86 (analogue)

[*Aries*] The Ram

I am a shaggy beast armed with ridged horns. I crop the fields' green grass in mouthfuls, but, as I go along, I am accompanied by a host of stars which climb in crowds to the lofty heights of heaven. I shake cities with the combat of my turreted head, and I hurl down towns and the high towers on their walls. I clothe men with the twisted thread in a robe. If I am preceded by the fifteenth letter [in the Latin alphabet], then I stand up as part of a house [*paries* = wall].

R. K-D 58

1. Symphosius 71 (analogue)

Well

I am water sunk a long way underground in the deep earth. I cannot flow unless channels have been dug out, and I work upwards drawn by someone else's labor.

2. Symphosius 72 (analogue)

Wooden Water-pipe

The earth hides a tree-trunk; the waters lurk in the ground. It is a little river-bed which doesn't have any banks. In the middle of the wood is what used to carry wood.

S. K-D 60

1. Symphosius 2 (probable source)

Reed

I am the riverbank's sweet mistress and the deep water's neighbor; I sing softly to the Muses. When I am bathed in black and grasped by a scholar's fingers, I am the tongue's messenger.

T. K-D 63 (and perhaps a portion of 14, 27 and 30)

1. Aldhelm 80 (analogue)

Glass Wine-cup

I flowed in a slow stream from the chinks of rocks when flames broke up the tough hearts of stones and the furnace gave free rein to the heat. Now my rounded form shines just like ice. In fact, many men want to clasp my neck with their right hands and to hold my slippery body in their fingers. But when I bring sweet kisses to their lips, laying them on the mouths which press close to me, I upset their minds and bring their staggering footsteps to a fall.

U. K-D 65 (and perhaps a portion of 25)

1. Symphosius 44 (probable source)

Onion

I bite those who bite me; otherwise I don't bite anyone. But many people are prepared to bite me who bite them. No one is afraid of my bite, since I don't have any teeth.

V. K-D 83

1. Symphosius 92 (remote analogue)

Money

First I was earth and hidden in the earth's fell recesses. Now flames have given me a different value and name. I am no longer called earth, though you can buy earth with me.

W. K-D 84

1. Aldhelm 29 (analogue)

Water

Who would not be astonished at the spectacle of my fate? Although I am strong enough to carry a thousand forest oaks, a tiny needle still ruptures a huge wagon [like me] immediately. The birds of the sky and the fish swimming through the seas acquired their life's origins from me at one time. It is agreed by law that a third part of the world should be mine.

2. Aldhelm 73 (analogue)

A Spring

I am very fast and I creep secretly through the earth's hollow caves, wheeling my curving circles in the windings of its veins. Although I lack life and sensation and am totally destitute as well, what number can account for, what list can cope with, the thousands of livings things I can endow with life? Neither the glowing sphere of stars [turning] through heaven, nor the sands of the wave-tossed sea make up their number.

X. K-D 85

1. Symphosius 12 (source)

River and Fish

On earth there is a home which echoes again and again

with a clear sound. The home itself resounds, but the silent guest (*or* host) makes no noise. Yet the guest (*or* host) and the home both run on together.

Y. K-D 86

1. Symphosius 95 (probable source)

One-eyed Garlic Seller

Now you can see what you can hardly believe: he has one eye but many thousands of heads. He sells what he has; where will he buy what he doesn't have?

Z. K-D 91

1. Symphosius 4 (analogue)

Key

I bring great power with my little strength. I open up closed houses, but I close opened ones up again. I protect the home for the master, but I am protected by him in turn.

XVII

THE DESCENT INTO HELL

Only the central section (lines 23b-76) of this poem, alternatively called *The Harrowing of Hell* and *The Descent into Hell*, actually deals with Christ's journey to release the prophets and patriarchs. Earlier sections, not clearly marked, portray the arrival of the two Marys at the sepulchre according to the Gospel of Matthew and then give a composite account of the Resurrection. The concluding sections have a series of lyrical invocations to Gabriel, Mary, Jerusalem and the river Jordan (which vividly recall the *Eala* apostrophes in *Christ I*) and a prayer for mercy through baptism in Jesus. Such a peculiar mélange of different narrative actions and poetic modes has led scholars to suppose there must have been an equally peculiar original. But since this has never surfaced, we must work on the straightforward assumption that the poem's central section "goes back ultimately to the second part of the apocryphal Gospel of Nicodemus (also called the *Acta Pilati*)" (*ASPR*, III, lxii).

True, scholars have also found traces of other influences. There are minor, intermittent similarities with the *Blickling Easter Homily* (No. VII), whose source Max Förster has identified as another freer version of the Harrowing of Hell, namely the Pseudo-Augustinian *Sermon 160* (*PL*, 39.2059-61). This sermon may have passed to the English through an Irish intermediary (see "Altenglische Preditquellen. I," *Archiv*, 116 [1906], 301 ff.; and Genevieve Crotty, "The Exeter *Harrowing of Hell*: A Reinterpretation," *PMLA*, 54 [1939], 352). The Pseudo-Augustine piece has strong connections with *Christ and Satan*, and is now recognized as a conflation of Eusebius Gallicanus' *Homily 12* and Gregory the Great's *Sermon 22* (see Appendix I, Item 3). Thomas D. Hill also notes the possible impress of the *Protoevangelium* ("Cosmic Stasis and the Birth of Christ: The Old English *Descent into Hell*, Lines 99-106," *JEGP*, 71 [1972], 382-9). Yet such tesserae of information do not constitute a mosaic which can account for the whole poem, and the second part of the *Gospel of Nicodemus*, in whatever form, is obviously the significant model, if not the actual source.

However, there is no proper critical text for this model: the so-called standard edition by Tischendorf, as M. R. James points out, is "an eclectic text not representing, probably, any one single line of transmission" (*The Apocryphal New Testament* [Oxford, 1953], p. 94). The Old English poet would almost certainly have known "the Early Latin Recension which translates the Greek *Commentaries of Nicodemus* and adds the account . . . of Christ's 'Harrowing of Hell' " (H. C. Kim, ed., *The Gospel of Nicodemus* [Toronto, 1973], pp. 1-2). This version is unavailable, and we have used Tischendorf's "Latin A" reconstruction, omitting the later chapters which belong to the Late Latin Recension, the earliest manuscript of which dates from the tenth century (see Kim, pp. 2 and 7).

The motif of the Harrowing of Hell occurs in many other Old English poems. If one accepted all the instances supposed by the exegetes, the following list could be considerably expanded: *Christ and Satan, The Dream of the Rood* (Entry V), *Christ I, II, III* (Entries VII, VIII, IX) *Guthlac B* (Entry X), and *Judgment Day II* (Entry XXI).

The Second Part of *The Gospel of Nicodemus* or Christ's Descent into Hell

Text: Constantinus Tischendorf, ed., *Evangelia Apocrypha,* 2nd ed. (Leipzig, 1876), pp. 389-409.

Joseph arose and said to Annas and Caiaphas, "Rightly do you wonder because you have heard Jesus was seen alive after death and ascended into heaven. Yet it is more to be wondered at that He did not rise from the dead alone, but caused many others who were dead to rise living again from their tombs. Many people have seen them in Jerusalem. Now hear me, for we all know blessed Simeon, the high priest, who received the infant Jesus with his own hands in the temple. This Simeon had two sons, full brothers, and we were all at their death and burial. Go, therefore, and see their tombs; they are open, for the brothers have risen. Lo, they are in the city of Arimathia, living together in prayer. In fact, men hear them crying out, although they talk to no one and are silent like the dead. Come, let us go to these brothers and bring them to us with all honor and respect. If we charge them, perhaps they will tell us about the mystery of their resurrection."

After they had heard this, they all rejoiced. Annas and Caiaphas, Nicodemus, Joseph and Gamaliel went out, but did not find them in their sepulchre. Yet when they went into the city of Arimathia, they found them there on bended knees devoting their time to prayer. Kissing them, they led them with reverence and in the fear of God to the synagogue at Jerusalem. When they had shut the doors, they took up the law of the Lord and put it into their hands. They charged them by the God Adonai and the God of Israel, who spoke to our fathers through the law and the prophets, "If you believe it is Jesus who revived you from the dead, tell us how you rose from the dead."

When Karinus and Leucius heard this charge, they trembled in body and groaned, being troubled in heart. They both looked to heaven and with their fingers made the sign of the Cross on their tongues. At once they both spoke, "Give us each sheaves of paper and let us write down what we have seen and heard." They gave it to them, and, sitting down, each wrote:

CHAPTER II

Lord Jesus Christ, the resurrection and life of the dead, permit us to speak of the mysteries you did through your death on the Cross, for we have been charged by you. You ordered your servants to tell no one the secrets of your divine majesty which you performed in hell. But after we were placed with all our fathers in the depths, in the shadow's gloom, suddenly the golden heat of the sun came and its royal-purple light shone upon us. Immediately the father of the whole human race, together with all the patriarchs and prophets, rejoiced, saying, "This Light is the Creator of eternal Light; this Light promised to send us His co-eternal Light." Isaiah cried out and said, "This is the Father's Light, the Son of God, just as I prophesied when I lived on earth, 'The land of Zabulon and the land of Nephtholim across the Jordan, of Galilee of the Gentiles, the people which sat in darkness have seen a great light, and those who dwell in the land of the shadow of death, upon them the light has shone.' And now it has come and shone upon us who sit in death."

While we were all rejoicing in the light which shone upon us, our father Simeon came and exulting said, "Glorify the Lord Jesus Christ, the Son of God, for when He was born an infant, I received Him with my own hands in the temple. Moved by the Holy Spirit, I confessed and said to Him, 'For now my eyes have seen your salvation, which you have prepared in the sight of all people, a light as a revelation to the Gentiles and the glory of your people Israel.' " Hearing this, the whole multitude of saints rejoiced the more.

Afterwards, a desert hermit came and everyone asked him, "Who are you?" Answering them, he said, "I am John, the voice and prophet of the most High, who came before the face of His advent to prepare His ways and give knowledge of salvation to His people for the remission of their sins. When I saw Him coming towards me, I was moved by the Holy Spirit and said, 'Behold, the Lamb of God, behold Him who takes away the sins of the world.' I baptized Him in the river Jordan and I saw the Holy Spirit descending upon Him in the form of a dove. I heard a voice from heaven saying, 'This is my beloved Son in whom I am well pleased.' Now I have gone before His countenance and come down to announce to you that He is at hand to visit us; the rising Sun, the Son of God, is coming from on high to us who sit in darkness and the shadow of death."

CHAPTER III

When father Adam, the first man, heard that Jesus was baptized in the river Jordan, he cried out to his son, Seth, "Tell your sons, the patriarchs and prophets, everything you heard from Michael, the archangel, when I sent you to the gates of paradise to entreat God to send you His angel, so he could give you oil from the tree of mercy and anoint my body when I was sick." Then, drawing near the holy patriarchs and prophets, Seth said, "When I, Seth, was praying to the Lord at the gates of paradise, lo, Michael, the angel of the Lord, appeared to me, saying, 'I am sent to you by the Lord; I am put in charge of the human body. And I tell you, Seth, do not oppress yourself with tears in praying and pleading for the oil of the tree of mercy to anoint your father, Adam, because of his body's pain. For you will never be able to receive it from the tree until the last days and times, when five thousand five hundred years have been completed. Then the most beloved Son of God will come on earth to raise up Adam's body and the bodies of the dead; He will come and be baptized in the Jordan. When He has emerged from Jordan's water, He will anoint all who believe in Him with the oil of His mercy; and this, the oil of mercy, will last eternally for the generation of those who are born from water and the Holy Spirit. Then, the most beloved Son of God, Christ Jesus, will descend to earth and bring our father Adam back into paradise to the tree of mercy.'"

When they had heard the whole story from Seth, all the patriarchs and prophets rejoiced with great exultation.

CHAPTER IV

While all the saints were rejoicing, behold, Satan, the prince and commander of death, said to Hell, "Prepare yourself to receive Jesus who boasts He is the Son of God; but He is a man who fears death and says, 'My soul is sad even unto death.' He has been my chief enemy and done me [great] harm; the many people I have made blind, lame, deaf, leprous and possessed He has healed with a word. And the people I brought to you dead He has taken away from you."

In reply Hell said to prince Satan, "Who is He so mighty, if He is a man afraid of death? For all those who are mighty on earth are subject to my power, including those you have brought [here] who were under your rule. If you are mighty, then, who is this Jesus, who opposes your power, though He fears death. If He is so mighty in His humanity, I tell you truly He is omnipotent in His divinity and none can resist His power. When He says He fears death, He wants to ensnare you, for you will have sorrow forever and ever." But Satan, the prince of Tartarus, said in reply, "Why do you hesitate and fear to admit this Jesus, your adversary and mine? For I have tempted Him, and stirred up my ancient people, the Jews, with zeal and anger against Him. I have sharpened a spear to pierce Him. I have mixed gall and vinegar to give Him as a drink, prepared a cross to crucify Him and nails to transfix Him. His death is at hand so I can lead Him to you, your subject and mine."

Hell responded, "You told me this is the man who took the dead away from me. I hold many here who took the dead from me while they lived on earth, yet they did not do it through their own powers, but through holy prayers. Their almighty God took the dead from me. Who is this Jesus, who has taken the dead from me through His own word and not through prayers? Perhaps it is the man who by the word of His command restored life to Lazarus whom I held dead for four days, stinking and decaying." In reply, Satan, death's prince, said, "It is the same Jesus." Hearing this, Hell said to him, "I charge you through your powers and mine, do not bring Him to me. For the time when I heard His word's command, I quaked and was overwhelmed with fear, and all my servants were troubled with me. Nor could we keep Lazarus, for he shook himself like an eagle and with lightning speed leapt up and departed from us. The earth, which was holding Lazarus' dead body, immediately gave it back alive. So now I know that the man who could do these things is God, strong in power and mighty in manhood, the Saviour of mankind. If you bring Him to me, He will free all those who are shut up here in this cruel prison and fettered in the unbreakable chains of their sins, and He will lead them to the life of His divinity forever."

CHAPTER V

While prince Satan and Hell were talking together about this, suddenly there came a voice like thunder and a ghostly cry, "Lift up your gates, princes, and you, eternal gates, be raised, and the King of glory will enter in." Hearing this, Hell said to prince Satan, "Leave me and get out of my house. If you are a mighty warrior, fight against the King of glory. But what have you to do with Him?" And Hell threw Satan out of his house, and said to his wicked servants, "Shut the stout bronze gates; put iron bars on them; resist vigorously, lest we who hold captivity be captured."

But when all the multitude of saints heard this, they said to Hell in a voice of rebuke, "Open your gates so the King of glory may enter." And David cried out, "When I was on earth, did I not prophesy to you, 'Let them thank the Lord for His steadfast love, for His wondrous works to the sons of men, He who has destroyed the bronze gates and shattered the iron bars. He has taken them from the way of their iniquity.'" And after this, Isaiah said likewise, "When I was alive on earth, did I not prophesy to you, 'The dead will rise up and those who are in the tombs will rise again, and those who are in the earth will rejoice, for their health is the dew which comes from the Lord.' And again I said, 'Death, where is your sting? Hell, where is your victory?'"

Upon hearing this from Isaiah, all the saints said to Hell, "Open your gates. Now you will be vanquished, [and made] weak and powerless." There came a great voice like thunder, saying, "Lift up your gates, princes, and you, infernal gates, be raised, and the King of glory will enter in." When he perceived that the saints had twice shouted this, Hell said, as if he did not know, "Who is the King of glory?" In reply, David said to Hell, "I know those words of acclamation, for I prophesied the same through His spirit. I say to you now what I said before, 'The Lord who is strong and mighty, the Lord who is mighty in war, He is the King of glory. The Lord looked down to earth from heaven to hear the groans of those in fetters and to free the sons of the slain.' And now, most putrid and stinking Hell, open your gates so the King of glory may enter." While David was saying this to Hell, the Lord of majesty arrived in the form of a man and lit up the eternal shadows and broke the unbreakable chains. The aid of His invincible strength visited us as we sat in the deep gloom of transgressions and in the deathly shadow of sins.

CHAPTER VI

When Hell and Death and their wicked servants saw this, they and their cruel ministers were struck with dread as they perceived the brilliance of such a great light in their own kingdom. At the sudden sight of Christ in their dwelling, they cried out, "We have been conquered by you. Who are you, sent from the Lord, to preside over our confusion? Who are you, who, without [being subject] to corruption's ruin, angrily condemn our power and have the incorruptible seal of majesty [upon you]? Who are you, so big and small, so humble and exalted, foot-soldier and commander, splendid warrior disguised as a servant, the King of glory both dead and alive, whom the Cross bore as one slain? You who lay dead in the sepulchre have come down to us alive; at your death all creation trembled and all the stars were shaken. Now you have been released among the dead and disturb our legions. Who are you who liberate the captives held bound by original sin and restore them to their former liberty? Who are you who pour a divinely brilliant and dazzling light over those blinded by the darkness of their sins?" Likewise all the legions of demons were struck by the same dread and together they cried out in fearful confusion, "Jesus, where do you come from, a man so strong and so splendid in majesty, so spotlessly noble and clear of guilt? For that earthly world which till now has always been subject to us and has paid tribute for our benefit, has never sent us such a dead man, never appointed such reward for Hell. Therefore, who are you who so fearlessly have crossed our borders? Not only are you heedless of our torments, but you are also trying to carry off everyone from our chains. Perhaps you are that Jesus who, as our prince Satan used to say, would receive the rule of the whole world through your death on the Cross.

In His majesty the King of glory then trampled on Death; and seizing prince Satan, He delivered him over to the power of Hell. But Adam He drew to His own brightness.

CHAPTER VII

Then Hell took prince Satan and said to him in great reproof, "O Beelzebub, prince of perdition and leader of destruction, the angels' scorn and the spitting of the just, why did you do this? What made you want to crucify the King of glory, whose death you had promised us would bring such great rewards? Like a fool, you did not know what you were doing. For behold, this Jesus has now chased away all death's shadows with the splendor of His divinity. He has shattered the prisons' strongholds, set the prisoners free and released those who were bound. All who used to sigh under our torments [now] insult us, and, as a result of their prayers, our realms are conquered, our kingdoms subdued. No human race fears us any longer. Moreover, the dead, who were never proud towards us, threaten us fiercely, as do the prisoners who could never be happy. O prince Satan, father of all the wicked, the unrighteous and the renegade, why did you want to do this? From the very beginning until this day people have despaired of salvation and life here, but now you cannot hear their usual bellowing. Not one of their groans resounds; nor can you find a trace of tears on any face. O prince Satan, possessor of hell's keys, the riches you acquired through the tree of sin and the loss of paradise you have now forfeited through the tree of the Cross. All your joy has perished. When you hanged Christ Jesus, the King of glory, you acted against yourself and me. From now on you will know how great are the eternal torments and infinite punishments you must suffer in my everlasting custody. O prince Satan, author of death and source of all pride, first you should have looked for something evil in this Jesus. Why, with no cause at all, did you dare crucify unjustly a person in whom you saw no guilt; why have you led someone innocent and righteous into our kingdom and [so] lost the guilty, the wicked and the unrighteous of the whole world?"

When Hell had finished speaking of this to prince Satan, the King of glory said to Hell, "Prince Satan will be under your sway for all ages in the place of Adam and his children, my righteous ones."

CHAPTER VIII

And the Lord put out His hand and said, "Come to me, all my saints, those who have my image and likeness. You have been damned because of a tree, the devil and death; now see the devil and death damned because of a tree." Immediately all the saints were united under the Lord's hand. Holding Adam by the right hand, the Lord said, "Peace be to you and all your children, my righteous ones." When Adam had cast himself at the knees of the Lord and entreated him with tearful supplication, he said in a loud voice, "Lord, I will magnify you, because you have sustained me and not favored my enemies over me. O Lord, God, I have called to you and you have healed me. Lord, you have led my soul from hell; you have rescued me from those who descend into the pit. Sing psalms to the Lord, all His saints, and praise the memory of His holiness; for there is wrath in His disdain and life in His good will." Likewise all God's saints knelt at the Lord's feet and said as one, "O Redeemer of the world, you have come. What you foretold through the law and your prophets, you fulfilled through your deeds. By your Cross you have redeemed the living, and through your death on the Cross you have come to deliver us from hell and death through your majesty. O Lord, just as you have set up the sign of your glory in heaven and erected your Cross, the sign of redemption on earth, so Lord, put the sign of your victory on the Cross in hell, that death may no longer have dominion."

The Lord extended His hand and made the sign of the Cross over Adam and all His saints. He took Adam by the right hand, and ascended out of Hell; all the saints followed Him. Then holy David cried aloud, saying, "Sing to the Lord a new song, for He has done marvellous things. His right hand and His holy arm have protected Him. The Lord has made His salvation known; He has revealed His righteousness before the face of nations." And the whole multitude of saints replied, "This glory is for all His saints. Amen, Alleluia."

After this, the prophet Habacuc cried out, "You went forth for your people's salvation, to set your chosen ones free." All the saints replied, "Blessed is He who comes in the Name of the Lord. God is the Lord and He has illumined us. Amen, Alleluia." After which the prophet Micheas cried out likewise, "What God is like you, O Lord, who remove iniquities and pass over sins? Now of your own free will you contain your anger as evidence that you are merciful. You turn away and pity us; you absolve our iniquities and have drowned our sins in the depths of the sea, just as you swore to our fathers in the days of old." All the saints replied, "This is our God for eternity, world without end. He will reign over us forever. Amen, Alleluia." Thus spoke all the prophets, recalling sacred things out of their praises. And all the saints followed the Lord, crying, "Amen, Alleluia."

CHAPTER IX

*The Lord took Adam's hand and delivered him to the archangel Michael; all the saints followed the archangel Michael and he led them into the glorious beauty [*gratiam*] of paradise. Two men, ancients of days, met them on the way. The saints asked them, "Who are you, who have not yet been dead with us in hell and have been placed in paradise in body?" One of them replied, "I am Enoch, who have been brought here by the Lord's word, and this man with me is Elias the Thesbite, who was taken up in a fiery chariot. We have not tasted death till now, but have been* *preserved for the coming of Antichrist. We will oppose him with divine signs and wonders, and be killed by him in Jerusalem; and after three and a half days we will be taken up again alive in the clouds."*

CHAPTER X

While Enoch and Elias were talking about this with the saints, behold, another wretched man arrived, bearing the mark of the Cross on his shoulders. When they saw him all the saints said, "Who are you? You look like a thief. Why do you bear a mark on your shoulders?" He answered them, "You have spoken rightly, for I was a thief who performed all manner of evil on earth. The Jews crucified me with Jesus and I saw the wonders of creation which occurred through Jesus' Cross when He was crucified. I believed Him to be the Creator of all creatures, the King almighty, and I pleaded with Him, saying, 'Remember me, Lord, when you come into your kingdom.' Forthwith He received my prayer and said to me, 'Truly, I tell you, today you will be with me in paradise.' And He gave me the mark of the Cross and said, 'Walk into paradise bearing this. If the guardian angel of paradise will not let you enter, show him the mark of the Cross and tell him, "Jesus Christ, the Son of God, who has now been crucified, sent me."' When I had done so, I related all to the guardian angel of paradise. Hearing this from me, he opened [the gate] at once, led me in and put me on the right side of paradise, saying, 'Lo, wait a while and Adam, the father of the whole human race, with all his holy and righteous sons will enter in after the glorious triumph of Christ's Ascension, [the triumph] of the Lord who has been crucified.'" When they had heard everything the thief said, all the holy patriarchs and prophets said with one voice, "Blessed is the Lord almighty, the Father of eternal goodness and the Father of mercy. You have given such grace to your sinners and brought them back again to the beauty [gratiam] *of paradise and to your quiet pastures; for this is certainly the most spiritual life. Amen, Amen."*

CHAPTER XI

These are the divine and sacred mysteries we have seen and heard, I, Karinus, and I, Leucius. We are not allowed to say more about God's other mysteries, as the archangel Michael warned us, "You will go to

Jerusalem with your brothers and pray, proclaiming and glorifying the Resurrection of the Lord Jesus Christ, who raised you from the dead with Him. You will speak with no man and you will sit like mutes, until the hour comes when the Lord will permit you to declare the mysteries of His divinity." The archangel Michael ordered us to cross over the Jordan to a rich and fertile place where there are many who rose again with us in testimony to the Resurrection of Christ the Lord. For we who rose from the dead were permitted only three days to celebrate the Lord's Passover in Jerusalem with our parents who were still alive in testimony to the Resurrection of Christ the Lord. We were baptized in the holy river Jordan and each of us received white robes. After three days, having celebrated the Lord's Passover, all those who had risen again with us were drawn up into the clouds; they were led across the Jordan and no one saw them any more. But we were told to remain in prayer in the city of Arimathia.

This is how much the Lord commanded us to tell you. Laud and praise Him; do penance that He may be merciful to you. Peace be with you from the Lord Jesus Christ, Saviour of us all. Amen.

After they had finished writing all this on separate sheaves of paper, they arose. Karinus gave what he had written into the hands of Annas, Caiaphas and Gamaliel, and likewise Leucius gave what he had written into the hands of Nicodemus and Joseph. And suddenly they were transfigured; they became white beyond measure and were seen no more. But their writings were found to be identical, not one letter more nor less.

When the whole Jewish synagogue heard all the wonderful sayings of Karinus and Leucius, they said to each other, "Truly, all this has been done by the Lord; blessed be the Lord, world without end, Amen." They all left in great anxiety, striking their breasts with fear and trembling, and each went away to his own home.

Everything the Jews said in their synagogue Joseph and Nicodemus immediately reported to the governor. Pilate himself recorded everything which the Jews had done and said concerning Jesus, and put it all down in the public records of his palace [*praetorium*].

XVIII

THE BATTLE OF MALDON

Byrhtnoth, ealdorman of Essex and leader of the English *fyrd* at Maldon, emerges from the medieval chronicles as much more important than the battle in which he fell. One of England's three most powerful ealdormen, he achieved a contemporary renown which persisted for some considerable time. E. V. Gordon writes, "it is remarkable testimony to Byrhtnoth's fame and popularity, to the impression he made on the people by his deeds and bearing, that he was still celebrated as a hero in the east of England in the twelfth century ("Introduction" to his edition [London, 1937], p. 20).

The battle itself receives appropriate notice in the *Anglo-Saxon Chronicle*, in the later Latin imitations of the *Chronicle* and in other monastic records. But, for patriotic reasons, the defeat suffered by the English at the hands of the Viking raiders did not elicit the same enthusiasm as the victory at the Battle of Brunanburh (see below, Entry XIX). Not long after the slaughter at Maldon in 991, the notices pay less attention to the battle than to Byrhtnoth's reputation for holiness. A good part of this reputation was a result of his generosity towards the monasteries, and much of our knowledge comes from the records of two rival foundations—Ely and Ramsey. The official history of each explains why Byrhtnoth left so much wealth to the community at Ely: supposedly the Abbot of Ramsey once turned down a request to feed him and his entire army as he marched (according to the Ely account) to the Battle of Maldon. Such matters have no bearing on the poem and we omit them; but they do indicate that accurate knowledge of the battle faded rather quickly and was replaced by propaganda.

A. MS F of *The Anglo-Saxon Chronicle*

(12th c.)

Text: Francis P. Magoun, Jr., "*Annales Domitiani Latini:* An Edition," *MS*, 9 (1947), 262.

991. In this year ealdorman Brihtnoth died at Maldon. And in this year tribute was first given to the Danes on the advice of Archbishop Sigeric, namely ten thousand pounds.

B. *The Life of Saint Oswald*

(late 10th or early 11th c.)

Text: James Raine, ed., *The Historians of the Church of York and Its Archbishops* (London, 1879), I, 456.

After not many months had elapsed [since a battle in Wessex where the Danes were beaten], another heroic battle occurred in the east of this famous region. The renowned ealdorman, Byrhtnoth, was in charge of the battle along with his fellow warriors. Who can trust that his style is elegant enough to describe how gloriously, how bravely, how courageously Byrhtnoth urged his war captains into the battle-line? He stood there, his tall height eminent above the rest, his hand sustained not by Aaron and Hur, but strengthened by the Lord's manifold love; for he was worthy. With his right hand he struck again and again, oblivious of the gray hair (like swan's down) on his head; for his alms and holy masses strengthened him. With his left hand he defended himself, mindless of his failing body; for his prayers and good deeds supported him. When he, the field's noble general, saw the enemy charging down and his own men fighting bravely—killing many of the enemy—he began to fight for his country with all his might. An uncountable number of the Danes and our own men fell; Byrhtnoth himself fell and the rest fled. The Danes were so incredibly wounded that they could scarcely man their boats.

C.1. Florence of Worcester, *The Chronicle of Chronicles*

(early 12th c.)

Text: Benjamin Thorpe, ed., *Florentii Wigorniensis Monachi Chronicon ex Chronicis* (London, 1848), p. 149.

991. In this same year, the Danes, led by Justin and Guthmund, the son of Steitan, ravaged Ipswich. Not long afterwards, Byrhtnoth, the vigorous ealdorman of the East Saxons, fought a battle with them near Maldon; but after an infinite number had been killed on both sides, the ealdorman himself fell. It was the Danes' fortune to prevail. Also in that year, on the advice of Sigeric, the Archbishop of Canterbury [*Dorubernensis*], and the ealdormen, Aethelward and Aelfric, the Danes were given ten thousand pounds of tribute money for the first time. This was so they would stop the incessant plunderings, burnings and killings of men (which they had committed time and again all along the seacoast) and keep a stable peace with them.

C.2.

Another account in almost exactly the same words is given by Simeon of Durham in the *Historia Regum*. See Thomas Arnold, ed., *Symeonis Monachi Opera Omnia* (London, 1882-5), II, 134.

D. Henry of Huntingdon, *The History of the English* (12th c.)

Text: Thomas Arnold, ed., *Henrici Archidiaconi Huntendunensis Historia Anglorum* (London, 1879), p. 168.

[A.D. 991] Elsewhere, Ipswich was plundered. The ealdorman, Byrhtnoth, opposed the Danes in battle with a considerable force, but was defeated. He himself was slain by the sword and his troops were driven back and destroyed.

E. *The Ely Book* (late 12th c.)

Text: E. O. Blake, ed., *Liber Eliensis*, Camden Third Series, 92 (London, 1962), 133-6.

62. *About the worthy leader, Brithnoth, who gave [various places] with their appurtenances to Saint Aetheldred.*

There follows a memorable account of Brithnoth, a remarkable and famous man, whose life and deeds receive no small praise in the English histories. With the reader's permission we will extract a few facts from them without paying any attention to style. It is a great subject that merited the account our ancestors gave of it, and, being feeble and inarticulate [by comparison], we cannot tell the story without being ashamed of our dry style. This famous man was leader of the Northumbrians and extremely brave. Because of the extraordinary wisdom and bodily strength with which he firmly defended himself and his men, everyone called him "ealdorman" in English, that is, an elder or leader. He was eloquent in speech, robust in strength, large of body, unremitting in war and campaigns against the kingdom's enemies, and bold beyond measure, neither regarding nor fearing death. Moreover, he honored Holy Church and God's ministers everywhere and gave the whole of his patrimony for their use. He always made himself a bulwark for the religious orders against those who tried to cause trouble in holy places. At one time certain nobles out of greed and madness wanted to expel the monks and put those whom Edgar and Saint Aethelwold had previously expelled back in the churches. This religious man took his place in the council and argued against them with great firmness: he said that there was no way in which he could tolerate the expulsion of those monks from the kingdom who had wholly preserved religion in it. As long as he lived, he devoted his life to defending his country's liberty, and he was totally committed to the stand that he would rather die than let injuries to his country go unavenged. At that time frequent Danish raids into England occurred. They used to come by ship and severely ravage various districts. Because of Brithnoth's great worth and trust, all the provincial commanders faithfully bound themselves to him as their leader, as though he were an invincible protector. In this way they could defend themselves against the enemy Danes with more security under his protection. Thus on one occasion, when the Danes had landed at Meldun and he heard about it, he met them with an armed force and killed nearly all of them on the bridge. Only a few of them escaped and sailed to their own country to tell the news. After this victory, ealdorman Brithnoth quickly returned to Northumbria. The Danes, who were extremely depressed by their news, once more fitted out a fleet. Led by Justin and Stectan's son, Guthmund, they hurried to England and landed at Meldun again four years later to avenge the slaughter of their men. When they reached the harbor, they heard that it was Brithnoth who had inflicted this slaughter. They immediately sent word they had come to avenge their men and would consider Brithnoth a coward if he did not dare fight them. Brithnoth's valor was roused by this news and he summoned his old comrades to the affair. With a few warriors, and led by the hope of victory and his own over-great spirit, he marched to battle, both taking precautions and hurrying to prevent the enemy army from occupying even one foot of land in his absence.

[Digression involving the Abbot of Ramsey and the church of Ely; the gifts made to the Abbot of Ely]

When he arrived, he was not worried by the small numbers in his own army, nor alarmed by the enemy's multitude. But he attacked the Danes at once and fought them savagely for a fortnight. On the last day, and with few of his men left, Brithnoth knew he was going to die, but this did not lessen his efforts against the enemy. Having inflicted an enormous slaughter on the Danes, he almost put them to flight. But eventually the enemy took comfort from the small number of Brithnoth's men, and, forming themselves into a wedge, rushed against him in one body. After an enormous effort, the Danes barely managed to cut off Brithnoth's head as he fought. They carried the head away with them and fled to their own land.

When the Abbot [of Ely] heard about the battle's outcome, he went to the battlefield with some of his monks, found Brithnoth's body and, taking it back to the church, buried it honorably. But in place of the head he put a round ball of wax, by which sign the body was recognized long afterwards in our own times and placed with honor among the others. This pious and active man lived in the days of the English kings, Edgar, Edward, King and Martyr, and Aethelred. He died in the fourteenth year of the reign of the same Aethelred, in the nine hundred and ninety-first year since our Lord's Incarnation.

XIX

THE BATTLE OF BRUNANBURH

Of the six poems scattered through the *Anglo-Saxon Chronicle*, only the *Battle of Brunanburh* requires documentation here. The other five—*The Capture of the Five Boroughs* (942), *The Coronation of Edgar* (973), *The Death of Edgar* (975), *The Death of Alfred* (1036) and *The Death of Edward* (1065)—contain allusions and descriptions too specific or too vague for background material to be of much help; and since they are minor poems, we have omitted them (see Preface).

The poem's contemporary popularity reflects the importance chroniclers accorded the battle itself. Alistair Campbell remarks in his edition (London, 1938) that all the English, Irish, Pictish and Welsh chronicles in the vernaculars or Latin which cover the tenth century in any detail have entries for the battle at Brunanburh (p. 53n); other brief allusions occur in a number of chronicles and charters (see Campbell's edition, passim). Of all the full Latin accounts, ranging from the *Chronicle* entry in MS F (938) to the early modern *Annals of Ulster*, we have left aside only the curious narrative in the *Chronicle of Croyland Abbey* which has been attributed to Ingulf: his facts, such as they are, derive from William of Malmesbury and the rest "is merely . . . a fabrication in honour of the Abbot [Turketul]" (Campbell, pp. 79-80).

Ingulf apart, the other documents make a unified impression: Brunanburh was the "great battle" in Anglo-Saxon history until the greater battle against the Conqueror at Hastings. Nevertheless, they do not always agree on important details, such as the site—thirteen different names are given for it. Essentially the facts are these: Anlaf, the Norse King of Dublin and son of

Guthfrith (not to be confused with his cousin Anlaf, son of Sihtric), invaded England in 937 to re-establish Norse control over York and Northumbria. Allied with Constantine, King of the united Picts and Scots, and also probably with Eugenius, King of the Strathclyde Welsh, he met Aethelstan at Brunanburh where he was beaten terribly. Anlaf and Constantine fled back to Ireland and Scotland. Woven in and among these facts are the various distortions, discrepancies and accretions that come from legend, historical confusions, scribal errors, fabrication for political ends, and, in the case of Henry of Huntingdon, total incompetence in reading Anglo-Saxon.

The dates for the battle are given as they appear in the texts; they do not always coincide with fact.

A. MS F of *The Anglo-Saxon Chronicle*

(12th c.)

Text: Francis P. Magoun, Jr., "*Annales Domitiani Latini:* An Edition," *MS,* 9 (1947), 26.

938. In this year occurred that great and famous battle at Brunanburh, when King Aethelstan and his brother Eadmund fought against Anlaf. With Christ's help, he was victorious and killed five kings and seven nobles from Anlaf's troops.

B. *The Nero Chronicle*

(12th c.)

Text: F. Liebermann, ed., *Ungedruckte Anglo-Normannische Geschichtsquellen* (1879; rpt. Ridgewood, N.J., 1966), p. 68.

938. In this year occurred that great and famous battle at Bruningafelda, when King Aethelstan fought against Anlaf. With Christ's help, he was victorious.

C. *The Vitellius Chronicle*

(12th c.)

Text: Liebermann, p. 88.

937. In this year occurred the battle at Bruningafelda, in which King Aethelstan defeated Anlaf.

D. Aethelweard, *Chronicle*

(late 10th c.)

Text: Alistair Campbell, ed., *The Chronicle of Aethelweard* (London, 1962), p. 54.

After thirteen years [of Aethelstan's reign], there was a tremendous battle against the barbarians at Brunandun; and from that time to the present it has commonly been called "the great battle." The barbarian troops were then overcome on all sides and could no longer prevail. Afterwards, Aethelstan drove them back beyond the ocean's shores; the Scots as well as the Picts also submitted. The fields of Britain were united into one; there was peace everywhere and universal abundance. Nor until now has a naval force come and stayed on these shores without a treaty from the English.

E. Florence of Worcester, *The Chronicle of Chronicles*

(early 12th c.)

Text: Benjamin Thorpe, ed., *Florentii Wigorniensis Monachi Chronicon ex Chronicis* (London, 1848), p. 132.

Anlaf, the pagan King of Ireland and many [other] islands, urged on by his father-in-law, Constantine, King of the Scots, entered the mouth of the river Humber with a mighty fleet. King Aethelstan and his brother, Prince Eadmund, met the enemy with an army at a place called Brunanburh. In a battle extending from daybreak to evening, they killed five kings and seven nobles, whom the enemy had assembled to help them. They shed more blood than had ever been shed before in any war in England. King Anlaf and King Constantine were forced to flee to their ships; and [Aethelstan and Eadmund] returned with great rejoicing. But, overcome by the great misfortune of their army's destruction, [Anlaf and Constantine] returned to their homes with a few men.

F.1. Simeon of Durham, *The History of the Church of Durham*

(early 12th c.)

Text: Thomas Arnold, ed., *Historia Ecclesiae Dunhelmensis* (London, 1882), I, 76.

Four years after [the subjugation of Scotland], that is, in the year 937 of our Lord's birth, Aethelstan fought at Weondune (which is also called Etbrunnanwerc or Brunnanbyrig) against Anlaf, the son of the former king, Guthred, who had come with six hundred and fifteen ships. With him against Aethelstan he had the troops of the aforementioned kings of the Scots and the Welsh [i.e., Constantine and Owen]. But Aethelstan relied on the protection of Saint Cuthbert and drove these kings from his realm, destroying a great number. He brought back a glorious triumph to his people. He was kind to his own, but everywhere terrible to the enemy. Shortly afterwards, he ended his life in peace, leaving the rule of the kingdom to his brother Eadmund.

F.2. Simeon of Durham, *The History of the Kings*

(early 12th c.)

Text: Thomas Arnold, ed., *Historia Regum* (London, 1885), II, 93.

A.D. 937. King Aethelstan fought at Wendune and put King Anlaf to flight along with his six hundred and fifteen ships, and also Constantine, King of the Scots, and [Owen], King of the Welsh, and all their many troops.

G.1. William of Malmesbury, *The History of the English Kings*

(early 12th c.)

Text: William Stubbs, ed., *De Gestis Regum Anglorum* (London, 1887), I, 142-4; 151-2.

(131.) Aethelstan's last battle was with Anlaf, Sihtric's son. In hopes of seizing the kingdom, Anlaf had crossed the border along with the aforementioned Constantine, who was rebelling again. Aethelstan deliberately withdrew in order to derive more glory when he conquered the arrogant enemy. The daring young [Anlaf] had penetrated far into England, his heart full of unlawful intentions, when he was finally met at Brunefeld by the most experienced generals and their strongest troops.

[On the eve of the battle, Anlaf, realizing the danger he is in, disguises himself as a harpist and visits Aethelstan's tent. When the English king discovers the deceit, he moves his retinue elsewhere.]

Ready for the battle, Anlaf advanced by night. He killed a bishop who had joined [Aethelstan's] army that evening and was unaware of what had occurred; because of the green field's level surface, he had pitched his tent there with his whole company. Marching on, Anlaf surprised the King, who had allowed himself to fall into a deep sleep, since he did not anticipate an enemy attack. But when [Aethelstan] had been roused from his bed by the great noise, he spurred his men on to battle as much as he could, given the night. At that point his sword accidentally fell out of its sheath. So he called upon God and Saint Aldhelm for help, although there was absolute panic and blind commotion everywhere. When he placed his hand on the sheath again, he found his sword there. Because of this miracle, the sword is preserved to this day in the kings' treasury. It is very grooved, as they say, on one side, but it can never be filled with gold or silver. Trusting in this gift from God, and at the same time attacking the Norwegian now that it was getting light, Aethelstan fought tirelessly the whole day long until evening and put [Anlaf] and his army to flight. Constantine, King of the Scots, fell there, a man of treacherous spirit and vigorous in his old age, plus five other kings, twelve nobles and nearly the whole assembly of barbarians. The few who did escape were preserved to receive the faith of Christ.

132. A strong tradition about this king persists among the English that no one more just or learned ever governed the realm. That he knew letters I discovered a few days ago in a very old volume where the author struggles with the difficulty of his subject and cannot express his thoughts as he wants to. In the interests of brevity I would append his words here, if they did not ramble on unreasonably in their praise of the prince. He has the kind of style that the king of Roman eloquence, Cicero, calls "bombast" in his book on rhetoric. The eloquence one can excuse because of the conventions of that age; and the good will toward Aethelstan, who was still alive, provides a reason for the excessive compliments. So I will add a few facts in a familiar style which seem to supply further documentation for his great reputation.

> [William continues with a long description of various events from Aethelstan's life. He quotes a passage from a Latin poem that treats the King's childhood and accession. Finally, William prepares to quote a second passage dealing with the Battle of Brunanburh by talking about Malmesbury.]

(135.) Aethelstan ordered Aelwine and Aethelwine, sons of his uncle Aethelweard, both of whom he had lost in the battle against Anlaf, buried there with due honors, and also declared that his own body would rest there too in the future. It is now time that we present the account of the battle from the poet from whom we have excerpted all this:

> Aethelstan had spent twelve years ruling his subjects justly and using his strength to subdue tyrants, when that plague of Europe, that noxious pestilence returned. The savage barbarian from the north now occupies the land; he tarries in the field. The pirate, Anlaf, has abandoned the sea and breathes his unlawful savage threats. The King of the Scots abetting, the northland grants a glad welcome to the demented fury. They boast aloud, they terrify the air with

their words. The local people retreat; the whole region gives way to their arrogance. Because our King, though steadfast and active in his youth, had retired for some time and passed long years in peace, they ravaged everything with their continual plundering. They oppressed the poor and set fire to their fields. In all the pastures the green grass withered; the blighted cornfields scorned the farmers' prayer. They had so many men on foot, so barbarous a mounted force; when they charged, their horses were numberless. The bad news of what was happening at last aroused the King. He did not want to be burned with a Northman's branding-iron because he had yielded his arms to a barbarian axe. There was no delay. Banners led the conquering divisions; Aethelstan unfolds a hundred savage standards to the wind. Ten times twice five thousand men in their raw strength accompany the banners as they lead the way to the stadium of battle. The noble renown of the approaching enemy terrified the plunderers; their clashing [arms] moved the robber hordes, so that they surrendered their booty and sought their own countries. But the remaining heap of men, who had been killed in that terrible massacre, infected the moist air with its foul stench. As just one man from so many thousands, Anlaf escaped death's destruction: this was fortune's noble gift to him. After Aethelstan's [death] he was to have a decisive impact on events.

G.2. William of Malmesbury, *The Deeds of the English Bishops*

(early 12th c.)

Text: N. E. S. A. Hamilton, ed., *De Gestis Pontificum Anglorum* (London, 1870), pp. 21; 144; 178.

(14.) When Aethelstan marched against Anlaf, he had Bishop Odo by his side to rouse him in prosperity and guide him in adversity. Wherefore on that sad night (as I described in the second book of the Royal Deeds), when Aethelstan was heedless of his own safety and the enemy almost caught him by surprise, and he had also lost his sword, Odo once called for was there. Although there was blind commotion everywhere, Odo offered up prayers to heaven and looked down and saw that the King's sword had fallen from heaven into the royal sheath—clearly a gift from the Lord. The sword's fall and return to Aethelstan immediately after Odo cried out had such an effect that the King did not hesitate to refer to Odo as the protector of his life and to appoint him Primate of Canterbury when Wulfhelm died.

. . .

(73.) The citizens proclaim [Theodred's] not wholly forgotten memory. They say he lived at the time of King Aethelstan and went with him to the battle against Anlaf, and was, along with Odo [Bishop] of Wilton, an intercessor and witness of the heavenly gift, which we described above.

. . .

(80.) [After he had been made bishop by King Aethelstan], they say Werstan was killed by the pagans in a battle undertaken by Aethelstan against Anlaf. For although, as we have said elsewhere, the King had deliberately withdrawn, the Bishop came with his army to the battle. Not expecting an ambush, he pitched his tent, because of the green field's level surface, in the place from which the King had retreated. Anlaf, who had discovered and explored the place on the day before, advanced at night ready for battle and killed Werstan without delay.

H. Henry of Huntingdon, *The History of the English*

(12th c.)

Text: Thomas Arnold, ed., *Henrici Archidiaconi Huntendunensis Historia Anglorum* (London, 1879), pp. 159-61.

(18.) In the year of grace 945, in the fourth year of his reign, King Aethelstan fought the greatest of battles at Bruneburh against Anlaf, King of Ireland, who had augmented his forces with Scots and Danes living in England. English writers have talked about the magnitude of this battle in a kind of poem which uses both strange words and figurative language. The verses are given here in a faithful translation so that, by rendering their eloquence almost word for word, we may learn from the majesty of their language about the majesty of this nation's deeds and courage.

19. "King Aethelstan, glory of leaders, ring-giver to his noblemen, along with his brother Eadmund, both of them illustrious from a long family line, used their sword's edge to strike in war at Brunesburh. The family offspring of dead Eadweard split the shield-walls and cut noblemen to pieces. It had been bred in them [as children] on their kindred's knees to defend their country's treasures and homes, its wealth and gifts, in frequent wars against hostile nations. Irish men and men on ships rushed forth to their doom. Hills resounded. Soldiers struggled from the time the sun rose, shining cheerfully, gladdening the deeps, the lamp of God, the torch of the Creator, till the time when this same noble leader hid itself in the west. Many men of Danish descent fell there, pierced by spears, shot through under their shields; along with them the Scots, wearied by war. But the West Saxons, who had been chosen before and were unwearied afterwards, laid low the troops of the enemy nation the whole day long. The Mercians were noble men; they struck down their [enemies'] spears and hurled sharp javelins with hard play of the hand. There was no safety for those who had sought this land with Anlaf across the sea's plains in a ship's bosom; they were going to die in war. Five young kings lay on the battlefield, struck down by swords, and seven of King Anlaf's generals. Scots fell without number and the pride of the Northmen died. To the strife of war they had brought with them not a few men, but with only a few the King sailed away in his ship on the surge of the sea, and inwardly he groaned. At the same time Froda, the Northmen's leader, and general Constantine with his comrades were both unable to boast about this contest of Mars, when they saw the wreck of their kinsmen, where their friends had fallen together, felled by war, in the same place as the commoners. [Froda] left his dear son on the battlefield, disfigured with wounds. Danish Gude could not boast, though he was gentle in speech and ancient in his wisdom. Anlaf himself and the remains of his army could not dishonestly tell the council of wisemen that his men had distinguished themselves in this enterprise, in the field

of battle, in the fierceness of the onslaught, when spears bored through [them]. But the mothers and their daughters-in-law bewailed those who had played at the dice of war with Eadweard's sons. Then in nailed ships the Northmen and ruined Anlaf sought their own lands over the deep flood in sorrow. Then both brothers returned to Wessex, leaving behind them the relics of war, men's flesh ready as food. So the black raven with its horned beak, the leaden toad, the eagle and the kite, the dog and the mottled wolf were fattened on these delicacies for a long time. There was never a greater war fought in this land, nor had such a slaughter occurred before this, since the time the Saxons and Angles (who were to drive the Britons away) came here across the wide sea. Famous as warmongers, they conquered the Welsh, put their kings to flight and seized their territories."

. . .

(32.) Aethelstan, Eadweard's son, ruled for fourteen years and fought the great battle of Bruneburh.

I. John of Fordun,
The Chronicle of the Scottish Nation

(14th c.)

Text: William F. Skene, ed., *Johannis de Fordun Chronica Gentis Scotorum* (Edinburgh, 1871), pp. 164-5.

(Book IV; Chapter XXII)

[William] tells us that Sihtric, who died a year later, gave Aethelstan an excuse for annexing Northumbria to his kingdom. Aethelstan soon besieged York and entreated the citizens to surrender with both prayers and [threats]. Finding that neither method worked as he had hoped, he withdrew. The people of Northumbria and Wales had now been faithfully joined for a long time to the Scots and Danes as one people; they would much rather have been subject to them than to the English. After Sihtric had died (as I said above), the Northumbrians gladly received his sons, Anlaf and Guthfrith, as their leaders. Joined immediately by Constantine, they attacked

Aethelstan with their whole army. Accordingly, in the thirty-sixth year of his reign, King Constantine, Anlaf and Guthfrith assembled an enormous army and ravaged all the southern English regions through which they passed, until they arrived at a place called Brounyngfelde, where Aethelstan had pitched his tents. [William] says that Aethelstan's last battle was with Anlaf, Sihtric's son, and with Constantine, King of the Scots, who crossed the border in hopes of seizing the kingdom. Aethelstan deliberately retreated in order to acquire more glory when he won. By then the attackers had crossed far into England. Suddenly, the battalions and battle-lines of both sides were engaged and there was a brutal conflict. Compared with others, it was by far the most savage battle that has come down to us in writing from the old days, or that is still remembered by the living. On the side of the victorious Aethelstan, the chief generals Aeldwine and Aethelwine died, and two others; also two bishops and many nobles. On the other side, Eligenius, Prince of the Deirans, died, together with three other princes and nine generals. Both sides had innumerable losses among the common people.

Chapter XXIII

That was an unfortunate day for the Scots, because the domains they had conquered either in the times of Gregory or up to then, and had also held for fifty-four years or more, they lost that day by right of conquest.

J. *Annals of Ulster*

(15th or 16th c.)

Text: William M. Hennessy, ed., *Annals of Ulster* (Dublin, 1887), I, 456.

(936 alias 937) An enormous battle, lamentable and dreadful, was cruelly fought between the Saxons and the Northmen, in which many uncounted thousands of Northmen died. But the King, that is, Anlaf, escaped with a few men. A great number of Saxons [also] died on the other side. Aethelstan, King of the Saxons, profited from the great victory.

XX

DURHAM

This late Old English poem can be classified as an *encomium urbis,* a type of literary exercise which Margaret Schlauch has demonstrated "reached the Middle Ages hallowed by centuries of practice in the rhetorical schools of Greece and Rome" ("An Old English *Encomium Urbis,*" *JEGP,* 40 [1941], 14). While *Durham* has no specific source, Prof. Schlauch identifies five works that closely parallel the Old English poem: "the anonymous praises of Milan and Verona, Alcuin's verse history of York, Paulinus on Aquileia and Alphanus on Monte Cassino" (p. 23). We have selected parts of Alcuin's poem on York to exemplify the several topics covered in *Durham:* "the grandeur of the city, its fortunate location, and the saints and holy relics for which it is celebrated" (p. 14).

Alcuin, *Verses on the Fathers, Kings and Saints of the Church of York*

Text: *MGH, Poetae Latini Aevi Carolini,* 1 (Berlin, 1881), 169-70; 177-8; 206.

(Lines 1-45)

O Christ and God, Power of the Highest, the Father's Wisdom, Life, Salvation, Maker, Restorer and Lover of men, God's only Tongue, you kind Giver of gifts! Give me intellectual presents; give words to a frail poet. Moisten my dull breast with a living stream, so my tongue may speak of your gifts. Without you no tongue can tell what should be told. In suppliance I also invoke you, citizens of Olympus, O saints, you mighty people, the Thunderer's divine race, you who bear heaven's victorious standards into the citadel and bring royal gifts to the heavenly king. For your sake He freely poured out His sacred blood on earth to save you from the shadows [of death] and lead you back with Him into the palace of God the Father. Inspire the meter for me, compose this poem with your prayers. For my mind hastens to sing the praises of my home and cradle of old, and briefly to describe in grateful verses the famous city of York.

The Roman army first founded this noble town with walls and towers by forcing the housecarls and their comrades, the native Britons, to labor hard—for at that time fertile Britain justly accepted the Roman kings who ruled the world's dominions. They did this so the city might become the universal marketplace of land and sea, a safe stronghold for the leaders of the realm, the empire's glory and a terror to hostile troops, and a welcoming haven for ships plying from the ocean's rim, where the sea-weary sailor might hasten to tie their prows with a long rope. The waters of the fish-filled Ouse flow through the city; along both banks flowery meads extend. Here and there the land is adorned with hills and woods. With fine locations, it is a beautiful and healthy place to live; and since it is fertile, it will have many farmers. Men gathered from diverse peoples and realms everywhere come here in hope of wealth, seeking riches from the rich earth, a place to settle for themselves, profit and a home. But when the Roman army departed, its provinces in general confusion, wishing to expel its savage foes and to defend its Italian kingdom and throne, then the lazy Britons took control of the city. Harried by virtually incessant raids from the Picts, they were eventually destroyed and submitted to the burden of slavery. They could neither defend their country with their own shields, nor recover their ancestral liberty with their swords.

(Lines 356-79)

After these miracles had occurred, the town became famous and fair peace was restored to the churches of Christ. Osthrida, King Ethelred's faithful queen and daughter of Saint Oswald's brother, ordered her holy uncle's relics covered with a sacred roof and buried with due honor. When the bones had been conveyed to the monastery, a neighbor from Lindsey was profoundly astonished at the miracle which took place: he saw a pillar of ethereal light above the bones of the saintly man gleaming up to heaven's arch throughout the night. At that time a large tapestry was draped over the relics; for at first the cruel monks refused to accept the bones and take them into the monastery because of their old enmity. They made them stay outside for the night. But when the monks saw the fire of the divine light, they begged to keep what they had previously rejected. In the morning, after washing the bones, they laid them in a sarcophagus they had prepared, and bore them with great honor under the roof of the church. Then they took care to bury the living riches in the ground. From that time until now, through the merit of such a great patron saint, many sick people have received there the gift of health if they have possessed the virtue of holy faith. It is enough if I touch upon one of these healings with my hastening plectrum, so that you may believe, devout reader, in the rest.

(Lines 1648-57)

A rude sailor, I have steered my ships with their fragile keels through the floods of the open sea and the treacherous shoals. I have brought back wares again, as is just, to the harbor of York, the city that nourished me, its own child, for itself, and in one way or another instructed me devoutly from my earliest years. So for her I have composed these rustic songs about her own fathers and kings and saints. Likewise, I pray that the saints whom I have mentioned in these verses, through their merits and prayers, may steer my skiff away from the whirlpool of the world towards the port of life.

XXI

JUDGMENT DAY II

De Die Judicii, a poem usually ascribed to Bede, but sometimes to Alcuin, provides the model for *Judgment Day II*. The poet has, however, Englished his Latin with such "careful literalness" that there is no more slavish translation in the corpus of Anglo-Saxon poetry, despite its expansion of 157 Latin hexameters to 306 alliterative lines (L. Whitebread, "The Old English Poem *Judgment Day II* and its Latin Source," *PQ*, 45 [1966], 645; see H. Löhe, ed., "*Be Domes Dæge,*" *Bonner Beiträge,* 22 [1907], 53-62, for a discussion of the slight variations that do occur). The MS actually introduces *Judgment Day II* by quoting the opening Latin verses and attributing them to Bede (*ASPR, VI,* lxx-lxxi).

This text and the analogues for *Christ III* (Entry IX) give the background for the lesser poem, *Judgment Day I*, for which no specific sources exist.

Bede, *The Day of Judgment*

Text: *CC*, 122.439-44.

While I sat sad and alone under the covering of a shady tree, among the flowering grasses of the fertile earth, with the branches echoing on every side from the wind's breath, I was suddenly disturbed by a bitter lament. I sang these mournful songs because my mind was sad when I remembered the sins I had committed, the blotches on my life and the loveless time of death, the great Judgment Day with its fearful trial, the strict Judge's eternal wrath towards the guilty, all humanity on separate benches, and the joys of the saints as well as the punishments of the wicked. When I recalled these things to myself, I said under the quiet murmur [of the leaves], "O eyes, I ask you now to open your warm fountains. While I strike my guilty breast with my fists, while I prostrate my limbs on the ground and call for the pains I deserve, I beseech you, do not spare your copious tears! Pour the salt drops down my sorrowing face! Reveal my sins with groaning voice to Christ, and do not hide any fault in my heart's cave! Let all be brought to light and declared openly: the fierce crimes of the heart, the tongue and the flesh. The soul's only salvation and the certain hope for him who grieves is to show his wounds tearfully to the heavenly Doctor. He is accustomed to heal the sick and free those in chains; He does not want to break us like quivering reeds with His right hand, nor quench us like the lampwick's faint smoke with water. Isn't the thief who hanged on the Cross an example for you of how much sin's true confession is worth? Until he was crucified, he was a wicked man who had committed evil deeds; but at the point of death, he cried out with words of prayer. With one word of faith he merited salvation and entered the open gates of paradise with Christ. I ask you, my spirit, why are you so slow to reveal yourself completely to the Doctor? My tongue, why are you silent when there is still time for forgiveness? The Almighty listens to you now with open ears. The day will come when the world's Judge will arrive and you must render an account of yourself. I urge you to prevent the Judge's wrath now with tears. Why do you lie in filth, O flesh, full of guilt and crime? Why don't you purge away your sins with plentiful tears and beg for yourself the comfort of a gentle remedy? While you have been given the grace to weep with incessant tears, it is pleasant to repent now and wholesome to weep. The eternal Judge will be mild if you submit your claim to Him now, but heavenly God will not deliver anyone from his crimes twice.

Do not scorn the times of forgiveness you have for certain.

Remember how great the torments are that await the wicked and how the high-throned, fearful Judge will come from the heights of heaven to give everyone his due. Remember what signs will precede Him: suddenly the earth will tremble and the mountains crumble down; the hills will melt and the sea confound mens' minds with its terrible roar; the sky will be covered sorrowfully with black shadows; the stars will fall and the sun grow dark in the crimson east; the pale moon will not uncover her nightly lamp, and signs threatening death will come from the sky. Having surrounded the heavenly King with its angelic hosts, the wakened might of heaven will suddenly arrive; sublime, He sits on His high throne, ablaze with light. When the crowds have been assembled from all regions, we are brought before Him so each may be judged according to his deeds. Remember the fear which will strike the hearts of everyone brought to the tribunal, and which will make them plead in vain. At that time the angelic troops will come with all the innumerable throngs of heaven, accompanying the King of the sky. All men alike will be forced to go there: those who are, have been, or will be in the future; and everyone's every secret will be universally revealed. What the heart or tongue or hand has done in shadowy caverns, what I am ashamed and afraid for anyone to know, everyone alike will then be allowed to know openly. The air will be filled with avenging flames; and fire, its reins broken, will rule everywhere. Where the air now spreads its empty lap, the fiery flame will pour its terrible thunder and hurry to avenge the fierce causes of crimes. Then avenging heat will not care to spare anyone, unless he comes there cleansed of every stain. Then the tribes and people will strike their guilty breasts with fists and all will stand there together: the proud man and the pauper, the strong man, the beggar and the rich man will all fear the same authority. The fire-belching river will torture men grievously and worms will gnaw at the inmost recesses of sinners' hearts. No one present will be able to rely on his own merits before the Judge; but a great terror will run through every breast and the wicked throng will be struck dumb at the same time with dread fear. What, flesh, what will you do, weeping at that hour? The hour you now rejoice to serve, alas, with wretched lust, will vex you then with the sharp stings of your luxury. Why aren't you afraid of the fiery torments which evil demons have long prepared for you, and which exceed the perceptions and descriptions of any man alive? No voice can declare the miserable punishments, the regions of eternal hell filled with black fires and the icy colds mingled with burning flames, the eyes weeping from the furnace's great heat on the one hand, and the teeth gnashing from the bitter cold on the other. With these wretched alternations the wretched wander forever in pitch darkness and night's obscurity. No voice sounds there unless it is the dreadful weeping all around, and no face is seen except for the faces of those in torture. Nothing is felt except the cold and the flames. The stench of overwhelming decay fills your nostrils and your lamenting mouth will be filled with flame-belching fire. With fiery teeth the worms will tear at your bones. Your breast will be tormented too with bitter thoughts about why the flesh briefly surrendered to its own desire and incurred eternal punishment in the black prison, where no spark of light shines on wretched men, where no peace or mercy, or indeed hope of peace, smiles upon those who weep. All comforts flee away. No one will be there to help you in your grievous afflictions; no happy face will ever be seen there, only pain and lamentation, gnashing of teeth and fear, trembling dread, weariness, sorrow, fierce indignation and listlessness, and souls wandering among the flames in the blind prison. Then this world's injurious pleasures will cease: drunkenness, banquets, laughter, wantonness, jesting, fierce desire, clinging lust, wicked passion, idle sleep, heavy torpor and lazy sloth. Now, delight seduces all the flesh and plunges the soul into the blind whirlpool of sins; then, it will sink wretches into the dark flames forever. How greatly and perpetually happy is the man lucky enough to flee from these disastrous punishments. He will rejoice together with the saints, world without end. United to Christ, he will live in the kingdoms of heaven where no night exists to snatch away the splendor of the pleasing light; and no grief or lamentation will come, nor feeble old age. No thirst is present there, no hunger, sleep, or any labor; no fevers, diseases, or injuries; no frosts, flames, weariness, sadness, anxieties, torments, catastrophes, bolts of lightning, storm clouds, winter, thunder, snow, hail, tempests, anguish, poverty, sorrow, death, accidents or need. Rather, there reign peace and love, goodness and wealth, and joy, happiness, virtue, light, eternal life, glory, praise, tranquility, honor and sweet concord. God Himself provides every good thing for all; God is always present. He cherishes, fulfills and honors all. He glorifies, preserves, esteems, loves, adorns and places the happy on heaven's high throne. He bestows celestial rewards and everlasting gifts in the midst of angelic hosts and sacred throngs, joined with the prophetic patriarchs and prophets. He bestows them in the midst of apostolic citadels and happy souls; in the midst of splendid fortresses and rosy triumphs. He bestows them in the midst of the white ranks and their maiden flower, ranks which the loving Mother of God, the holy Virgin Mary, in shining raiment, draws through the Father's blessed kingdoms. He bestows them in the midst of the saints of the Church, its fathers and sons, and in the midst of the heavenly senate with its celestial peace.

What, I ask, can we consider harsh in this world, when it permits us to live with the heavenly throngs, to rejoice always on the blessed thrones of those above and to bless the Lord Christ forever? May Christ keep you safe for my sake, my dearest brother [Acca], and make you always and forever happy. Following your commands, lo, I have sung songs of lamentation for you. I ask you to do what you promised faithfully to do: commend me now to Christ with your prayers, I who have sung for you. Live happy in God and say farewell to the kind brothers, Father Acca; remember your anxious, fearful servant, and commend me in your bounteous prayers to Christ.

XXII

THE METRICAL CHARMS

When the Rev. Oswald Cockayne first collected all the materials comprising the magico-medical lore of the Anglo-Saxon era, he subtitled his three-volume anthology, "The History of Science in this Country before the Norman Conquest" (*Leechdoms, Wortcunning and Starcraft of Early England* [London, 1864-66]). But the science has been more aptly described by Charles Singer as "a medley of remedies, charms, invocations, prescriptions and prayers" (J. H. G. Grattan and Charles Singer, *Anglo-Saxon Magic and Medicine* [London, 1952], p. 28). From this medley come the twelve metrical charms, so called because they share some of the characteristics of Anglo-Saxon prosody, though they are not uniformly written in verse (or even in Old English, since Latin tags often appear at particularly auspicious moments).

The sources are likewise various and constitute a mixture of debased classical medicine, classical superstition, Teutonic magic and Christian ritual (see Grattan and Singer, pp. 23-79). Many of the surviving Old English charms have analogues in other Germanic languages, particularly in Old High German. But, while Latin prayers and fragments are everywhere present, Latin charms themselves provide only remote analogues for the English incantations; as Godfrid Storms remarks, "we find agreement in the way of details, such as the number three, silence, excrements, plants, colours, and so forth; we do not find parallel charms" (*Anglo-Saxon Magic* [The Hague, 1948], p. 121).

Three Latin charms are close enough to warrant inclusion: 1. *The Prayer of Mother Earth* is a pagan charm surviving in medieval MSS from the sixth century on (Grattan and Singer, p. 45); it contains material of interest for Charms 1 and 2. 2. One of many bee charms has been selected to go with Charm 8 (see Austin E. Fife, "Christian Swarm Charms from the Ninth to the Nineteenth Centuries," *JAF*, 77 [1964], 154-9, for a brief survey). And 3. the *Lorica,* attributed to Gildas, is "of the same date and in the same spirit" as Charm 11 (Grattan and Singer, p. 70; see also F. P. Magoun, Jr., "Zu den ae. Zaubersprüchen," *Archiv*, 171 [1937], 25).

A. K-D 1 and 2

The Prayer of Mother Earth

Text: Alexander Riese, ed., *Anthologia Latina*, I, 1 (Leipzig, 1894), 26-7.

You will sing this song as follows:

Holy goddess, Earth, nature's mother, who create and renew all things every day, you alone give peoples your protection. Divine arbitress of the sky, the sea and the universe, through you nature is still and falls asleep. Again, you restore the light and make night flee; you hide away Hell's shadows and unending chaos; you contain the winds and rains in their proper season. When you please, you scatter and confuse the seas and put the sun to flight and rouse the storms. Again, when you wish, you bring forth jocund day. With eternal fidelity, you bestow the foods that nourish life; and, when the soul departs, we will take refuge in you. Thus, whatever you give them, all things return to you. You are rightly called Great Mother of the gods, because you have conquered the powers of the gods with your kindness. You are truly the mother of men and gods, for without you nothing can either mature or be born. You are great, queen and goddess of the gods. Goddess, I adore you and invoke your power. It is easy for you to give me what I ask you, and I will render you thanks, goddess, as you deserve. Hear me properly, I beg you, and favor my undertakings. What I ask of you, goddess, give me willingly. Every one of the herbs your majesty produces you give to all peoples for the sake of health. Now grant me your medicine; may it come to me . . . with your powers. Whatever I make from these herbs, may the result be good. May each person to whom I give these herbs accept them from me. May you make them healthy . . . . Now, goddess, I beg that your majesty give me what I humbly request.

B. K-D 8

Latin Bee Charm

Text: Godfrid Storms, *Anglo-Saxon Magic* (The Hague, 1948), p. 139.

So the bees won't abandon the hive, inscribe the following on a lead plate and put it where the bees leave the hive:

In the Name of the Father, the Son and the Holy Spirit. I charge you bees, you handmaidens of God, who do God's work, you faithful little bees, fear God. Do not take to the woods, do not fly away from me, do not try to escape. May Abraham keep you here; may Isaac keep you here; may Joseph [Jacob] stop you flying away. I charge you through the Virgin Mary, God's Mother, and I charge you through Saint Joseph to settle in the spot I tell you. Bees! I charge you through the Father, the Son and the Holy Spirit not to take the liberty to fly away from a son of man.

Then say the Lord's Prayer and the Creed.

C. K-D 11

The Lorica of Gildas

Text: J. H. G. Grattan and Charles Singer, *Anglo-Saxon Magic and Medicine* (London, 1952), pp. 130-46.

Help me, One-God-in-Three; have mercy on me, Three-in-One-God. It is as if I were in danger of a mighty sea; please help me, so neither this year's death nor the world's vanity will drag me away with them. I ask the same from the high powers of the celestial army: let them not leave me to be torn apart by my enemies, but defend me still with their strong weapons and precede me in the battle-line—the army of the heavenly host, the cherubim and the seraphim with their thousands, Michael and Gabriel with theirs. I want the thrones, the virtues, the archangels, the principalities and powers and angels to defend me in dense array, so I may overthrow my enemies. Next I beseech the rest of the champions, the patriarchs, the sixteen prophets, the apostles who pilot Christ's ship and the martyrs, all of them [God's] athletes. Also I entreat all the virgins, the faithful widows and confessors, so that through them salvation may encompass me, all evil pass away from me, Christ conclude a firm pact with me, and fear and trembling terrify [hell's] hideous throngs. God, with your power and invincible protection, defend me on all sides; with your safe shield protecting every part, keep both my body's flanks protected, so that the foul demons cannot hurl their darts into my sides, as they usually do. Defend the crown of my head and my head and hair, my eyes, forehead, tongue, teeth and nostrils, neck, back, side, loins, thighs, internal fat and two hands. Be a helmet of safety, therefore, for the top of my head with its hair, brow, eyes and the three parts of my brain, nose, lip, face, temple, chin, beard, eyebrows, ears, cheeks, lips, the septum between the nostrils, the nostrils, the pupils and irises, the eyelids, eyebrows, gums, breath, jaws, gullet, teeth, tongue, mouth, uvula, throat, larynx, the frenum of the tongue, headpan, brain, cartilage and neck. Be present, merciful [God], with your protection. Also, be the safest lorica for my limbs and guts, so you may beat away from me the invisible points of the shafts devised by hateful enemies. As a strong lorica, cover my shoulders, God, along with my shoulder-blades and arms. Cover my elbows, along with the forearms and hands, fists, palms, and fingers with their nails. Cover my spine, my ribs with their joints, back, and the sinews with their bones. Cover my skin and blood along with the kidneys, hips and backside with the upper thighs. Cover my legs, calves, the [other] parts of the thighs with their sockets, knee-joints and knees. Cover the ten branches growing together and the twice five nails that complete them.

Cover my ankles with the shanks and heels, my legs and feet with their soles underneath. Cover my chest, collar-bone, breast-bone, nipples, stomach and navel. Cover my belly, loins, genitals, bowels, and the heart's vital parts. Cover the three-sectioned liver, the groin, scrotum, kidneys and the great gut with its caul of fat. Cover my tonsils, thorax with lung, veins, lobes and gall with midriff. Cover my flesh and groin with its marrow, and the spleen with the twisting intestines. Cover my bladder, the fat, and all the numberless kinds of internal structures. Cover my hairs and the rest of my physical parts whose names I may have perhaps omitted. Cover all of me along with my five senses and their ten well-made entrances, so that from soles to crown I may not be sick in any internal or external part; and no plague, fever, weakness or pain may drive life from my body, until, God granting, I grow old and can erase my sins with good deeds. Leaving the flesh thus behind, I may have the strength to escape the depths [of hell] and fly to heaven, and, God being merciful, be carried joyfully to the consolations of His kingdom. Amen.

Appendix I

Notes on Additional Latin Sources and Analogues

1. *Exodus*

Until the publication of Samuel Moore's article, "On the Sources of the Old-English *Exodus*," *MP*, 9 (1911), 83-108, scholars were satisfied that *De Transitu Maris Rubri*, Book V of Avitus' long biblical poem, was the source of *Exodus*. Moore demolished that belief and inaugurated the search through patristic commentaries which still flourishes. In 1912 James W. Bright suggested that the source was the twelve "prophecies" read at the baptismal service for Holy Saturday ("The Relation of the Caedmonian *Exodus* to the Liturgy," *MLN*, 27 [1912], 97-103). Although this general thesis did not win acceptance, his suggestion that the poem may be, in some way or other, about baptism continues to find partisans.

Subsequent scholarship has followed Sir Israel Gollancz in maintaining that the *Exodus* poet was acquainted with the works of the Fathers and intended his poem as an allegory of "the way of life" (*The Caedmon Manuscript of Anglo-Saxon Biblical Poetry* [Oxford, 1927], p. lxxxiii). Since Gollancz, critics have divided over the presence and extent of this allegory. Edward B. Irving, Jr., the most recent editor, is reluctant to accept the existence of a specific, continuous and coherent allegory, but acknowledges that the poet "is certainly . . . much more learned than I had once thought him to be"; he cautions us nevertheless that the poet did not adopt "structures of meaning," despite his free borrowing of details ("*Exodus* Retraced," in *Old English Studies in Honour of John C. Pope*, ed. Robert B. Burlin and Edward B. Irving, Jr. [Toronto, 1974], p. 209). In short, apart from the Bible and particularly Exodus 13 and 14, no single model has yet been discovered for the poem as distinct from some of its ideas and phrases.

For the general background, several works are of note:

1. Josephus, *Antiquitates Judaicae*; see *The Latin Josephus*, Vol. I: Introduction and Text, The Antiquities: Books I-V, ed. Franz Blatt (Copenhagen, 1958); see Fred C. Robinson, "Notes on the Old English *Exodus*," *Anglia*, 80 (1962), 364, et passim.
2. Tertullian, *De Baptismo, CC*, 1, 1.277-95; see J. E. Cross and S. I. Tucker, "Allegorical Tradition and the Old English *Exodus*," *Neophil*, 44 (1960), 126n.
3. Jerome, *Liber interpretationis hebraicorum nominum, CC*, 72, 57-161; see Fred C. Robinson, "The Significance of Names in Old English Literature," *Anglia*, 86 (1968), 14-58.
4. Augustine, *Enarrationes in Psalmos, CC*, 39.989-90; see James W. Earl, "Christian Traditions in the Old English *Exodus*," *NM*, 71 (1970), 552.

Predictably, most biblical commentaries provide allegorical interpretations of the Exodus, the Flood and the Sacrifice of Isaac. A good review of the details can be found in Irving's "*Exodus* Retraced" and also in his "New Notes on the Old English *Exodus*," *Anglia*, 90 (1972), 289-324.

2. *Daniel*

The Old English *Daniel* paraphrases rather freely the first five chapters of the Book of Daniel. Whether the Song of Azarias (lines 279-332) and the Song of the Three Children (lines 358-408) are integral parts of the original poem has long been debated. The biblical texts of both Songs are in the Vulgate (Dan. 3.24-90), but in the apocrypha of Protestant Bibles. Robert T. Farrell makes a strong case for contributions of the Songs to the unity of the poem ("The Unity of Old English

Daniel," *RES*, 18 [1967], 117-35). However, the Song of the Three Children in *Daniel* depends more on an adaptation found in a Latin Canticle than on the Vulgate text (see Sherman M. Kuhn, ed., *The Vespasian Psalter* [Ann Arbor, Mich., 1965], p. 156, for the Latin text of the Canticle with an Old English interlinear gloss). Farrell's suggestion that *Daniel* may have been influenced by Hippolytus of Rome's third-century commentary on the Book of Daniel falls outside the purview of this book, since Hippolytus wrote in Greek and no Latin translation of his commentary is known before the twelfth century ("A Possible Source for Old English *Daniel*," *NM*, 70 [1969], 85n).

3. *Christ and Satan*

Whether or not a convincing argument can be made for the unity of *Christ and Satan*, the poem certainly falls into three separate parts: I. The Lament of the Fallen Angels; II. Christ's Descent into Hell, Resurrection, Ascension and Second Coming; III. The Temptation of Christ.

In 1925 Clubb justly remarked of Part I that "In any strict sense of the word, the laments of the fallen angels in lines 1-365 cannot be said to have a source" (Merrel Dare Clubb, ed., *Christ and Satan: An Old English Poem* [New Haven, 1925], p. xxiv). The poet does, however, draw upon the rich apocryphal and patristic materials that constitute the hexameral tradition (see Entry I). Clubb also calls attention to Gregory the Great's *Homily 34* on the Gospels (*PL*, 76.1246-59); to a passage from Aldhelm's *De Virginitate* (lines 296-302 of a portion usually called *De Octo Principalibus Vitiis*, in *MGH*, *Auctores Antiquissimi*, 15 [Berlin, 1919], 464); and to Aldhelm's Lucifer riddle (*CC*, 133.498-9). But he finds only negative evidence for the poet's knowledge or use of these texts. Thomas D. Hill (*PQ*, 48 [1969], 550-4) and Charles R. Sleeth (unpublished edition of *Christ and Satan*) both find echoes of the *Visio Pauli* in the poet's description of hell (see M. R. James's translation of the *Visio Pauli* in *The Apocryphal New Testament* [Oxford, 1953], pp. 525-55).

The analogues for Part II are more identifiable, though their precise relationships to the poem remain obscure. *The Gospel of Nicodemus* is unquestionably the ultimate source (see Entry XVII), but details of Christ's descent into hell and other events in His life on earth after the Crucifixion derive from a homiletic tradition. *Blickling Homily* 7 bears a marked resemblance to Part II and its sources are known. A large part of the homily depends on Pseudo-Augustinian *Sermon 160* (*PL*, 39.2059-61), which is now recognized as a conflation of Eusebius Gallicanus' *Homily 12* and Gregory the Great's *Sermon 22* (see *PLS*, 2.850). Other aspects depend on *The Book of Cerne* (see *The Prayer Book of Aedeluald the Bishop, commonly called The Book of Cerne*, ed. Arthur B. Kuypers [Cambridge, 1902], pp. 196-8). And Grau proposed that the section on the Resurrection, Ascension and Last Judgment depends on a version in Bodleian MS Hatton 116 ("Quellen und Verwandtschaften der älteren germanischen Darstellungen des Jüngsten Gerichtes," *Studien zur Englischen Philologie*, 31 [Halle, 1908], pp. 194-6). These several dependencies of *Blickling Homily* 7 are complicated enough, but their tenuous connection with Part II is even more so. Again, Clubb's conclusions must go substantially unchallenged: "It is altogether probable that some homily . . . furnished a model for many of the structural features of *Christ and Satan* 366-664. However, that homily must have been very different from either the Pseudo-Augustinian, Hatton, or Blickling Homily, if it was in any very vital sense a source of the section as a whole" (p. xxxvi).

Part III relies on Matthew 4.1-11, though here too the Gospel story cannot account for all the details. Clubb flatly admits he cannot discover anything analogous to the episode following the actual temptation when Satan returns to hell and suffers the punishment Christ imposed on him—to measure hell with his hands (p. xli). As a final note to the source material in his unpublished edition, Professor Sleeth calls attention to the thirteenth hymn in *The Vespasian Psalter* (ed. Sherman M. Kuhn [Ann Arbor, Mich., 1965], pp. 159-60). The hymn shares many topics with the poem, especially, as Sleeth points out, "the combination of Christ as Creator with the harrowing of hell and the last judgment" (p. 116).

4. *Homiletic Fragment I*

Krapp characterized this fragment as "a loose amplification of Psalm 28" (*ASPR*, II, xxxix); but recently Neil D. Isaacs has argued that "only lines 9-15a closely parallel the passage from Psalm 28" (*Structural Principles in Old English Poetry* [Knoxville,

Tenn., 1968], p. 100). Thomas D. Hill finds a patristic source for the poem's central metaphor of "the bee with its honeyed mouth and poisoned tail" in Gregory's *Homiliae in Ezechielem*, *PL* 76.879-80 ("The Hypocritical Bee in the Old English *Homiletic Fragment I*, lines 18-30," *N&Q*, 213 [1968], 123).

5. *Azarias* (see Item 2. *Daniel*)

6. Poems of Common Wisdom

Two of the poems that properly belong here have been treated above (see Entry XIV for *The Gifts of Men* and *The Fortunes of Men*); and the remaining six—*Precepts, Vainglory, Maxims I* and *II, The Order of the World* and *Instructions for Christians*— formed a mixed group. Even so, the eight poems are no more than a sample of the wisdom literature represented in many Anglo-Saxon poems, as Morton W. Bloomfield demonstrates ("Understanding Old English Poetry," *AnM*, 9 [1968], 22).

Though the various stages in its development have given rise to considerable differences in poetic expression, wisdom literature is universal and its ultimate source religious (see Lynn L. Remly, "The Anglo-Saxon Gnomes as Sacred Poetry," *Folklore*, 82 [1971], 147-58). Ecclesiastes, Ecclesiasticus, Psalms, Proverbs and the Book of Wisdom provide the most obvious biblical instances.

With two clearly Christian poems, *Vainglory* and *The Order of the World,* scholars have turned to John Cassian, Gregory the Great, Ambrose, Augustine, Cassiodorus and Bede for parallels (see Catherine A. Regan, "Patristic Psychology in the Old English *Vainglory*," *Traditio*, 26 [1970], 324-35; and Bernard F. Huppé, *The Web of Words* [Albany, N. Y., 1970], pp. 2-61). Blanche Colton Williams' *Gnomic Poetry in Anglo-Saxon* (New York, 1914) is still a standard work and contains useful comparisons between Old English and Old Norse gnomes; it treats the biblical and Latin sources very sketchily, however.

7. *Widsith* and *Deor*

In any strict sense, these two poems do not have a Latin background. However the references to ancient Germanic peoples and geography can often be identified by consulting Latin historians—Tacitus, Jordanes, Gregory of Tours and Saxo Grammaticus, for example. The reader should consult Kemp Malone's editions for the specific details: *Widsith,* rev. ed. (Copenhagen, 1962); and *Deor,* 4th ed. (London, 1966). See also Malone, "An Anglo-Latin Version of the *Hjađningavíg,*" *Speculum,* 39 (1964), 35-44.

Murray F. Markland raises the possibility that *Deor* and the Alfredian *Boethius* are related in theme ("Boethius, Alfred, and *Deor,*" *MP*, 66 [1968], 1-4; see also, Whitney F. Bolton, "Boethius, Alfred and *Deor* Again," *MP*, 69 [1972], 222-7).

8. *Alms-Giving*

For its source the central image in this nine-line poem has Ecclesiasticus 3.33, "Water quenches a burning fire and almsgiving makes atonement for sins" (see L. Whitbread, "The Old-English Poem *Almsgiving,*" *N&Q,* 189 [1945], 3). Joseph B. Trahern, Jr., points out that "the first sentence of the poem is a paraphrase of the beginning of Psalm xl," and that the organization of the whole derives from patristic tradition ("The Old English *Almsgiving,*" *N&Q,* 214 [1969], 46); he claims the poet follows the *Exposition of the Psalms* by Cassiodorus (*CC*, 97.372-4). In a later article, Carl T. Berkhout suggests the poet relies on the patristic conception of almsgiving as a release from purgatory and as a symbol of baptism ("Some Notes on the Old English *Almsgiving,*" *ELN*, 10 [1972], 81-5).

9. *Pharaoh*

Krapp and Dobbie state that this short and badly mutilated text should "be classed with the Anglo-Saxon dialogues of the question and answer type, such as *Solomon and Saturn,* in verse and prose, and the prose *Adrianus and Ritheus*" (*ASPR,* III, lxiii). Joseph B. Trahern, Jr., has shown that a basis for the specific question in the Old English poem can be seen in the popular *Jests of the Monks*: "How many thousand Egyptians pursued the sons of Israel?—1800" ("The *Ioca Monachorum* and the Old English *Pharaoh,*" *ELN*, 7 [1970], 165).

10. *The Lord's Prayer I*

Three poetical versions of the Lord's Prayer exist in Old English; the first "follows the Latin original [Matt. 6.9-13] very closely, with no additions to the sense" (*ASPR*, III, lxiii). See also Item 20.

11. *Homiletic Fragment II*

Lines 6-7 are reminiscent of the Christian idea of the declining world in its sixth age (see J. E. Cross, "Aspects of Microcosm and Macrocosm in Old English Literature," in *Studies in Old English Literature in Honor of Arthur G. Brodeur*, ed. Stanley B. Greenfield [Eugene, Ore., 1963], p. 12). Lines 8-10 have their source in the Epistle to the Ephesians 4.5-6 (Joseph S. Wittig, "*Homiletic Fragment II* and the Epistle to the Ephesians," *Traditio*, 25 [1969], 358-63).

12. *Judith*

Verses 12.10-16.1 of the apocryphal Book of Judith are the source for this Old English poem; and echoes of verses 9.14, 17 and 10.16 also occur (see B. J. Timmer, ed., *Judith* [London, 1952], pp. 14-6). Two critics have interpreted the poem allegorically, on the basis of the standard patristic commentaries (Jackson J. Campbell, "Schematic Technique in *Judith*," *ELH*, 38 [1971], 155-72; and Bernard F. Huppé, *The Web of Words* [Albany, N.Y., 1970], pp. 114-89). Both identify Judith as a type of the Church, and Holofernes, her adversary, as a type of the devil; both list more or less the same commentaries in support of their interpretation:

1. Ambrose, *Liber de viduis, PL,* 16.258-60.
2. Two Pseudo-Augustinian sermons on Judith, *PL*, 39.1839-41; see *PLS*, 2.841-2.
3. Prudentius, *Psychomachia, CC,* 126.153-4.
4. Dracontius, *De laudibus Dei, MGH, Auctores Antiquissimi,* 14 (Berlin, 1905), 105.
5. Aldhelm, *De Virginitate, MGH, Auctores Antiquissimi,* 15 (Berlin, 1919), 316-7.
6. Rabanus Maurus, *Expositio in Librum Judith, PL,* 109.539-92.

13. *The Paris Psalter*

The Anglo-Saxon translator of the one hundred metrical psalms (51-150) preserved in MS Fonds Latin 8824, Bibliothèque Nationale, Paris, "used the Roman version of the Psalter, which was losing ground to the Gallican in the late tenth or early eleventh century" (Kenneth Sisam and Celia Sisam in *The Paris Psalter*, ed. Bertram Colgrave, [Copenhagen, 1958], p. 17). Since the modern Vulgate derives from the Gallican Psalter, the reader should consult an edition of the *Psalterium Romanum* (see Robert Weber, ed., *Le Psautier Romain et les autres anciens psautiers latins* [Rome, 1953]; also *PL*, 29.124-420).

Commentaries on the Psalms existed from the earliest patristic period and their influence on various Old English renditions has long been noted (see Johannes Wichmann, "König Aelfred's Angelsächsische Übertragung der Psalmen I-LI excl.," *Anglia*, 11 [1889], 39-96; and James Douglas Bruce, "The Anglo-Saxon Version of the Book of Psalms commonly known as *The Paris Psalter*," *PMLA*, 9 [1894], 43-164). John D. Tinkler has recently made an extensive survey of their influence, and finds "ample evidence in both the prose and metrical portions that medieval commentary upon the psalms lies behind many of the most difficult and seemingly far-fetched additions" (*Vocabulary and Syntax of the Old English Version in the Paris Psalter* [The Hague, 1971], p. 12). Tinkler provides a convenient list of the commentaries (p. 11), although it must be revised to take account of recent patristic studies:

1. Augustine, *Enarrationes in Psalmos, CC*, 38-40.
2. Pseudo-Jerome, *Breviarium in Psalmos, PL*, 26.863-1382 (see *CPL*, 629).
3. Cassiodorus, *Expositio Psalmorum, CC*, 97-8.
4. Pseudo-Bede, *In Psalmorum Librum Exegesis, PL*, 93.483-1098 (see *CPL*, 1384).
5. Anselm of Laon, *Commentarius in Psalmos, PL*, 116.193-696 (formerly attributed to Haymo of Halberstadt; see *PRM*, p. 57).
6. Bruno of Wurzburg, *Expositio Psalmorum, PL*, 142.49-530.

The *Enarrationes in Psalmos* attributed to Remigius of Auxerre

(*PL*, 131.149-844) belongs to the twelfth century and thus falls outside our period (see *PRM*, p. 58).

14. *The Meters of Boethius*

The Meters of Boethius pose a special problem because their direct source is the Old English prose translation of the Latin text (*ASPR*, V, xxxvi). Whether Alfred himself turned the prose into verse remains in dispute, but the two texts do afford a rare glimpse of an Old English versifier at work. (For a discussion of the ways in which the prose has been reworked, see Larry D. Benson, "The Literary Character of Anglo-Saxon Formulaic Poetry," *PMLA*, 81 [1966], 337-41; and John W. Conlee, "A Note on Verse Composition in the *Meters of Boethius*," *NM*, 71 [1970], 576-85.)

Ultimately the poems may derive from Boethius' Latin meters, but the early medieval commentaries on Boethius' *Consolation* have clearly influenced both the prose and metrical parts of the translation throughout (see G. Schepss, "Zu König Alfreds 'Boethius'," *Archiv*, 94 [1895], 149-60). Ironically, the specific commentary discussed by Schepps was first identified as belonging to Remigius of Auxerre (see H. F. Stewart, "A Commentary by Remigius Autissiodorensis on the *De Consolatione Philosophiae* of Boethius," *JTS*, 17 [1915], 22-42; and E. T. Silk, ed., *Saeculi Noni Auctoris in Boetii Consolationem Philosophiae Commentarius* [Rome, 1935], pp. 305-43, for discussions and the text of selected portions). But Remigius must be dismissed on chronological grounds (see, for example, Brian S. Donaghey, "The Sources of King Alfred's Translation of Boethius's *De Consolatione Philosophiae*," *Anglia*, 82 [1964], 28-9).

As a substitute, scholars have suggested a commentary preserved in a Brussels manuscript and sometimes attributed to John Scotus Erigena (see H. Silvestre, "Le commentaire inédit de Jean Scot Érigène au mètre IX du livre III du *De Consolatione Philosophiae* de Boèce," *RHE*, 47 [1952], 44-122; and Dorothy Whitelock, "The Prose of Alfred's Reign," in *Continuations and Beginnings*, ed. E. G. Stanley [London, 1966], pp. 82-3). Another commentary found in a manuscript at St. Gall has also been suggested (see Donaghey, pp. 45-6). Finally Kurt Otten posits the existence of "a commentary which is closer to Remigius than to the St. Gall, but which is either lost or remains unknown to us" (*König Alfreds Boethius* [Tübingen, 1964], p. 155).

For a list of the medieval commentaries on Boethius, see Silvestre, pp. 46-7, and P. Courcelle, "Étude critique sur les commentaires de la *Consolation* de Boèce (IXe-XVe siècles)," *Archives d'histoire doctrinale et littéraire du moyen âge*, 12 (1939), 5-140.

15. *Waldere*

The mutilated text of *Waldere* makes it difficult to assign action and speech with assurance; however, there is little doubt that the Old English does preserve a portion of the Walter of Aquitaine legend. The epic *Waltharii poesis*, often (but not always) ascribed to Ekkehard I of St. Gall, provides the fullest version of this legend. Though scholars are not in total agreement about the nature of the relationship between the two poems, they now agree that the Anglo-Saxon does not derive directly from the Latin (see Karl Langosch, "Die Vorlage des *Waltharius*," in *Festschrift Bernhard Bischoff*, ed. Johanne Autenreith and Franz Brunhölzl [Stuttgart, 1971], p. 240).

The standard edition of the *Waltharii poesis* is by Karl Strecker in *MGH, Poetae Latini Medii Aevi*, 6, 1 (Weimar, 1951), 24-83. A good translation along with translations of other versions of the legend and excellent bibliographical references may be found in F. P. Magoun, Jr., and H. M. Smyser, *Walter of Aquitaine: Materials for the Study of his Legend*, Connecticut College Monographs, No. 4 (New London, Conn., 1950), pp. 3-37.

16. *Solomon and Saturn*

Except for two brief articles by Thomas D. Hill, the fullest commentary on the background of *Solomon and Saturn I* and *II* remains Robert J. Menner's lengthy introduction to his edition (*The Poetical Dialogues of Solomon and Saturn* [New York, 1941], pp. 1-70). He points out that "A lost *Contradictio Salomonis* has been supposed by many writers to be the actual source of the Old English dialogues" (p. 24); but adds that "no Latin texts resembling either dialogue in content have as yet been discovered, for the later [mainly 12th-14th c.] Latin dialogues of Solomon and Marcolf . . . have little in common with the Old English poems. One may hazard the guess that even if Latin sources should be found they would contain only a part of the material of the Old English dialogues" (p. 26).

Hill's articles are: "The Falling Leaf and Buried Treasure: Two Notes on the Imagery of *Solomon and Saturn*, 314-22," *NM*, 71 (1970), 571-6; and "Two Notes on *Solomon and Saturn*," *MÆ*, 40 (1971), 217-21.

17. *The Menologium*

Dobbie's summary of scholarship on the sources of the *Menologium* is useful but in need of revision. He writes, "it is unlikely that the poet . . . used any sources beyond the ecclesiastical calendars in missals and other liturgical books readily available to him" (*ASPR*, VI, lxv). John Hennig has demonstrated that the Old English *Menologium* falls within the tradition of the Irish *félire* ("The Irish Counterparts of the Anglo-Saxon *Menologium*," *MS*, 14 [1952], 98-106). He remarks that the "'metrical martyrologies' . . . are not martyrologies in the traditional sense," being devotional rather than liturgical (p. 106); and he concludes that the *félire* constitutes "the backbone of the European tradition of 'metrical martyrologies', of which the Anglo-Saxon *Menologium* and its Irish counterparts . . . represent the naturalistic trend which survived in secular calendars" (p. 106). See Entry III for analogues to *The Fates of the Apostles*, which also depends upon the martyrologies.

Two metrical martyrologies are frequently cited as Latin analogues to the *Menologium* (see *ASPR*, VI, lxi):

1. The *Martyrologium poeticum*, once ascribed to Bede (*PL*, 94.603-6).
2. Wandalbert of Prüm's ninth-century *Martyrologium* (*MGH*, *Poetae Latini Aevi Carolini*, 2 [Berlin, 1884], 578-602).

18. *An Exhortation to Christian Living*

L. Whitbread characterizes the structure of *An Exhortation* as "a loosely connected series of miscellaneous urgings to repentance and temperate living . . . [based on an] assembly of conventional clerical formulas garnered from various sources" ("Notes on Two Minor Old English Poems," *SN*, 29 [1957], 125)! The poem has affinities with the literature of the Last Judgment, and the reader should consult Entries IV, IX, XIII and XXI for analogues.

19. *A Summons to Prayer*

Max Förster identifies this short macaronic poem as a prayer of intercession, representing the closing section of a verse paraphrase of the *Confiteor* and the *Misereatur* from the Mass ("Zur Liturgik der angelsächsischen Kirche," *Anglia*, 66 [1942], 41).

20. Poems of the *Benedictine Office*

Metrical versions of parts of the liturgy and the Psalms belong to a compilation put together by Aelfric and Wulfstan for the use and instruction of monks (see James M. Ure, ed., *The Benedictine Office* [Edinburgh, 1957], pp. 25-46). The group includes *Lord's Prayer III, Gloria I, The Creed,* and *Fragments of Psalms*. Ure would also link *Lord's Prayer II* with the *Office* (p. 54), though L. Whitbread strongly disagrees ("The Old English Poems of the *Benedictine Office* and Some Related Questions," *Anglia*, 80 [1962], 37-49). The renderings of the Lord's Prayer, the Gloria and the Creed repeat their Latin text line by line and then paraphrase and comment metrically in Old English. The Psalm fragments are, apparently, drawn from the same source as those preserved in *The Paris Psalter* (Ure, pp. 17-9; see Item 13). Ure's edition contains a useful survey of the liturgical and historical backgrounds contemporaneous with the Benedictine revival of the late tenth and early eleventh centuries (pp. 58-66).

21. *The Kentish Hymn*

This is "a conflation and paraphrase of passages from the *Te Deum* and the *Gloria in excelsis*. . . . Some phrases in the *Hymn* appear to have been suggested or reinforced by reminiscence of the Nicene Creed" (Geoffrey Shepherd, "The Sources of the OE *Kentish Hymn*," *MLN*, 67 [1952], 395-6).

22. *Psalm 50*

As Dobbie points out, *Psalm 50* "in general follows the patristic interpretation of this Psalm as David's expression of penitence for his sin against Uriah and Bathsheba (II Samuel xi-xii)" (*ASPR*, VI, lxxx). See Augustine, *Enarrationes in Psalmos, CC*, 38.599-616; and Pseudo-Jerome, *Breviarium in Psalmos, PL*, 26.1030-4.

23. *Thureth* and *Aldhelm*

No specific sources for either of these poems have come to light, but one could extend C. L. Wrenn's comments on *Thureth* to cover *Aldhelm* as well. He writes, "this *halgunboc* [Pontifical or coronation service book] is here personified by the same kind of prosopopoeia that we find in the *Riddles*" (*A Study of Old English Literature* [New York, 1967], p. 192). In both poems a book speaks: in *Thureth* it requests "prayers for the well-being of Thureth, who had it made" (Wrenn, p. 192); in *Aldhelm*, it praises the saint who wrote the tract (*De Laudibus Virginitatis*) which follows. See Entry XVI, especially the analogues under F. and O.

24. *The Seasons for Fasting*

Although Kenneth Sisam suspected that *The Seasons for Fasting* may have been translated from Latin ("*Seasons of Fasting*," in *Studies in the History of Old English Literature* [Oxford, 1953], p. 51), there is no proof that any specific Latin source exists. A more recent study has discovered "echoes" of the Bible and Gregory the Great's *Regulae Pastoralis Liber* in the poem (see Hans Schabram, "*The Seasons for Fasting* 206ff. Mit einem Beitrag zur ae. Metrik," in *Britannica: Festschrift für Hermann M. Flasdieck*, ed. Wolfgang Iser and Hans Schabram [Heidelberg, 1960], pp. 222-8).

On the problem of the dates for the Ember weeks, the reader should consult the works noted by Dobbie (p. xciii): H. Henel, *Studien zum altenglischen Computus* (Leipzig, 1934), 60-4; B. Fehr, *Die Hirtenbriefe Aelfrics* (Hamburg, 1914), pp. 240-1; and K.

Wildhagen, *Texte und Forschungen zur englischen Kulturgeschichte* (Halle, 1921), pp. 68-77.

25. Caedmon's *Hymn*

Several scholars have found traces of the liturgy and patristic works in this poem by a supposedly unlettered scop; they note in particular the impress of the Common Preface of the Mass (Sir Israel Gollancz, *The Caedmon Manuscript of Anglo-Saxon Biblical Poetry* [Oxford, 1927], pp. lx-lxi; Bernard F. Huppé, *Doctrine and Poetry* [New York, 1959], pp. 108-9; and Geoffrey Shepherd, "Scriptural Poetry," in *Continuations and Beginnings*, ed. E. G. Stanley [London, 1966], p. 9). Gollancz also remarks that the poem resembles the *Alenu* prayer of the Jewish synagogue (p. lxi).

Huppé emphasizes the importance of the commentaries on the opening verses of Genesis, and suggests a Trinitarian interpretation. He receives support from Morton W. Bloomfield, who also adds new material ("Patristics and Old English Literature: Notes on Some Poems," *CL*, 14 [1962], 41-3). See the headnote to Entry I for further information.

N. F. Blake suggests that in composing his *Hymn* Caedmon owed more to the psalms than to the traditions of Germanic poetry; he speaks of the "Hymns of praise" that occur towards the end of the Psalter, in particular Psalms 144 and 145 ("Caedmon's Hymn," *N&Q*, 207 [1962], 243-6).

P. L. Henry calls attention to the similarities between Caedmon's *Hymn* and the Old Irish *Lord of Creation* (*The Early English and Celtic Lyric* [London, 1966], p. 212).

26. Bede's *Death Song*

Bede's *Death Song* has analogues in the texts depicting God's judgment, both of the individual soul and of all souls on the Last Day (see Entries IV, IX, XIII and XXI). While scholars have located no source for this short piece, several have drawn connections between it and Christian tradition: see Bernard F. Huppé, *Doctrine and Poetry* (Albany, 1959), pp. 78-9; Ute Schwab, "*Ær—æfter*: Das *Memento Mori* Bedas als christliche Kontrafaktur: Eine philologische Interpretation," in *Studi di letteratura religiosa tedesca in memoria di Sergio Lupi* (Florence, 1972); and Howell D. Chickering, Jr., who relates the scriptural quotations from the *Epistola Cuthberti de Obitu Bedae* (in which the *Death Song* appears) to the poem ("Some Contexts for Bede's *Death Song*," *PMLA*, 91 [1976], 91-100).

27. Metrical Epilogue to the *Pastoral Care*

As C. L. Wrenn notes, all the metrical prefaces and epilogues were "probably suggested by Latin practices" (*A Study of Old English Literature* [New York, 1967], p. 191); and yet only the Metrical Epilogue to the *Pastoral Care* has received much attention.

Jackson J. Campbell and James L. Rosier point out that "The metaphorical meaning of water in this poem is drawn ultimately from the story of Christ and the Samaritan woman told in John 4. Water there is the symbol of the spiritual grace of the Holy Ghost" (*Poems in Old English* [New York and Evanston, 1962], p. 79). Neil D. Isaacs follows this metaphor through Gregory's original ("Still Waters Run *Undīop*," *PQ*, 44 [1965], 545-9).

Correcting certain details in Campbell and Rosier and in Isaacs, J. E. Cross calls attention to John 7.38 as the source for the central metaphor and gives additional patristic references ("The Metrical Epilogue to the Old English Version of Gregory's *Cura Pastoralis*," *NM*, 70 [1969], 381-6).

Appendix II

The Old Saxon Genesis

Text: Otto Behaghel, ed., *Heliand und Genesis*, 8th ed., rev. Walther Mitzka (Tübingen, 1965), pp. 233-4.

(OE lines 790-817a; OS lines 1-26a)

"Alas, Eve," said Adam, "you have now sealed both our fates with evil. You can see dark hell gaping in greed; you can hear it roaring in the distance. The kingdom of heaven is not thus aflame. This land was the most beautiful of all and our Lord willed us to possess it if you had not succumbed to the devil—he counselled us to this evil deed so we violated the command of the Lord, the King of heaven. In our affliction we may grieve over our fate, since the Lord Himself commanded us to arm ourselves against such punishment, the worst of harms. Hunger and thirst oppress me now—the bitter deed—and we were both free of them before. How shall we live now? How shall we exist in this world, now that the wind comes in turn from west or east, from south or north? Darkness gathers, a hail shower drives down from the sky: they come together—it is very cold. At other times the bright sun burns and blazes from heaven. We stand here thus naked, unprotected by clothes. There is nothing here in front of us: neither shade nor shelter, nor cattle provided for food. We have made almighty God, the Ruler, angry with us. What shall become of us now? Now I regret that I ever asked heavenly God, the Ruler, for this . . ."